CW00922683

HALF SEAS UNDER

The author in 1945. Photo by Howard Coster.

Ruari McLean

HALF SEAS UNDER

SEAMAN SUBMARINER CANOEIST

Thomas Reed Publications

A DIVISION OF THE ABR COMPANY LIMITED

In memory of Richard Blackwell, DSC

The right of Ruari McLean to be identified as the author of this work has been asserted by him in accordance with the Copyright, Designs and Patents Act 1988

Published by
Thomas Reed Publications
(a division of The ABR Company Limited)
The Barn, Ford Farm
Bradford Leigh, Bradford on Avon
Wiltshire BA15 2RP
United Kingdom

First published in Great Britain 2001

British Library Cataloguing in Publication Data
A CIP catalogue record for this book is available from the British Library

Designed and typeset by Nicholas Jones and David McLean
at Strathmore Publishing Services, London N7
in 'Minion', designed by Robert Slimbach

Printed in Great Britain by Biddles Ltd, Guildford

ISBN 0 901281 27 1

CONTENTS

FOREWORD

Beneath the surface of wit and wonderful lightness of touch used by Ruari McLean to describe his wartime experiences in submarines and with the Combined Operations Pilotage Parties (COPP) lies a story of true heroism and dedication.

Winston Churchill told Parliament in 1942 that 'of all branches of His Majesty's Forces none faces grimmer perils than the submarines'. He was right. One in three of British and Allied submariners lost their lives during World War II, with the Royal Navy losing five out of its six minelaying submarines. To stand into danger with one's own countrymen is one thing, but to be exposed to that danger in a foreign submarine carries an additional piquancy. Sub-Lieutenant McLean's appetite for adventure and his ability to get on with his fellow man carried him through, and he was fortunate to serve an outstanding Submarine Commanding Officer of FS *Rubis* and their gallant crewmembers. Lieutenant de Vaisseau Henri Rousselot was the most decorated Allied officer, with a DSO and a DSC and two Bars, all awarded for his many successful minelaying sorties between 1941 and 1944. His ship's company received three DSCs, one with a Bar and another with two Bars, and eleven DSMs, one with a Bar. Seven of his men were mentioned in Despatches. The reader should be in no doubt that FS *Rubis* was in the thick of things!

COPPs played a vital role in establishing the groundwork for Allied amphibious operations, and once again the dangers involved are nicely understated by the modesty of the Author. The journey to the objective carried its risks regardless of the mode of carriage, and the various phases of deployment, transit, getting ashore, conducting the surveys, and finally getting the results home to those who needed them, were all extremely hazardous. Many COPPs did not return.

Because of the public fascination for stories about the German U-boat, too often the contribution of the Allied Submarine Services to ultimate victory in World War II is forgotten, and I doubt that many people will have even heard of the COPPs and their magnificent work. *Half Seas Under* is thus an important book historically, as well as a brilliant read.

Commander Jeff Tall, OBE RN
Director
ROYAL NAVY SUBMARINE MUSEUM

ACKNOWLEDGEMENTS

This book is entitled *Half Seas Under* because the phrase 'Half Seas Over' used to be commonly applied to someone who had had too much to drink. And a lot of this book happens 'Seas under'.

I am most grateful to Commander J.J. Tall OBE RN, Director of the Royal Navy Submarine Museum in Gosport, for continual help and encouragement, and for the Foreword he has written for this book. I am also grateful, for help and advice, to Mme Maggie Rousselot, widow of Admiral Rousselot who commanded the Free French submarine *Rubis*, Admiral Jean Mathey in Paris, Allan Brunton-Reed my publisher, John Beaton my editor, Nic Jones and son David McLean for their endless help and skill in designing and producing this book, my daughter-in-law Mary McLean for typing most of it, my daughter Catriona McLean, Fianach Lawry, the National Library of Scotland, and many unnamed Dundee photographers who photographed the crew of *Rubis* after our triumphant return from Norway in August 1941. Also to the editors of *Manchester Guardian*, *Men Only*, *London Opinion*, and some naval periodicals for kindness in allowing me to reprint some drawings and excerpts from articles I wrote for them many years ago.

Ruari McLean

Part 1

SEAMAN

*… an old lady answered
"Foe!"*

*… I joined the Home
Guard …*

*… and a rich supply of
unprintable stories …*

*… nearly punctured an
Admiral …*

*Before joining the Navy, I was a sentry in Park Crescent, in the Home Guard,
in the London War Reserve Police Force, and finally in the Royal Navy.*

1

JOINING THE WAR

I had never particularly wanted to join the Navy, until it turned me down; then I wanted to join it very much indeed. Now I was standing at its front door, the wrought-iron gates of Royal Naval Barracks, Portsmouth. Inside, hundreds of men in blue, wearing khaki gaiters and boots, were rushing about – marching and counter-marching, presenting arms, lunging with bayonets, taking off their caps, trotting in squads. Other groups in singlets were vaulting over wooden horses or swinging their torsos in circles. All that I had done at school. Round the perimeter, I could see the flicker of red and yellow flags and signal lamps practising the Morse code. I had done that in the Boy Scouts. The air vibrated with the barking of orders, the crash of booted feet, the rattle of rifle-butts – all familiar, from the army-training parade ground at school. But beyond, there was a high wall, and above it I could see the grey masts of ships. That was new. I walked inside.

The first thing that happened to new recruits in late 1940 was Joining Routine, a sort of game for twelve or more players, which took about two days. We were issued with gas-masks, and then put in a gas chamber to see if they worked. We were then given hammocks (called 'ammicks), which turned out to be more complicated than they looked; an elderly sailor showed us how to tie the 'nettles' (the pieces of string connecting the canvas you lie in to the ropes by which it is suspended), make the wooden 'stretchers' which keep it open at both ends, and then how to sling it as taut as possible, for sleeping in comfortably. Having done that, you learned how to 'lash up and stow' the 'ammick in the morning. Then we were issued with blue serge uniforms for northern waters, white 'duck' uniforms for the tropics, a tin hat-box, a ditty-box (in peace-time, a small wooden lockable box for private possessions, but in the war, a small cheap attaché-case), a pen-knife, and a kitbag. Then we visited another hut, where two elderly sailors actually cut the names of each man in our class in reverse on little wooden blocks, so that we could stamp them on any of our friends or possessions that could take it. I had been learning about printing before I joined the Navy, and here it was again. So far, the barracks seemed a very nice place, staffed by kind elderly pensioners.

On the third day, we met our first Gunner's Mate.

Chief Petty Officer Jack Brayne was a fair example. He was short, but

Napoleonic. He was a great performer. For a long time, I believed everything he said. He could play on a class of New Entries standing in front of him like a wind running over green grass. He would ask a question, and smile at you, and you would be lulled and smirk back, proud to be so favoured … and then you would realise that the smile had faded, and you were being stared at by icy and hostile blue eyes, like a snake's.

He had a few things to say about the Navy in general and Gunner's Mates in particular, which of course we believed. For example, that the best anti-aircraft gun in the world at that moment was the Bofors, and that he personally had gone over to Sweden to test it and bring back the first ones for the Navy. And that, as far as drill went, we had come to the right man. Before the Guards had gone over to Paris earlier that summer with the King and Queen, they had come to him to get their final polishing. And his eyes flashed, and he was so like a ramrod himself, that even now I almost believe it.

He had the squad moving like one man very quickly, in a sort of combination of fear and hypnosis.

Every morning the whole barracks went to 'divisions'. This ritual was quite impressive – at a distance.

First, markers went out on the parade ground and took up their positions. The rest of us stood round, with cigarettes hidden in palms, chattering. Then, at a bugle-call, we all rushed out and fell in, by classes, with much shuffling, head-turning, and shouting by the Gunner's Mates. Gradually the whole vast parade ground shuffled and squirmed itself into straight lines, and in a series of yelps, the classes were brought to attention, to be reported correct. The climax of the ritual came when every class and every division had been reported correct to the Chief Gunner's Mate of the barracks, a paranoid who was later court-martialled for telling a destroyer captain on his own bridge how to handle his ship. The Chief Gunner's Mate then stared at the parade like a puffed-out king cobra, ready to strike at any moment; and periodically, to demonstrate his all-seeing eye, he stiffened, quivered and screamed: 'Stand STILL there! Howe class, rear rank, number seven, stop picking your nose, you've had your breakfast haven't you?' Then, with a final glare, having awed eight thousand men into silence and near asphyxia, he spun round, took three stamps up to the Duty Officer, a young Lieutenant, and saluted, nearly knocking him down. After that, the Lieutenant's subsequent report to the Commodore appeared casual.

The order was then given 'Off Caps!', and eight thousand seamen stood bareheaded and sang the sombre naval hymn

'O hear us when we cry to thee
For those in peril on the sea.'

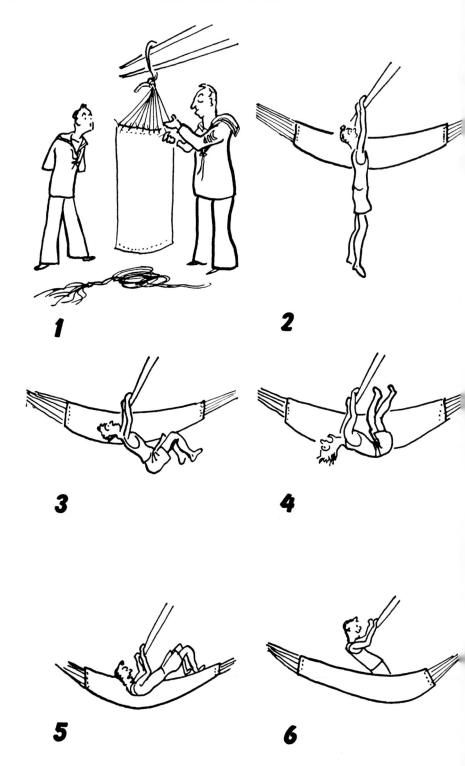

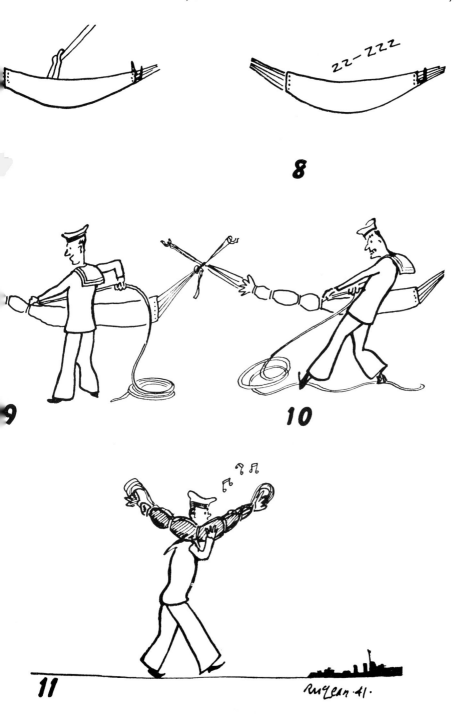

'Ammicks.

Freelance sweeping.

'Swinging the lead, sir …'

while the wind blew their collars up against the backs of their necks, and the Gunner's Mates in front of their classes turned their heads and snarled, out of the sides of their mouths, 'Sing, you bastards'.

There was a hymn, and a prayer, and then the parade marched past the Commodore, taking the salute on the dais, while the Royal Marine band played lilting airs like 'You're in the Navy' and 'Sussex by the Sea'. The Gunner's Mates trotted beside us like brazen-voiced sheep-dogs, barking injunctions to look in on the wheel, to throw those chests out, and to swing those arms.

*　*　*

The collars which blew up round our necks on the parade ground were a significant part of our uniform. They were detachable and worn like a back-to-front bib, with tapes which came under one's arms and were tied across one's stomach. The collars were dark blue when new, but by much scrubbing and washing the colour would gradually fade, and therefore showed that one was no longer a 'new' sailor. The collar also showed other qualities. On a good sailor the blue collar would be well ironed, and the white tapes would be clean (it required some skill when washing to prevent them from becoming tinged with blue from the rest of the collar). A bad sailor's collar would not be ironed and the tapes would be grubby.

After the collar came the jumper. It was skin-tight; and for the first three days I could neither put it on nor take it off by myself. We had a complicated time-table, and had to change our clothes several times a day. Chief Petty Officer Brayne had told us that the greatest sin in the Navy was to be adrift, i.e. late. For my first few days in the Navy I was therefore very unhappy. I rarely knew where I was supposed to be at any given time, nor could I get in or out of my clothes by myself. I was in the middle of a very large and noisy ant-hill, consisting of several thousands of men, who all seemed to know where they were going, and did not greatly care if they trod on me on the way. Gradually I learned my new life without really notic-ing that I was doing so; and when I suddenly discovered the knack of getting in and out of my jumper by myself, life became easier.

The second sin in the Navy, said C.P.O. Brayne, was to be dirty. If a man was dirty (he added cheerfully), his ship-mates would soon scrub him down: soap was cheap in the Navy. The thing the Navy didn't have, at least in Portsmouth barracks, was plugs in its washbasins. This was an added technical complication in the morning fight to get washed and shaved in the middle of a scrum, without losing one's washing equipment or clothes in the mêlée. We solved it by carrying corks.

We learned a lot of other things quickly too.

We learned the badges, ranks and ratings of the Navy. We learned to obey an officer at the double, and a Gunner's Mate at the treble. We learned to stand with our hands behind our backs, like seamen, not with our hands on our stomachs, like expectant mothers. We learned how to wash our collars in cold water and to keep the tapes white. We learned how to live with all our possessions in a kitbag and a small attaché-case; and in particular we learned how to keep our No. 1 suit and other best clothes in a kitbag without getting them crumpled. We learned the first beginnings of the basic principles of being ship-mates, but that lesson was not really to be learned until we went to sea. We learned how to lash up and stow a hammock, first of all in under ten minutes and finally in under one minute. And we learned that, whatever C.P.O. Brayne said, the first commandment in the Navy is: Thou Shalt Not Be Found Out; and that the second is: Thou Shalt Always Look Busy.

We were getting on.

'*Thanks, Stripey.*'

2

ORDINARY SEAMAN

Shortly after joining the barracks I was sent before the Commander and asked if I wanted a commission. I said that I hadn't thought about it, but I supposed I did, eventually. The Commander then said that it was a pity that I was a telegraphist, because the telegraphists had to spend six months training in barracks before they went to sea, and I would have to do at least three months at sea before I could be recommended for a commission. Would I like to change over to Ordinary Seaman? That way, I could get to sea in six weeks.

He didn't ask why I was a telegraphist. The reason was that, at my medical examination for the Navy, I was found to have one good eye and one so bad that I was rejected. As I went out of the door of the Naval recruiting office, it occurred to me to say 'I have a cousin who is a Lieutenant-Commander, does that make a difference?' The recruiting officer, actually a senior colour sergeant in the Royal Marines, said 'Why didn't you say that before?' He looked down a list and said 'Well, I can make you a steward or a telegraphist'. I ascertained that telegraphists wore bell-bottomed trousers, and chose that. The Navy is a family business, which is not so stupid as it may sound.

So I said to the Commander, yes sir, thank you. He replied that he would speak to the Captain of the Signals School, but he was afraid that I would have to do a month's probation as a telegraphist, and then be recommended.

One month later, I became an Ordinary Seaman. From then on, a 'white paper' would go with me wherever I went, on which my superior officers had to note my 'officer-like qualities' or 'O.L.Q.', if they found any. But I wanted to become a seaman first.

The telegraphists, mostly from white-collar jobs, tended to be serious types. The seamen were wilder, and preferable.

The barracks at that time, late 1940, was an overcrowded, antiquated, nefarious, seething factory of sailors. The noise was continuous. Out of doors, there were all the barracks noises, and all the dockyard noises. Inside, apart from the shouting, singing, whistling, stamping and swearing of however many men there might be in the room, there was the barracks loud-speaker system. It could hardly ever stay silent. There would be a pop, and then the words 'D'ye hear there? D'ye hear there?' and then an instruction or a message, or an appeal to an individual to report to somebody's office. Occasionally volunteers were piped for, and that was more interesting.

One morning we were having instruction in knots and splices on a mess-deck, and next to us a class of Newfoundlanders was being lectured by a Gunner's Mate on discipline. Suddenly the loudspeakers popped and began their monotonous 'D'ye hear there? D'ye hear there?' 'Volunteers are required for …' Before we could hear what for, the entire class of Newfoundlanders had disappeared out of the door, while the Gunner's Mate screamed after them in vain; 'Come back! Come back! You're under training! You can't volunteer!'

The Newfoundlanders were conspicuous for their strong physique and the fact that several of them had a decidedly Red Indian cast of countenance: hooded slanting eyes, hook noses and straight jet-black hair. They looked hard and dangerous.

One day our mess was changed, and we found ourselves sharing with the New-foundlanders. My heart sank. When two strange classes shared a mess, the first class to get upstairs off the parade ground at dinner-time collected all the food and usually – it had already happened to us – ate it.

On the very first morning, we were kept late on the parade ground. When we were released, I dashed upstairs (I was Class Leader, and had a certain responsibil-ity in the matter). The Newfoundlanders had not only laid all our places at the table as well as their own, but had also served out all our dinners. That, I soon found out, was like them. We actually got more food while messing with them, for they had managed to return the figure of sixty-two men in the mess, instead of fifty. I was lucky enough to serve later with two of them in my first ship.

Training took all day. There were occasional breaks in which one could, at a rush, get one's hair cut, fetch one's washed clothes out of the drying rooms, or smoke a cigarette. In the evenings, if not on air raid duty, one could stroll around, carrying a book. It was hardly ever possible to read a book in the barracks, but I found it comforting merely to hold a book. At night, if one did not have shore leave, there was one's hammock. There was also the job, which came round in rotation, of being room-sentry.

The Navy was generous with leave, but you could not just walk out of the barracks when you wanted to. You had to 'go ashore' in a 'Liberty Boat'. Liberty Boats went ashore at certain fixed times. To go ashore by Liberty Boat, you parad-ed, were inspected, and were marched out through the gates. There was, of course, no actual boat.

The sirens seemed to have a habit of going about 5 p.m., particularly on holi-days, when more than a quarter of the barracks would be catching trains to go on long week-end leave. We all had to go down into the trenches and seethe, until the all-clear, while the trains rolled out of Portsmouth Station without us. It was a stupid rule, and later, when the bombing increased, the authorities were only too anxious to send all men not on duty away from the place. But at that time the volcanic fury of those waiting to go on leave had to be contained. (Those on duty in the barracks were of course quite pleased.) When the all-clear went, there was an ugly rush to secure a position in the front row of the Liberty Boat. The only time I ever knew discipline to break down completely in the barracks was when the sirens sounded while the libertymen were actually marching out of the gates. Once outside, you did not have to shelter, and could race to the station, so there was a wild stampede for the gates, impossible to stop, of sailors muttering; 'F– 'itler, f– the officer of the watch, and f– everybody, I'm going to catch the 6.40!'

Leave was administered by the Leave Hut, which was, therefore, one of the most important places in the barracks. I heard later that it was possible to buy leave, but I never did discover how much it cost. The currency was probably rum or tobacco.

Of secondary importance was the Drafting Office. All ships in the Fleet were supplied with men through one of the three great Naval barracks, namely Portsmouth ('Pompey'), Devonport ('Guz') and Chatham ('Chats'). The barracks' prime job – virtually their reason for existence – was to keep the ships manned. If the Fleet required sixteen seamen-stewards and five volunteers for submarines, then sixteen men from here to the right became seamen-stewards and five men from there to the left volunteered for submarines, regardless of what they had already signed on as or wanted to be. And vice-versa.

The Drafting Office was always an interesting sight. At any one moment it might have a thousand men milling round it, dragging kitbags and carrying hammocks, like giant bananas, on their backs. The thousand men might be a unit, like the ship's company of a battleship about to be commissioned; much more likely they would consist of four leading seamen for a destroyer, fifty stokers for a fleet aircraft-carrier, three E.R.A.s (Engine-room Artificers) and a hundred Naval Airmen on passage to train in Canada, alongside sixteen signalmen for Stornoway, two leading telegraphists for Colombo, six electricians, two Maltese stewards, twenty-two sick berth attendants, two Asdic operators, one blacksmith, one carpenter and one sailmaker for the *Nelson*, and seven seamen-stewards for a trawler, trying to volunteer for the Fleet Air Arm. And so on. The Drafting Office was where we would all come to in the end, to get our chits when we had finished our training, and were going to sea.

The third important place in the barracks was the Seamen's Divisional Office. This was where personal matters were dealt with.

I went there once on some trivial affair. It was a snug little room, with a coal fire and several tables loaded with papers. Beneath the papers lay numerous bottles of red ink, which the Navy loves, and scraps of ancient blotting-paper. On top of the papers lay cigarettes, cups of tea, and a railway time-table. On the walls were pinned coloured vulgar postcards, pictures of film stars, careless talk posters, lists of fire-watchers, lists of duty week-ends, lists of trains to London, and lists of lists. The proprietor of this little home from home was a Chief Petty Officer with sharp eyes and a creased face (and forty years of sea service). He was assisted by a 'stripey' – a three badge Able Seaman.

'Nice soft job you've got,' I thought. 'Nice long way from the rolling deep you are. Probably haven't been to sea for years. Probably get home every night. Probably get a cup of tea from the Wrens every hour. And you probably treat the seamen like dirt,' I said to myself.

There was a long queue of men waiting to see the Chief and I joined it at the back. The Chief was at that moment being questioned by a young seaman who looked anxious and unhappy. At first I could not hear what they were talking about, but I was sure the seaman was being bullied. Then I heard the Chief saying: 'Compassionate leave? You must have a letter from a doctor saying your presence is vital'.

The seaman murmured something. 'But y'know, you're better not there. Honest, son, you're better as far away as possible, in the Med or somewhere.' I was puzzled. 'I know,' went on the Chief, 'because I've got two myself. Well, one's bigger'n me now, in the *Rodney*. And I can tell you, son, you can't do anything to help. They won't let you in, you know. Y' can't help her. Y're only in the way. You stop here, son, and don't worry. She'll be all right. It's happened before in the world. And if the doctor wires for you, y'can go straight off and no-one can stop you even if you're on draft to a ship. All right? Just don't worry. OK?'

The seaman nodded, his face still troubled.

'Well, that's the rules. But take my tip. She'll be all right. And come and tell me when you're a proud father. All right?'

The other men in the office smiled. So, at last, did the young seaman, and went out.

I went out too. I'd forgotten what I'd come in for. It didn't matter much anyway.

The Chief didn't see me go. He was on to his next case; and before black-out that evening he had to send three hundred men on leave, take in two hundred and fifty new entries, make arrangements for receiving seventy-five survivors, and help seven seamen whose homes had been bombed; two whose parents had died; four Canadians who had hit a policeman; and sixteen Australians who had lost all their luggage, and were now outside whistling 'Are you happy in your work?'

3

A SEMBLANCE OF SAILORS

The war came closer to us in September.

We had just sat down to dinner, roast beef and potatoes, when the sirens went. We had to leave our dinners on our plates and rush downstairs to take shelter in the trenches beneath the parade ground. The duty cooks stayed behind and returned the food to the ovens. After a few minutes, the all-clear sounded and we rushed upstairs again. Then, just as we lifted our knives and forks, the sirens wailed again. This time, men grabbed their roast potatoes, meat and gravy in their hands and stuffed them in their pockets – after filling their mouths – as they hurried downstairs.

Up in the blue fields above us, one of the decisive battles of the world was being fought. Its only effect on us was to spoil our dinners.

Then, as we waited impatiently in the air raid shelter trenches, we got more closely involved.

A first-class air raid developed over our heads as quickly as a thunderstorm in the tropics. Within minutes the whole circus was going full swing – bombs, guns, machine-guns, and the roar and zoom of planes. Each noise, easily heard, was analysed by the sailors sitting on wooden benches in trenches beneath the parade ground. Every man was an expert. 'That's a Spitfire.' 'That was the dockyard pom-pom!' 'Sounds like the *Manchester*'s six-inch!' 'Them's bombs.' 'Coo! Cannon-fire! Saucy bastards!' Some more bombs fell in the distance. Or were they bombs?

We were still arguing when an unmistakable bomb fell close; then – I cannot remember any noise -the walls of the trench, which were concrete, suddenly bulged in and out like a piece of india rubber. A blast of air rushed through the trench, followed by the rattle of fragments coming down above our heads, and then the seeping smell of cordite. It had missed us, but not by much. Various rumours about where it had hit were circulating instantly, but within a few minutes the all-clear sounded, and we filed out and up to the parade ground.

After every previous raid, we had looked round hopefully when coming out for any signs of smoke or damage, but had never seen any. This time, there was enough visible mess to satisfy the most avid sensation-monger. Smoke was going up from a dozen places and the whole parade ground was covered with bricks and stones and rubble. But we could see no crater. And the barracks building seemed intact. We fell in, and the Commodore addressed us from the dais. He said 'Three bombs have fallen on Royal Naval Barracks. One behind the wardroom, one outside the carpenter's shop, and one by the flagpole. The only casualties are two men slightly wounded.' (A spontaneous cheer). 'Cooks to the galley!' (A terrific cheer. The cooks broke from the ranks and doubled away.) 'Now don't talk about this in the town tonight. And this afternoon we must roll up our sleeves and clear away the mess. Dismiss parade'.

At that, there was a rush to the flagpole. There was the crater, quite a beauty. The bomb had fallen about thirty feet away from our trench. The massive white flag-pole lay splintered like a pencil. The flag locker was not to be seen, but the flags which it had contained were now adorning a nearby tree, like gipsies' wash-ing. The crater – the first many of us had seen – was admired by all, and the size of the bomb rapidly rose to at least two thousand pounds. It had fallen about twenty feet from the base of the clock tower, which had rocked like a cornstalk, and before it had finished rocking, a Petty Officer, who was stationed at the top, manning a Lewis gun with two seamen, had telephoned H.Q. to report the bomb's position.

That three bombs could have fallen on those crowded barracks without killing anyone seemed hardly credible.

After dinner, every man in barracks changed into overalls, and fell in for tidy-ing up ship. The wreckage flung round by the bombs was scattered far and wide. There was a large amount of glass roofing in the barracks, much of which was damaged. It was decided to break it all. I was in one of the roof parties. We sat astride a roof from which we could gaze out over the dockyard and at girls passing in the street below. Every now and then we hit a piece of plate glass with a hammer. It was a most satisfying afternoon. Sometimes we pushed out complete panes and watched them turning over in the air as they fell, to shiver into fragments on the ground below.

By supper-time, we were all black with grime and cobwebs, but the job was finished. Those of us not on duty went into the town, where we heard a sad tale of civilian casualties. I went to a cinema and saw Walt Disney's *Pinocchio*, which I had seen before. The smell of gloom and air raids was in my head when I went in; but when *Pinocchio* started, with that aerial view of the old roofs of a medieval town, sleeping in blue and snow-sparkling moonlight, I immediately felt I was away on a magic carpet. The shattered roofs I had been climbing over became the unreal ones. In those days of destruction, here was something they could not destroy; story-telling would outlive this war, and the next, and the one after that.

> *But the dreams their children dreamed*
> *Fleeting, unsubstantial, vain,*
> *Shadowy as the shadows seemed*
> *Airy nothing, as they deemed,*
> *These remain.*

Afterwards I spent the night in Aggie Weston's Temperance Hostel, where you got a cubicle (roofed with wire netting, they trusted nobody) a bed, and a Bible beside it. I fell asleep trying to remember all the toy clocks in that tantalisingly short glimpse of the old toy-maker's shelves. There was a farmyard, with a cock crowing; three fiddlers in an orchestra; a boy being slippered for stealing jam; a young man presenting a bouquet to his sweetheart …

A few days later, I had a Saturday afternoon off and went to the top of Portsdown Hill. Smoky Portsmouth was laid out in the late afternoon sunshine below me. Beyond lay the English Channel, streaked with dark cloud-shadows and pools of sunlight.

Then the sirens sounded faintly in the city. In a few minutes, thirty or forty German aircraft came over, like silver butterflies in the sunlight. They sailed serenely through the myriad puffs of the anti-aircraft guns. Then I noticed a line of smoke columns climbing slowly up, right across the town – where the bombs had fallen. Within five minutes the whole town was blotted out by dense smoke. The raiders turned away towards Southampton. I saw one plane dive on another, (very far away), and a parachute drift out. Gradually the cloud thinned out over Portsmouth and the individual fires could be seen. They were soon put out. No attempt had been made to bomb the dockyard, an enormous area. The raid had been on the town, but quite indiscriminate. A cinema full of sailors and children was hit.

* * *

Time was passing. Gradually we began to take on at least the outward semblance of sailors. The major part of our lessons were from the Gunner's Mates.

Many of the Gunner's Mates who instructed us were pensioners, men who had done their time in the Navy, retired, and got jobs ashore. They had become police sergeants, or lock-keepers, or guv'nors of public houses. Now, most of them were back at sea, and the rest were sweating up and down the parade ground of naval barracks, drilling people like me.

Besides discipline and bad language, they taught us – or began to teach us – something about their philosophy – only they didn't call it that. They did not tell us, for example, that Nelson wrote, in his prayer before Trafalgar, 'and may Humanity after Victory be the predominant feature in the British Fleet'; but a Gunner's Mate did say it to my Class, in September 1940: 'The important thing to notice about the recent action in the Med is not that the Navy sank some Eyetye warship, or ice-cream boat, but that it stayed there, for two hours afterwards, picking up survivors …'

It was the civilisation of the Navy that they were instructing us into – or trying to. But they sighed, when they saw that some of us couldn't even tie a clove hitch after four attempts.

And they were not so severe, those Gunner's Mates. They pretended to be holy terrors, but they really behaved more like nursemaids with children. Long after I went to sea, I used to remember the Duty Gunner's Mate coming round in the morning shaking our hammocks and shouting – almost tenderly – 'Wakey-boo! Wakey-boo! Change here for another day! C'mon, me 'earties!'

But there were times when they put on a terrible act of being men of iron. For example, when we went to Whale Island for gun drill.

For a week beforehand, C.P.O. Brayne built up a fearsome picture of this place, 'the Gunnery School of the world'; where everything was done at the double, where Captain Bligh of the *Bounty* would have been considered kid-gloved, and where, if you were adrift even five seconds, it would be better if you had not been born.

'In Whale Island', said Brayne, 'I shan't shout at you – I shall rave; and you won't run – you'll fly'.

I pictured a place like Sing-Sing; and was surprised, when we got there, to find an establishment of beautiful red-brick Georgian houses, among trees. Typically Navy, every building was white-washed all round for a height of exactly two feet from the ground, and of course everything was meticulously tidy. It was unfortunate about the fall of leaves in Autumn: but any carelessness that occurred at night was instantly swept up at dawn.

In the gun batteries, discipline was as they said. Sometimes a cartridge or shell is defective, and a gun mis-fires. Then the gun's captain screams out 'Still!' and every man freezes. The lives of everyone round the gun may depend on split-second obedience to this order.

We did only twelve-pounder drill, as most of us (we were told) were going to trawlers. The gun's crew consisted of six men, each with his position and job. We took each in turn until our reactions were automatic. We had to shout strange phrases, like 'Tompion out, bore clear!' and 'Still! Misfire! Carry on! Strikers gone forward!' Right till the end, most of the class had not the foggiest idea what the phrases meant, or even what the right words were. They bawled out something and hoped for the best. It was the most strenuous exercise most of us had ever had. In the middle of it, we got inoculated for typhoid. During the next day's gun drill, several of the class fainted.

We had hardly recovered from the combined effects of gun drill and inoculations, when the war stepped even closer. We got our draft chits to sea.

7 p.m *SORRY I CAN'T COME TO THE FLICKS TO-NIGHT — I'M GOING TO WORK!*

8 p.m *NOW, SHALL IT BE NAVIGATION OF GUNNERY FIRST!*

8·15 *OH WELL! JUST ONE GAME THANKS!*

8·45 *THIS REALLY MUS BE THE LAST GAME !*

9 p·m ·· *MUST N'T MISS THE NEWS!*

·40 *GOOD HEAVENS! TIME FOR MY BATH!* 10·50 *DON'T KNOW HOW YOU FELLOWS WHO GO ASHORE EVERY EVENING EXPECT TO PASS!*

4

SHIP'S COMPANY

There was a scrap of paper on the messdeck table, with my name on it, and the word *Windsor*; my first ship. What was she? The bystanders were most helpful. They thought she was a flak ship on the river Itchen, a minesweeper, a cruiser, the flagship of the China Fleet…

We drew warm clothing; a balaclava, blue scarf, blue woollen gloves, and long grey woollen pants.

Next day a trail of men, like ants, carrying hammocks, kitbags, and attaché-cases, met at the Heavy Gun Battery. The new ship's company of HMS *Windsor* had a sight of each other for the first time. By 3 p.m. the gear was stowed in lorries and the men in motor coaches. We left Portsmouth in a drizzle and an air raid. We were going to join our ship, which I now knew was a 1918 V. & W. class destroyer, in the East India Dock, London.

Never have I known sober men behave so uproariously as we did on that trip. It was not that we were looking forward to our future: it was just sheer relief at leaving R.N.B. We behaved like a released chain gang; we leaned out of our windows, waving and cheering to every girl or woman we passed. The ones who smiled back got a redoubled ovation.

It was the first time most of us had seen London since the blitz started: there were cheers or groans as familiar landmarks – mostly pubs – were found to be still there – or gone.

The coach drivers got lost somewhere in Millwall. When at last we found the right dock, and got out of the coaches, it was pitch dark and raining hard. We were on a lonely quay, littered with pools of rain, rats, ropes and old packing cases. A destroyer's side loomed in the darkness. We lugged kitbags and hammocks up a very slippery plank and forward to the seamen's mess deck, and had the first sight of our new home: an improvement on barracks anyway. We were given some tea, slung our hammocks and turned in early.

*　*　*

HMS *Windsor* was just completing a refit after some severe damage from bombing in the Channel. She had made seven trips to Dunkirk, and most of the old hands on board were wearing army greatcoats, left behind by soldiers too tired to care.

Next morning the Captain called everyone aft 'for the new chaps to have a look at me'. He was a young Lieutenant-Commander, very like the destroyer captain in Noël Coward's film *In Which We Serve*. (He was killed in action on a Northern convoy a year later, leaning down from his bridge to encourage the men on 'B' gun just below him.) He told the ship's company something about the programme. He said he thought it would be night work again, mostly in the Channel. We would be moving down to Sheerness in a day or two to ammunition ship, and would then have a practice shoot, as we were at least two shoots behind the rest of the Flotilla. As an afterthought, he added that the Germans were using a new sort of mine, the 'Acoustic', or as he preferred to call it, the 'Wibbly-Wobbly'. There was no method of sweeping it, yet. The *Campbell* (our Flotilla Leader) had set off seven the other night. They generally exploded some way astern, but the rule about always wearing life-belts at sea would be more strictly observed. That was all.

The day before we sailed, I had leave and went ashore, with a ship-mate called Tom. First we went to see Rupert Curtis, a pre-war friend who was waiting to join the Navy and who had an office in Bouverie Street. (By night he served in the River Fire Brigade.) A time-bomb was due to explode next door. His typists had refused to move out. All he could do was to move their desks to the furthest away corner of the office.

Then we went to check on a church and a pub.

The church was all right. It was St Dunstan's-in-the-East, designed by Christopher Wren, the one with a spire on four thin legs which looked to the builders so weak a support that it is said Wren's daughter sat in a chair beneath it when the scaffolding was taken away, to convince the workmen that it was safe. 'She'd probably be an Air Raid Warden today', I said 'and engaged to a DFC (Distinguished Flying Cross)' sighed Tom. And when we went to look inside, we got a shock, because the church had been turned into a lunch canteen and was full of girls having lunch, and laughing, and whistling at us. 'Let's go' said Tom hurriedly, 'and find the "Prospect of Whitby"'.

Before the war, we had both of us often come to this pub on summer evenings, to sit on its balcony and watch the shipping in the Lower Pool. There had been the tramp steamers, that might be going up-stream to Hay's Wharf or downstream to Hong Kong; and lighters being neatly handled in the strong tide, and police launches and sailing-barges and still the occasional rowing boat, surviving from the numbers there must have been when, not so long ago, there were no petrol engines and no bridges between London Bridge and Westminster.

Then there were all the noises of the river: the loud ones like raucous sirens, and

rattling anchor chains, and seagulls and riveters and empty barges banging together on their moorings; and the smaller, subtler ones, like mewing ships' kittens,
and bargees whistling *Rose Marie*.

After sunset, we used to go into the bar where the men sat in blue jerseys, with
beer mugs clenched in gnarled fists, smoking clay-pipes. They never condescended to speak to us.

Now, we were back in Wapping, and the world had changed. Tom and I were
ourselves in blue jerseys, and our hands, if not yet gnarled, were no longer soft and
white. And silver balloons flew above the city, and many streets were heaps of rubble. Yet somehow no-one needed cheering up. The barmaid, for example, was
wearing Royal Air Force wings across her bosom. 'Her morale is clearly sky-high'
murmured Tom. 'Let's go back and pick up Rupert.'

Rupert, looking very glamorous in fireman's uniform, had arranged a supper
party for us in Soho with three of his girl-friends. It was great fun, and afterwards
we walked back to deposit the girls at their flat in Bayswater. It was not my first experience of being bombed, but my first in the West End of London. As we went up
Regent Street, and along Oxford Street, the whole thing seemed, in such familiar
places, unreal and unbelievable. An orange glow from fires in the East End suf-
fused the sky behind us; flashes from the Hyde Park guns continually lit up the
street. Once a flare hung dangerously above us for interminable minutes; the Anti-
Aircraft shells winked among the stars, and the full moon shone serenely above all,
like a queen at a very rowdy party.

Just beyond Marble Arch there came a wheee … we flung ourselves down. Two
bombs fell close. One of the girls jumped to her feet and laughed, but a policeman
on his tummy behind us snarled 'Geddahn!' and we pulled her down as the debris
came rumbling round us. Some of the pieces of masonry on the street ahead of us
were quite big enough to kill.

We trod on delicately. The pavement was thick with broken glass. A gas main
was blazing round the corner, casting a lurid glow into the sky; and a woman was
sobbing. Rupert hurried us on: the rescue squads were already there, and the Fire
Brigade soon would be.

Just as we reached the front door of the flat there was another whistle … we
dived for the steps. Three bombs fell in the next street. In answer to our questions,
the girls said no, they didn't mind sleeping alone, and never went down to the shel-
ters; they preferred their flat, with the flowers in the window, and the view over the
square. If a bomb had their names on it …

They asked when we would be in port again, smiled, and said good-night.

We got back to the ship at last. Everyone who had been ashore returned drunk,
but only one man, a stoker, fell into the dock. The duty part of the watch fished
him out.

We sailed next day. As we dropped down the river, I looked back to London, to the ships, towers, domes, theatres, and temples, and to the girls. Who would be under fire from nightfall onwards? We might not be; but the girls almost certainly would be. A curious war.

We anchored at Sheerness. For the first time, I was sent to empty a bucket of potato peelings over the side of the ship, a satisfying manoeuvre if one remembers to do it to leeward and not lose hold of the handle.

S/Lieut RNVR

Destroyer men.

I just had a bath.

5

I JUST HAD A BATH

To find the seamen's mess deck in a destroyer, you walk for'ard until you are in the bows, beneath 'A' gun. In the middle of our living space was a donkey engine used for raising the anchors, which emitted a powerful stench of oil. In the narrowest part of the bows was the equally smelly paint locker. In the only open space on the floor was the hatch leading down to the mess deck of the stokers, who lived below the waterline, and the forward Ammunition Store. At the side were steel pens, the so-called hammock 'nettings' (a term surviving from wooden ships) in which the hammocks were piled when not slung. Here we reclined when off duty during the day. When I slung my hammock at night, my face was close up against the deck above; my nose practically fitted into the furrow of a shell or bomb fragment which had come through the ship's side at Dunkirk.

We were in three messes of ten men, each ruled by a Leading Seaman. I count-ed myself lucky; most of my ship-mates were members of the Navy by profession. Later on in the war, most of the seamen in a small escort destroyer, like the *Windsor*, would be 'Hostilities Only', i.e. amateurs like me.

The Leading Seaman of my mess was called Lofty. He was six feet six inches and of exceptional physique. He had a broken nose. His wife had once been ill, and he needed money to pay the doctor's bill; so he got compassionate leave to look after her, and fought for six consecutive nights in an East End boxing booth. When he returned on board the doctor promptly gave him a fortnight's leave, on account of his face. Lofty, with his hair matted and his teeth bared, could look like Boris Karlof, but was in fact as gentle as a lamb. He never slept in a hammock; he slept, rolled up in an army overcoat, on the lockers, and if he fell off, he continued sleep-ing on the deck. When I had to wake him, to go on watch, I used to shake him violently for several minutes without disturbing him at all. On evenings in harbour, he used to sit at the mess table, with a tiny paint brush concealed in his fist, and paint flower patterns, carefully following the movements of his brush with his protruding tongue. He copied his flowers from cigarette cards; and when the designs were finished, they were posted to a textile manufacturer in the East End of London, who sent him ten shillings and sixpence for every accepted design.

Then there was Wiggy, who was the Captain's servant, and, in action, the cap-tain of the 12-pounder. He was a curly red-haired cockney reservist, who had served twelve years in the Navy and left it before the war; he could talk anybody, particularly women, into doing what he wanted, and then talk himself out of the consequences.

Also in my mess were two Newfoundlanders, Bob and Jim. Jim was a fisherman with thick black hair and a red face. He had postponed marrying his girl in order to come and help us out. Bob, curly-haired, and with looks as good as many film stars, was a less simple ex taxi-driver from Halifax.

Ginger, the youngest in the mess, was as tough as Lofty, though a quarter the size. He had just got his first good conduct badge, for three years 'undetected crime'. Though only twenty, he had been round the world twice, had fought on land in Palestine, and had had some shrapnel through his jaw at Dunkirk. He had a most powerful, almost inhuman, voice, raised frequently in argument, admonition or anecdote.

Of the two other Leading Seamen, one had come to the *Windsor* after ten years in the Royal Yacht. He was taciturn, but scrupulously just. The other was a Tynesider, and one of those men whose hair will never lie flat, but always sticks straight up; consequently he never looked tidy, but he was tough and efficient.

Our first war patrol was the anti-invasion run on the East Coast between Sheerness and Harwich. We were at action stations all night. I was on 'Y' gun, right aft, and therefore shielded from the worst of the wind: even so, we were bitterly cold. In the morning we went to two watches, and I became a bosun's mate. One of my duties was to go down to the engine room to take a reading of the sea temperature to record in the log. I had to open a hatch in the iron deck and climb down into the engine-room; the clammy heat met me like a barrier, and I loathed going through it. I didn't like being in the engine room much at all, considering what it would be like if we hit a mine or were torpedoed, but passing from the clean cold into clammy heat revolted me physically. Why the sea temperature couldn't be ascertained by telephone, I never understood.

Bosun's mates' other duties included obtaining the 'wet' and 'dry' temperatures from thermometers outside the wardroom flat, and piping routine announcements like 'Up Spirits' or 'Special sea-duty men to your stations!' as ordered. An inexperienced bosun's mate in *Windsor* once asked the petty officer on the bridge what he should do next, and was told succinctly 'Wet and Dry', so he went through the ship blowing his bosun's whistle and bawling 'Wet and Dry!' until restrained.

Apart from such activities, I stood in the wheelhouse and did nothing, which was enjoyable. At about 0930 it was a lovely sunny morning. I had to go up to the bridge to deliver a message, and was watching the destroyer ahead, when suddenly the sea astern of her erupted in a spout of water, and she disappeared. When the water subsided, she was still afloat, emitting clouds of steam, but listing and turning in a circle. It had not taken long for us to become acquainted with the acoustic mine.

The mine had exploded some way astern and the ship suffered no casualties. We had to tow her into Harwich, and then we returned to Sheerness, where I found I had been awake, quite strenuously, for thirty-six hours; and slept.

We did some more night runs, gradually shook down as a crew, and learned to loathe Sheerness. Then we sailed one morning in a hurry, and when at sea were told we were sailing for the Clyde. We sailed in line ahead with two other destroyers. The weather was perfect, and during the afternoon, when off watch, I lay on the quarterdeck, near my gun, and read poems in the *Week-End Book*; only later did I realise that the quarterdeck is reserved for officers. However, no-one sent me packing. All that disturbed me was the Action Stations Alarm Bell clanging twice; once for an aircraft which turned out to be friendly, and once when someone leant against the button by accident.

It was during the aircraft alarm that it came home to me for the first time that I was not in a pleasure steamer, out for fun, but in a warship very seriously at war. I gazed, from the slit in the shield of 'Y' gun, on to a rail of depth charges, and suddenly realised that each of those canisters was packed very tightly with high explosive and all round me, clipped to the deck, were four-inch shells, not toys or dummies, but dealers of real death; and that I was in a very small ship with very thin sides in the middle of the North Sea, and I sincerely wished I wasn't.

These thoughts came as quite a shock, rather like the shock I had had during the second week of the war, when I was at the pictures and saw a news-reel of French and British soldiers walking along a trench and I suddenly realised that those men were not on manoeuvres but were actually at war. Now I realised for the first time that I was really in the war myself, and I didn't like it; it was like feeling permanently cold, and not having any extra clothes to put on. I indulged in strong self-pity for a few weeks and then forgot about it.

So the ship ploughed north, with the land rarely visible on the port side; usually hidden in mist or cloud. Then we turned west, and then, one evening at about 1800 we rounded Cape Wrath. Grey clouds trailed over a brassy yellow sky; the sea, heaving endlessly, was steely blue, and the mountains grey and eternal-looking. The Scotsmen in the crew came out and sat on deck and sang 'Will ye no come back again' and 'Annie Laurie', till cookie appeared and emptied a bucket of tea-leaves and potato-peelings to windward of us.

To my disappointment, we passed down the West Coast of Scotland at night. I was in the wheelhouse, and navigating the Minch at fifteen knots in pitch darkness seemed to be tricky work.

During the night, I had my first important commission. The quartermaster at the wheel sent me below to make cocoa for him and the look-outs. I had to go down to his mess, which was below ours, and hunt around in semi-darkness amid snoring petty officers for the right fanny and the right cocoa and sugar and milk;

and then carry the cocoa-fanny and the cups back up all the steel ladders to the wheelhouse. Luckily, cocoa was one of the two things I knew how to make in a kitchen; and I made it thick as molten lava. It was received with grunts: but I knew that if anything had been wrong with it I should soon have been told, and the word would have gone round that I was as useless as I looked.

We arrived at the mouth of the Clyde just as dawn was breaking. I could imagine no more beautiful ending to a voyage. We steamed slowly up the river between hills whose shapes and colours were of an indescribable softness; and ahead of us, sunlight and shadow chased one another slowly over the slopes of Ben Lomond. Snow lay on the higher hills.

Inside the boom lay the greatest collection of shipping I had ever seen in my life. There were ships of every nation and of every size, from liners, now troopships, loaded with troops, to small Dutch coasters. It was not something I was allowed to write home about, but it would have done the civilian population good to see it. We moved slowly through it all and picked up a buoy off Gourock.

About noon, leave was piped for my part of the watch, until midnight. After a hasty wash in a bucket, I put on my 'number ones' and went ashore in the first Liberty Boat. I went alone, as my particular friends were either catching up with their laundry, or in the duty watch. I caught a bus to Glasgow. It was Sunday. I wondered what to do, and took a turn along Sauchiehall Street. My nautical roll was genuine, as I had not yet got my land legs. I hoped that people were nudging each other as I passed and saying 'There goes a real sailor. Tough as nails. Real salty!' The last part would have been true. But the tang of the sea was getting too strong, I thought. So, having treated the citizens of Glasgow to the sight of a real sailor (who'd been at sea for two whole days) I entered the North British Hotel, and ordered a bath.

The bathroom exceeded my most picturesque dreams. It was immense. Its walls were (or I thought they were) made of marble. It had stained glass windows, which glowed with assorted marine fauna. The floor, covering a considerable acreage, was entirely cork. The fittings were not of mere chromium, but appeared to be of Homeric red bronze – or perhaps copper. The bath itself, within walking distance of the hand-basin and clothes hooks, was made of streaky green marble, like gorgonzola.

An ancient but motherly dame took me to the bathroom, turned on the water, and fetched me three towels, smooth, medium and rough. I half expected her to stay and bathe me, like Odysseus' old nurse – and discover the scar. But with a solicitous look round, as of someone who has laid a feast, she left me. The water was, of course, scented.

I lay back in that bath and dissolved two days of dirt and discomfort in a dream. It was really nothing, but seemed something then, to have completed my first voyage. The steam curled upwards; I broke surface with my toes, and they were the

Great Barrier Reef. All I needed was a celluloid goldfish ... fish, fly-replete in depths of June ... surely the God of Baths, too, is squamous, omnipotent and kind. The steam eddied away with my thoughts.

When I dressed at last, tipped the motherly dame, and descended to the foyer, the bill for the bath did not leave very much in my pockets. Stepping into the street, and conscious that I now smelt less of ozone than of attar of roses, I bought some chips (I couldn't afford the fish) and returned slowly to the ship.

At midnight, the mess deck was recounting its adventures ashore. Nobby had had a fight with some so1diers, probably commandos, judging by his condition. Ginger and Lofty had found a cinema open on the Sabbath and seen Dorothy Lamour in *Jungle Love*. Wiggy had a bruise on the bridge of his nose which came, he said, from making love to an air raid warden who refused to take off her steel helmet.

Someone sniffed my scented person and asked what I'd been up to.

'Me? Oh, I just had a bath.'

They obviously did not believe me.

On a destroyer mess deck.

6

INTO THE ATLANTIC

The worst misadventure, while we were in the Clyde, was what happened to the motor-boat's crew. They were sent ashore to collect some stores, broke down, and could not get the thing started again till after dark. They then set out for the ship, which was about a mile from the shore, and got lost. After touring for hours round that vast anchorage, and asking pathetically 'Are you OUR ship?' to every shape that loomed out of the darkness at them, the engine broke down again. They drifted ashore some hours later and arrived back next morning under tow, frozen and miserable. A special issue of wardroom whisky was administered by the First Lieutenant when he had verified the strict accuracy of their story.

We spent one day on a practice submarine hunt, with a real submarine, which was interrupted by a real hunt, for a mythical U-Boat, and were joined by two new Asdic ratings.

Next day we sailed at dawn, with two other destroyers, a cruiser and the old aircraft-carrier *Argus*, known to the Navy as the 'floating ditty-box', because that was just what she looked like, having no bridge superstructure on her flight deck. We were to escort her to about 16° west, and then return.

At sea we were free to wear what we fancied. Half a dozen of the men had army trench coats, left behind by soldiers brought back from Dunkirk. One man had a French soldier's coat. Most of the rest of us wore dirty old duffle-coats, often in rags. I did not possess sea-boots, and in any case, would never have worn them at sea, having been told how quickly a man drowned in them. I wore outsize gym-shoes, with three pairs of socks and sea-boot stockings, which kept my feet warm enough.

We had good Atlantic weather: sunshine and steely clouds, seagulls and rough seas which piled past revealing that dark blue colour that suggests infinite depths, so much deeper-looking than the green of the North Sea.

The first day out I was sick as a dog, like nearly everyone else. I was not sick again, but the smell of oil and steam coming from the capstan engine in the middle of the mess deck always threatened to turn my stomach. When I came off watch, I usually slipped straight into my hammock. By the third day, conditions on the mess deck were dirty. The ship leaked everywhere that destroyers usually do, and in some other places as well, which we couldn't trace. As the ship rolled to port,

Going on watch, destroyer's mess deck.

A game of cards on a destroyer's mess deck.

a tide of filthy black water rushed across the deck, carrying with it a flotsam of dried peas and cabbage leaves. As the ship rolled to starboard the black wave rolled back, beneath the hammock netting. The lowest hammocks were soon soaked. Every seventh roll or so, the peas were joined by a piece of raw red meat, which was to be No. 3 Mess's dinner. Every time it fell off its shelf it was hastily retrieved by Lofty or Ginger, if they were there: they were the only persons who wanted to eat it. 'Wish you were in the army, chum?' asked the regulars of us civilians, studying us keenly to see if we could take it. I couldn't explain just how much I preferred being there to being in a tank, or in a trench … Soon, I am glad to say, they forgot to think of us as civilians. But only Jim, the Newfoundland fisherman, was indistinguishable from the real thing; or better.

So the voyage went on. Up, up, up went the bows. Then down, down, down, down, till one crammed one's stomach back in one's throat. Crash went the bows on the 'pavement'. Then up and up and up …

My stomach never wanted the daily roast beef and potatoes. I lived mostly on oranges and Bovril and toffees. The Canteen Manager (an employee of the Naafi, and therefore permitted to wear a moustache) was a bad sailor, and when he opened his little shop he was always far too ill to care how many toffees we each took for a penny. We never bought toffees when it was calm.

During the third night, the destroyers parted company with the carrier and the cruiser, and we set course for home, by different routes. At this time the seas were so heavy that we could not steam at more than twelve knots. Up and up and up went the bows … then down and down and down and CRASH! on the 'kerb-stone'. Then up and up and up … and all the while she was rolling venomously.

On the fourth night we had a promise of action. The liner *Empress of India* had been attacked by a Focke-Wulf aircraft about 150 miles to the north of us, and we were ordered 'with utmost despatch' to her assistance. As the same thing had recently happened, in nearly the same position, to the liner *Empress of Britain*, and she had been subsequently torpedoed and sunk, it behoved us to find her before the U-Boats did.

During the following afternoon, the Captain asked for a volunteer to go up to the crow's nest, but just as someone was going up, we saw our *Empress* from the deck. I read in the papers later how the Focke-Wulf had near-missed her with bombs, and then machine-gunned her, while the Maltese quartermaster at the wheel had manoeuvred the ship lying down.

We steamed ahead of her, and every now and then made energetic-looking sweeps to port and starboard, like a child swerving on a bicycle. No U-Boats offered us contacts. Towards evening three Anson aircraft appeared and kept us company for a little, and a very fine sunset developed. I posted myself as a voluntary look-out on 'Y' gun in order to watch it.

Next morning we left her to cross the Irish Sea under the protection of Coastal Command, while we put in to Lough Foyle, to oil.

The only memories I have kept of Londonderry are of the coldest wind I have ever known in my life, like a whip lash; and of a small boy who came on board on Tuesday with the previous Sunday's papers. Having sold one to every member of the ship's company, he still had one paper left. It was saturation point; he had to leave without selling it.

'Will you wipe while I dry?'

7

INTERLUDE IN DOCK

The Atlantic in November is unfriendly to old destroyers, and the *Windsor* was a veteran of 1918. We already had six inches of water in the mess decks, and the rumour-mongers on board said there were tons and tons of water loose in the engine-room. Perhaps they were right; for it was soon confirmed that we were going into dry dock. But where? New York? California? No such luck. We wallowed back round Cape Wrath and Duncansby Head and arrived in Grimsby. The members of the crew who happened to live there were overjoyed, and the rest said well, it could not be worse than Sheerness.

Seven days boiler-cleaning leave was piped for each watch; the starboard watch (that meant me) went first. Armed each with a free railway ticket, a ration card and an advance of pay, hurriedly provided by the Sub-Lieutenant, the Coxswain and the ship's writer, those going on leave swept off the ship and ran to the station like hens running to be fed. I took Jim the Newfoundlander home with me to Oxford, and we found it strange to be drinking tea out of china, instead of condensed-milk-brew out of tin mugs, and to have adequate cutlery, instead of looking for forks in the bilges, and then eating with fingers, penknives and screwdrivers.

It was over too soon, and we returned to the equally novel, and strangely enjoyable, experience of living on board a ship in dry dock.

The stokers were pretty busy, but the seamen had an easy time. Our routine was like this: at 0730 we got out of our hammocks and had breakfast, in one motion; at 0800 we fell in and scraped the upper deck for an hour or so, and then went and made a cup of tea in the galley. We would then be chased out of the galley by the Chief Bosun's Mate, and carried on scraping till Stand-Easy, when we made a cup of tea. Then we carried on scraping till 1130, when the pipe 'Up Spirits!' meant that those entitled went to collect their tot of rum; and those not entitled made a cup of tea. After that, it was agreed that it was not worth while doing any more work before dinner. After dinner, there was a cup of tea, and then a sleep till about 1530, when Liberty men fell in, after, of course, having a cup of tea. A pleasant life.

Grimsby turned out to be a warm-hearted, hospitable place and no-one who went ashore had to wander. Every sailor seemed to get adopted by some family in the town, and there were football matches, parties and dances. When the men returned on board, late at night, they would recount their exploits, first of that day,

'Leave' (courtesy The Draconion).

then of other days in other ports. Even Ginger, the youngest, could hold us spellbound with old scandals and high adventures, in all the seven seas … 'Alex in '33
… the storm at Cannes Regatta when Nobby was adrift among the flower-girls …
we was stranded at Odessa three days and a middy (Midshipman) brought off a
bear … When Lofty fought that marine in Oslo … in the seventh round, no, the
sixth … he went down in the *Courageous*, best middleweight I ever saw … Gib in
'34 … Torquay last summer, and the Home Fleet Boxing Finals … up the Suez
Canal at twenty-five knots, that time the Eyetye Fleet came out, during the
Abyssinian business, the Arabs on the banks cheered us like f – till the wash hit
them… there's a street in Hong-Kong where you could buy any part of a British
warship; they once stole a 12-pounder gun screwed to the quarter-deck, and the
marine sentry swore no-one had passed him … Tientsin … the Japs shot Dusty
and Ginger at the barrier, the funeral was five miles long … I knew a girl in Singa-
pore, and her mother said … Remember that girl in 'Frisco? In Leith? In La Linea?'

Their lives had not been dull.

One night I had a minor adventure myself. Half the crew were on leave. Half the
rest were at a dance. The rump, the duty watch, the Cinderellas, were sitting all
together in the mess.

It was a cosy, domestic scene. The stove was going full blast, and above it, on
lengths of string, hung an interesting collection of seamen's smalls, which their
owners had just washed. Music-hall was coming through on the loudspeaker. The
nine o'clock news had just announced a record number of enemy planes shot
down. All we lacked was a glass of beer.

I was, in theory, writing a letter. Beside me Bob and Jim were reading letters. Jim
showed me a letter he had just had from a Newfoundland friend in another ship,
part of which I copied out then and there. It ran 'You ask if there will be another
armistice don't worry boy there will be one signed by and bye we will close Hitler's
bluddy eyes for him O good he wont know dinner from breakfast he will be so
bluddy frightened.'

Across the way in No.2 Mess, an elderly A.B. and the Leading Seaman were having an argument. It arose from the sermon page in a Sunday newspaper, and was
on whether crashed German airmen should be picked up out of the water or not.
The Leading Seaman said leave 'em. Stripey said, you should pick them up, and
then push them back in again, and then machine-gun the bastards. Stripey had
fought against Germans in two wars.

Forward in No. 1 Mess, a curious game was being played with matchsticks, half-
pennies, and a pack of cards. It looked highly complicated, but consisted merely in
turning up the highest card of the round. Lofty was beaming with his broken-
tooth grin, having just won sixpence. Ginger was using his stentorian lungs to
inform the chap beside him that it was his f-----g turn, and Stripey added that he'd

seen a fellow do just that to a Jerry they'd shot down coming back from a raid on London, and the Captain had sent him back to barracks.

I turned to look at Jim, who was earnestly chewing gum, and at Bob, who was trying to decide which of four girls in Halifax he was going to write to next. It was a pleasant life in dry dock: if only we had some beer …

At that moment MacGregor, one of the Scotsmen in No. 2 Mess, who was reading the Glasgow *Bulletin*, exclaimed that it was St Andrew's Night! There was not a drop of alcohol on board, and he was duty watch, and ye canna, he said, ye canna let by St Andrew's nicht with no a drink. The 'Three Jolly Mariners' he added, was no' far away. 'We cannot all go,' said the Leading Seaman primly, 'that would be breaking ship. But we could send somebody.' MacGregor immediately volunteered. 'No fears, we'll send a teetotaller' said the Leading Hand. 'Or nearly one' he added, looking at me. 'Who's deck sentry? Oh, him. Who's duty P.O.? Well, get cracking.'

It was an order. I plucked up my courage and went below to the P.O.'s mess. 'Chief, permission to go ashore for a minute and get some water?' (There was no tap working on board: drinking water was fetched from a tap on the wharf). 'I'll collect it in some empty bottles.' The Chief Stoker had not been born yesterday, but he was in a good mood. 'Yes.'

In three minutes, I was off the ship and stumbling over rails, under ropes, and round railway tracks, to get to the dockyard gates, with three empty bottles in my pockets. I soon got to the pub, pushed open a door, and found that foolishly I had come into the senior Lounge Bar, instead of the Jug and Bottle. It was too late to go back. I walked to the bar, produced the empties, and asked for them to be filled. As the bottles were given back to me, I saw to my horror a naval officer detach himself from a group and walk over to me. An RNR Lieutenant, small and ugly. Avoiding action was impossible. 'What've you got there?' he asked. I mumbled something feeble, smiled ingratiatingly, and tried to edge away. He grasped me firmly by the arm, and felt all over. 'What've you got there? You've got beer. How many bottles have you got? One, two, three –' 'Four, five, six,' said I, helping, 'seven, eight,' said the Lieutenant, seriously. 'I'm going to arres' you, and I'm going to arres' Molly for selling it to you. Molly! Molly!' He was holding on to me, I realised, for support, but I could not get out of his clutch. 'The guv'nor sold it to me, not Molly,' I said. 'Guv'nor!' squeaked the Lieutenant, 'I'll arres' him, and I'm going to sock you! I'm going to sock you good n' hard! I'm Benson of the Boom Defence, and I'm a tripehound – the bigges' tripehound there is. Ask anyone if Benson of the Boom Defence isn't the biggest tripehound there is.'

He said everything very slowly and repeated it six times. 'Yes, I'm a tripehound, and you an' me, when we're here, are jus' one, d'ye see, jus' one, you 'n' me.' He then ordered a round of beers for me, himself, Molly, and the Guv'nor, and launched into his life history. Then he presented me with four pint bottles of beer in a paper

When I go on leave

*it's grand to know I can
take a girl out to dinner*

knowing that it will cost only 5s. each, plus the extras . . .

Plus the extras . . .

plus the extras.

bag, for the fellows on board to drink his health, then he wanted to go to the Gents. I seized my chance and piloted him, not to the back door, but to the front door by which I had come in. It was pitch dark outside. I left him in the street, swearing as he searched for an electric light switch, and, weighed down by seven full bottles, I staggered to the ship. The sentry, as I passed him, shut his eyes.

The fury of the mess deck, who thought they could have trusted me not to stay drinking in the pub, was allayed when I told my story and produced the beer. But the Chief Stoker wanted to see me, to ask why I had been two hours getting water from a tap two minutes away.

I wondered if the Chief would be insulted, if I took him a bottle as a peace offering. I need not have worried.

Grimsby was a pleasant interlude. On one sunny day, we washed all the flags, and dressed the ship overall to dry them. I found a door open in the nearby 300 foot Dock Tower and climbed to the top and on to the balcony. The town was shrouded in smoke, out of which poked chimneys, roofs, spires and cranes. Below me, wrinkled water crawled in the dock basins and there was a toy destroyer – the *Windsor*, with all her flags flying. Later, to get the fishes-eye view, I went down to the bottom of the dry dock and crawled under the *Windsor*, among barnacles, and pools of water, and smells. She seemed vast there, yet thin as a sardine.

At last the time came to move on. It was a satisfying process to stand on the deck and watch the water gushing into the basin, and feel her become waterborne again, and see the timber props float away: likewise two of our fenders, while Lofty cursed black and blue at whoever had failed to secure them. At noon, we sailed, and outside the harbour picked up a convoy to escort to Sheerness.

We were now in a different system of watches, and I found myself on the pom-pom (anti-aircraft) gun with Lofty. The pom-pom was mounted in a sort of small band-stand amidships. We were able to sit down, muffled to the eyebrows, wrapped in tarpaulins. We huddled together for warmth, and watched the full moon rise out of a bank of mist. As the moon's face, climbing, turned slowly from red to silver, Lofty surprised me by saying 'You know, I believe the moon is God's face.' Lofty's next remarks were less poetic. They were on the subject of Sheerness.

Going on leave.

Shopping on leave.

8

TOO MUCH LEAVE

The sun dissolved slowly in mist, faintly red, as Sheerness became invisible astern. A convoy of fifty laden ships went past us, steaming up to London River: little coasting steamers, whose skippers faced storms, mines, dive bombers, E-boats and coastal guns, wearing bowler hats.

It was December; we were out on another night patrol; no-one was happy. In an hour, the ship would go to action stations, and remain so till dawn. Meanwhile, I was bosun's mate, and had to go down to the engine room, to obtain the Mean Revolutions and the Sea Temperature, and ask if they would dry Lofty's jersey that he had just washed.

When I came up, I stood on the iron deck for a few minutes, gazing at the moon, half full and well up in the sky to starboard. It was a quiet night, with few stars showing: probably it would be foggy later: E-boat weather. Wiggy, the Captain's servant, came along from aft, carrying a jug of steaming coffee up to the bridge. 'Any gash?' I murmured automatically, and we looked at the night for a few seconds together. Suddenly there was a roar and a great black seaplane zoomed over our heads from behind us, clearing the funnels by a few feet. Just as it passed, an object fell out of it and dropped in the sea about fifty yards away: it raised a splash, white in the moonlight, while the seaplane disappeared in the mist. Some seconds elapsed, then BOOM! the bomb exploded, in a great fountain of water.

Wiggy and I went on our way up to the bridge. 'Bit slow, weren't you?' said Wiggy to the starboard look-out and Lewis gunner, as we passed him, and 'See that drop, Sir?' to the Captain, as he handed him the jug of coffee. The officers were arguing whether it had been a Dornier or a Heinkel. The Lewis gunners and pom-pom crew, now fully awake, were pointing their guns fiercely at a completely empty sky.

So we steamed on, through the dark night, into a numbing wind. The men on the forward guns were exposed. In the small part of their brains not too cold to think, they were wondering why they had joined the Navy, and when that cocoa was coming up, and whether, if they died of cold before it reached them, anyone would notice. The look-outs, on the wings of the bridge, were also too cold to do anything but think of phrases for their next letters home; 'Dear Mum, thank you for the jersey. Could you send another six?'

But I was in the wheelhouse, which was snug. Click, click, went the gyro repeater as the ship's head swung away, or back again to our course. Wiggy, a great talker, was holding forth. Occasionally the Captain's voice came down the voice pipe from the bridge above, with an order for the wheel, cutting across his narrative. Apparently, Wiggy had had more leave during the past few months of war than he could remember having had in all his service in peace-time in the Navy.

'I got two lots of survivors' leave during the Norwegian business. Call it luck. Then I goes back to barracks, and to fill in time I put in for compassionate leave, and 'ow I got it is another story. Then I joins this 'ere ship. We does seven trips to Dunkirk, and gets Dunkirk leave. Then we gets a week's boiler-cleaning. And then, first time out, a Dornier drops a bomb on us off Dover, and we 'ave to dock; four weeks leave for each watch. Fine! But you can get too much leave. Twelve weeks now I been going with the same party, and this last time I had to promise I'd marry 'er on my next leave. Now we're back at sea, an' I 'ope we blooming well stay there!'

Wiggy opened his mouth to describe his latest 'party'. But at that moment we altered course, and the ship lurched so far over that everyone had to hold on for dear life. Then Wiggy was sent to get some more coffee for the Captain; and there was only the clicking of the gyro, and the monotonous voice of the quartermaster repeating his new courses, and the creaking of the ship as she rolled.

The destroyer steamed on.

Then, just before we went to our nightly routine of Action Stations, I came off watch, and went below to put on some more warm clothes. I was sitting on the lockers taking off my shoes, and the people who had seen the seaplane incident were describing it to those who had not, when suddenly; BANG! – all the lights went out; the collapsible tables folded with a crash; everyone was thrown on to the deck.

I made for the door. Someone slipped in the darkness. There was chaos and curses. Something serious has happened this time, I thought. Everyone was muttering 'No panic!' and scrambling like mad. Once out on deck we could see we were not on fire, anyway. Smoke, or steam, was rising from fractured pipes. Had we been torpedoed? 'Action Stations' was ordered and I went to my gun without shoes, gloves, coat or balaclava.

The quarterdeck was drenched with water. Our turn had come to meet an acoustic mine.

People came bustling around examining things and looking for damage. Two depth charges had gone overboard, luckily set at 'safe', and nearly everything I could see was slightly bent. The first serious damage discovered was two rum-casks which had been stove in. Then it became known that the engines were too seriously shaken to run again. The ship lay wallowing and rolling in the swell, while a great black ring of oil fuel spread and spread round her.

HMS *Garth*, the destroyer in company with us, was ordered to tow us into Harwich. It took three and a half hours' toil to get the tow fixed up, while our Captain fumed and cursed; only he and the navigator knew then that we were drifting on the edge of a British minefield. Lower deck was cleared and all hands were ordered on the fo'c'sle, which enabled me to pick up my shoes on the way. The scene on the fo'c'sle was eerie. The capstan was not working, so everything had to be done by hand. The watery moon did not do much to lessen the darkness. The deck was greasy and covered with shackles of iron chain, steel hawsers, capstan bars, and the immensely thick manila towing-cable. And there must have been upwards of sixty men, including all the stokers, of whom few really knew what they were doing. The Chief Bosun's Mate was in charge, and the First Lieutenant acted as liaison between him and the Captain, watching impatiently from the bridge. The cables parted four times before we got under way, and how no-one fell overboard in the mêlée, I cannot imagine. At one moment of discouragement or laziness the Captain himself came storming down from the bridge to see what was holding us up, hauled on a rope himself, and got everyone rushing about again with new life.

At last the tow held and *Garth* took us at about three or four knots to Harwich. Dawn brought no Dorniers. Our luck held, and so did the tow, until a tug came out from Harwich to relieve *Garth*. This tug was a madman: when the tow was transferred to him, with three shackles of chain and a wire and a grass, he steamed off at about ten knots at right angles to us, to bring our head round. The tow came

Wheelhouse.

out of the water, tautened, and snapped in a second. Next time he took up the strain more cautiously, and the tow held.

It parted again later, but eventually, at about four in the afternoon, we tied up alongside. We were all out on deck, filthy, tired, and smiling. The Canteen Manager preened his moustache and gazed appreciatively at the solid grey houses and the dry land. He nudged Wiggy, who was standing beside him.

'Mm'mm – nice drop o' leave out of this with any luck, eh, Wiggy?'

Wiggy's reply was rather strained.

The Ditty Box.

9

CAPTAIN OF THE HEADS

In a destroyer, certain jobs are performed by seaman ratings, who on account of these jobs are not liable for ordinary routine work on board. The jobs include those of Ship's Writer, Ship's Postman, Tanky the Captain of the Hold (used for stowing gear of all kinds), and Captain of the Heads. The 'Heads' are the lavatories, which used to be in the heads, or bows, of wooden ships.

To be Captain of the Heads at sea was not a pleasant job, as I found out once when given a broom and bucket and told to clean them out; but when the ship went into Chatham Dockyard for repairs, the Captain of the Heads went on leave, and for some reason I was awarded the job in his absence. Since the ship was alongside a quay in the dockyard, the seamen's heads on board were liberally dosed with Izal disinfectant and locked up, and the ship's company bidden to use the dockyard heads on the quay alongside. It was of these that I now found myself in command.

They were an interesting example of Victorian naval architecture. They were laid out in streets. In the first street there were six doors; one was marked CAPTAIN, one marked COMMANDER and four marked WARDROOM. All these doors were fitted with locks and keys. The Captain's compartment had a polished oak seat, brass nails, enamelled fittings, and an ornate air hole cut in the door. The other five compartments had polished deal seats and three plain circular holes in each door.

The next street had six doors, all marked WARRANT OFFICERS. These doors had locks but no keys, unpolished deal seats, and one plain round air hole in each door.

The next street had six doors, all marked PETTY OFFICERS. These doors were of distinctly inferior quality, had bolts instead of locks, and no air holes.

Then there were three streets for the ship's company, each with a double row of cubicles, so that the occupants sat facing one another. Each cubicle had a pair of half-size swing doors which did not fasten, and non-raising seats. I had the whole village to look after, and was given a broom, a bucket, and a bottle of Izal.

Luckily, they were in fairly good condition and did not take long to clean. I made the job last the whole morning, and then found that it had to last the afternoon as well.

The next day, I was given an assistant, and after sweeping out the place we

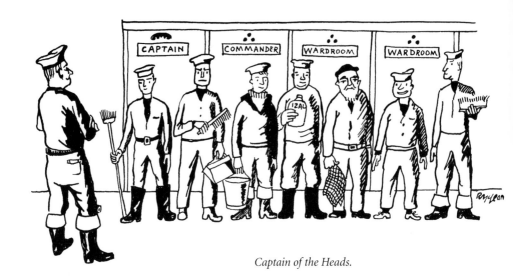

Captain of the Heads.

played cricket. The next day, because the Chief Bosun's Mate could not think up enough jobs for everybody, I got two assistants; it was then that we discovered that there was a bathhouse nearby, a beautiful warm building with hot water. I took it under my command, and we spent a happy day shaving, showering, and washing out our dirty clothes at leisure.

Finally, the Chief Bosun's Mate getting desperate, I was given seven assistants. We decided to form a syndicate, provide suitable reading matter and paper, and charge admission. Then the real Captain of the Heads returned from leave, and I was demoted. The Chief Bosun's Mate offered me a place in the care and maintenance party, which was a real favour; it was a select small band who would stay on board in some comfort and idleness, while the ship was repaired in dock and the rest of the ship's company were returned to barracks to join other ships.

However, I had now completed three months' sea-time, and found myself sent before a Selection Board and recommended for the officers' training course at *King Alfred*. But I had to have another medical test, and my defective eyesight was rediscovered. I was put in the 'Special Branch', who were not allowed to keep watch at sea, and wore a green stripe beneath the gold braid on their sleeves. I rebelled at the time, but later found it was wise. Looking through binoculars at night for hours as a watch-keeper is a great strain, and one eye, however good, is not enough.

THE MAKING OF A NAVAL OFFICER···

HMS *Windsor*.

10

FAREWELL TO THE LOWER DECK

On my first day back in Portsmouth Barracks, I came across Rupert Curtis, whom I had last seen in fireman's uniform. He was now dressed as a new entry, an extremely new Ordinary Seaman. He had leave to go ashore that night, but hearing that I was on duty in a fire-fighting party, he asked if be could join me: if there was going to be an air raid, it was better to have something to do. That was easily arranged. When, as expected, the bombs started falling, he imperceptibly but effectively took charge of our sector, because he knew so much better then the rest of us exactly what to do. Little splashes of light, like stars in the darkness, suddenly spangled the buildings all round us: the first load of incendiaries. Rupert quickly decided on the priorities for sand and stirrup-pumps, and no-one questioned him.

At last there was a lull, and the fire-watching parties flopped down, mopped their brows, and lit cigarettes. Rupert said, 'Now's the time to refill everything, and get ready for the next lot. I can't give orders round here, I'm a new boy!' Then heads began popping up from the trenches all over the parade ground, and one, close to us, wore a steel helmet bearing the three gold stripes of a Commander. Rupert ran over and said to it, I think, 'Sir, could you please give orders to these chaps to use the lull to refill all the buckets and sandbags?' And the face beneath the helmet actually replied 'Oh no, I couldn't do that, I'm only a Paymaster-Commander …'

Rupert started doing it himself, and I followed him, and gradually others joined in. So the night wore on. It was a long raid. At one point, Rupert and I were up on a roof which was burning, and to get a grip on the tiles, we took off our boots. Later, I was fascinated to find that the reason my feet were so warm was because my socks were on fire. Water cured that. By daylight, the worst fires were out, but damage was extensive, and sixteen sailors had been killed in a trench.

As many men as possible were sent home or to sea, that day. Rupert went to sea. He never rose to command a battleship, which he deserved; but three years later he commanded the two flotillas of LCI(S) (landing ships) that took Lord Lovat's No.1 Commando to the Normandy beaches; and not long after that, he was promoted to Commander, RNVR, which was quite a step from being an Ordinary Seaman.

* * *

51

When the last remaining *Windsor* men in the barracks met one night, there was a final party. We went to the theatre, got drunk, insulted some Military Policeman, chanted the name of our ship down echoing side-streets, and parted, brimming over with love for each other which we were all sure we would never, all our lives, forget. I never heard of any of them again. But whenever I think of them, I think of a drawing by Pont in *Punch* in 1939 of two oil-skinned sailors leaning against the wind; the one is saying to the other 'What's the meaning of this word "decadent", Willie?'

The next day, I went with forty others, to HMS *King Alfred*. Whatever regrets any of us had about leaving the Lower Deck, we had, as usual, none at all about leaving the Naval Barracks; and it was a blithe bus ride along the downs to Hove. The *King Alfred* appeared as a bright new building on the sea front. It had been built as a luxury hotel, and converted by the Navy before ever being used.

Within five minutes of arrival, we were paraded and issued with white bands to go round our caps, to show that we were now 'Cadet Ratings'. Then we were inspected by the Captain, a large venerable man who looked like Noah. The Captain made a brief speech on the life of new responsibilities on which we were embarking, and then called us to attention and ordered 'Off Caps'. Then he solemnly read out the Articles of War, which consisted of a large number of offences, for which the penalty in each case was death, and stalked away.

The Cadet Ratings were shaken.

The next thing that happened was the arrival of a brisk young Commander, rubbing his hands and grinning, who said, 'Well, well, well, well, cheer up! What are you all looking so glum about?' This was the Training Commander, and he outlined to us the organisation of the 'ship', and the training programme. We were then dismissed.

At dinner that evening, I compared the meal with our last supper in barracks. Twenty-four hours previously, we had been gobbling hash on a long oilcloth-covered table, on which cocoa lay in pools, and bread in tatters. Slung above our heads were the hammocks we would shortly sleep in. The supper plates were washed up on the table by the duty watch, with swearing and splashing, in a pail of tepid and greasy water, and were dried, if at all, on dish cloths of uncertain ancestry and no future.

Now, in HMS *King Alfred* how different was the picture, how elevated the tone! In a sumptuous dining hall, which had been designed as a ballroom, a company of elegant Cadet Ratings were making incredibly refined conversation across tables loaded with napery and silver. Menu cards with a genuine choice of dishes could be inspected with an off-hand air, and the order given (we could hardly believe our eyes about this) to waitresses. The tables of the Cadet Ratings were separated from those of the real officers by a thick tasselled rope, which no rating might cross; but the organisation and food on both sides were the same. And the washing-up was actually done for us. It was like stepping out of the dungeons of the Chateau D'If to become the Count of Monte Cristo. Occasionally, very occasionally, a rude word or gesture from the previous life was let slip, but the offender was instantly made aware of his faux pas by the horrified expressions of his neighbours. It was wonderful.

The fifty men composing my 'Special Branch' class were of all kinds. Besides seamen, there were signalmen and telegraphists, writers and stokers, E.R.A.s, sick berth attendants and a cook. We were of many ranks and seniorities; and we all had something wrong with us. We had done our sea-time in trawlers and torpedo boats, destroyers, sloops, cruisers, anything; and had then been discovered to have colour-blindness, or defective sight (my case), or fallen arches. One had been for twelve months coxswain of a wreck-recovery vessel; another had served three months in a battleship and then been discharged with the Commanding Officer's verdict that he would never make a seaman, but he might conceivably make an officer. (He did.)

We had a strenuous programme of work, and were under observation the whole time by the training staff, to see if we possessed the necessary officer-like qualities, known officially as 'O.L.Q.'. O.L.Q. was the keystone of the arch. However much technical knowledge a man had, it availed him nothing if he had insufficient O.L.Q., and, conversely, if he was considered to have O.L.Q., he could pass with less technical knowledge. What exactly O.L.Q. consisted of was never defined, and was made little clearer when one studied the people who were judged by the authorities to have plenty.

And so the courses continued, and finally ended, and I was among those who became officers. It was inevitable: it was duty. But I often wondered whether the wardroom would be a better place to live in than the Lower Deck had been.

O   L   Q

I thought of some lines I had recently read in Synge's Introduction to the *Play-boy of the Western World*: 'Anyone who has lived in real intimacy with the Irish peasantry will know that the wildest sayings and ideas in this play are tame indeed, compared with the fancies one may hear in any little hillside cabin in Geesala, or Carraroe, or Dingle Bay.' Fancifulness of all kinds lingers still in the Navy. Sailors are a rare combination of the superstitious dreamer and the man of action. Per-haps their strongest flow of poetry was in their swearing. It was not a Lost Art on the Lower Deck. I wished I had half the imaginative vocabulary of some of the Petty Officers who at various times had given me their Collected Words.

I had found the men in seamen's jerseys to be real; I feared that some of those in officers' shirts might be stuffed.

Honouring those who remained, inclined to blame myself for leaving them, it was with deep regrets that I eventually took my commission and said FAREWELL TO THE LOWER DECK.

Part 2

SUBMARINER

11

SECRET BOOKS

Towards the end of the course at the *King Alfred*, we began wondering what sort of jobs we would get. The top cadet, they said, would be joining the staff of the Admiral commanding Iceland. Most of the rest of us would become training officers at New Intake Establishments. 'Special Branch' officers (like me) did not go to sea, they said.

I could not believe this. It was like telling a small boy in an orchard that all the apples were reserved for the farmer's family. Surely I could have *one*?

Eventually I heard, quite accidentally, that Liaison Officers in allied submarines did not keep watch, and could be in the Special Branch. Two of us applied, and when we passed out, neither top nor bottom, we got this job, a perfectly good sea-going appointment.

We were immediately sent to HMS *Dolphin*, at Fort Blockhouse, the senior submarine establishment in the Royal Navy, to attend a shortened submarine officers' course.

Fort Blockhouse was known, we found, to be the most expensive mess in the service; but it was an experience to be there. A Royal Marine Band played up and down outside our cabin windows between 0800 and 0830, we fed like princes, and I had a Royal Marine servant who was prepared to wash out my underclothes (but not starch my white collars).

We studied complicated diagrams of High Pressure and Low Pressure Air Lines, rushed through the principles of the Trim, took one look at the Angle of Attack, and went down to the swimming baths to try the Davis Submarine Escape Apparatus. After splashing about on the bottom, and finding that we could really breathe under water, we progressed to the Tank. In this, you are locked into a small chamber on the ground floor, and put on your D.S.E.A. (Davis Submarine Escape Apparatus). The chamber is then flooded, just like a sunken submarine. The water creeps up round your neck, over your face, and then, when the water pressure inside equals that outside, you unclip the escape hatch and float up to the surface forty feet above.

When you reach the surface, there is a strong temptation to tear the mask off your face and breathe deep gulps of fresh air. If you do that, you sink, as you are weighted down by the steel bottles of compressed air and oxygen on your back.

The correct drill is to turn the tap off which feeds oxygen into your mask, and open another tap which inflates a life-jacket. When that is full you turn everything off and can then remove your mask in safety. My brother Liaison Officer and I reached the surface together. He immediately ripped the mask off his face, and began sinking. I turned off the one tap and turned on the other, but forgot to turn it off again, so that my life-jacket inflated till it burst; and I, too began to sink. Two patient instructors at the top of the tank leaned over and grabbed their pupils by the hair before they drowned.

That completed our course, which had lasted four weeks. I then had a daydream, which consisted of a drama enacted in the control room of an allied submarine lying on the bottom of the North Sea, close to the German coast. The allied officers and crew had all collapsed from lack of oxygen. Weak, but determined, I took command and, knowing which knobs to turn, brought her back unscathed – carrying out a successful attack on the *Scharnhorst* on the way. The day-dream was interrupted by a signal which appointed me as British Naval Liaison Officer to the Free French Submarine *Rubis*, at Dundee, and told me to go up there, quick.

So I got up to Dundee, quick – and had to wait. The *Rubis* was away at sea.

I was allotted a bed in what had previously been the Dundee Orphanage, but was now a home for naval officers. I found that I had a Wren, not a Marine, to look after me: she was called Minnie, and she brought me tea in the morning, which my Marine never did.

To fill in time, I decided to give myself a course in Electricity and Wireless. I found a Naval Wireless/Telegraphy handbook, and opened it. Early on, I found the following:

For a toroidal coil, *i.e.*, a coil wound on an iron anchor ring, the formula for an iron-cored solenoid, viz.,

$$L = \frac{4\pi N^2 \mu A}{l} \times 10^{-9} \text{ henry}$$

is very nearly correct, if the cross-section of the ring is circular, and small in dimensions compared with the length of the ring.

It was 'henry' that got me – and finished my attempts to learn about electricity. The telephone rang. I seized it. 'The *Rubis* is just coming up the river now. She'll be alongside in ten minutes. Are you ready?'

I slid out of my chair. By the time I had run down to the dock, she had rounded a bend in the river and was in view. She was small, but she had abnormally wide saddle tanks, because she carried sixteen mines down each side. She had an unusually large conning tower, because, being French, it contained a cooking galley below the bridge. She was flying the tricolour. She was the Free French submarine *Rubis*. We had not previously met.

The *Rubis* had a flat wooden deck (which no British submarine had) on which the seamen were getting ready to heave lines ashore. Running about between their feet I could see a black and white mongrel dog with short legs and a long tail, whose name, I already knew, was Bacchus, and who, I later heard, had been born in a submarine.

When the submarine was secured alongside, a plank was put across and the Captain came down it first, followed closely, at a gallop, by Bacchus, who was greeted by cries and whistles from the French spare crew on the jetty.

The Captain was a tall dark-haired young man called Henri Rousselot. I was introduced to him and to Bacchus, but they both had other more important things to do at that moment than attend to their new and very junior Liaison Officer; so I looked around for the man I was relieving.

He was, like me, a Sub-Lieutenant RNVR – and an already trained, watchkeeping submarine officer. When I first saw him, he was climbing out of the conning-tower, carrying a roll of charts and a large piano-accordion. When he found out who I was, he welcomed me like a long-lost brother – he had a very charming smile – and handed me the charts. He congratulated me on taking over his job which, he said, consisted mostly of sleeping and consuming excellent French cooking and wine. He would, he said, have loved to tell me more about my duties, but as soon as he had had a bath he would have to rush off on leave. I, being a completely new Sub-Lieutenant, and, as I had frequently been told, the lowest form of marine life found under flat stones at low tide, did not dare to contradict him. But the Staff Commander came up at this moment and reminded him that he had all the Secret Books to hand over to me. Could the said Books be mustered in his Office at 0900 the next morning? We agreed they could.

Sub-Lieutenant Christopher and I spent the evening together, chiefly in the bar of the North British Hotel, and I laughed more during that evening than I had done for a very long time. But, at the end of it, I knew little more about this man than I had done at the beginning. He was dark and handsome and one of the most vital people I have ever met. His white collar was filthy, his tie ragged, and he slouched: all deliberately, to annoy senior naval officers. It was from others that I learned he had been a journalist, had taken part in the Spanish Civil War, had been a pacifist, and wrote poetry. After being a pacifist, he joined the Navy as an Ordinary Seaman, and had been awarded the DSM (Distinguished Service Medal) while serving in a trawler in the Norwegian campaign. Then he had volunteered for submarines, had done the Submarine Officer's Training Course, and was now hoping to be appointed to a British boat. All I learned from him was that he was an extremely good raconteur and took nothing naval very seriously. We laughed the whole evening, particularly about the coming muster. Christopher assured me that musters of Secret Books were always a complete farce.

In this spirit, and despite severe hangovers, we approached the C.B. (Confidential Books) Office next morning. We were early, and Christopher, hoping to impress the Wrens, Pat and Marjory, entered the room on his hands and knees. But the Commander had also arrived early and was watching him, no less attentively than the Wrens, from his desk at the far end of the room. Christopher, more than anyone I have ever known, had *sang froid*. His transformation from a clown into a naval officer looking for something on the floor was instantaneous.

The seriousness with which I myself was ready to approach the Secret Books was thus undermined from the start. It received a second blow a minute later, when I picked up a volume of Admiralty Instructions on Security and found it was illustrated by the *Punch* humorous artist Fougasse.

The muster began. The room in which it took place had started life as a Victorian drawing-room and ran, long and narrow, down to a bow window which overlooked the River Tay and the docks. In the bow window, glowering like an irate Victorian parent, sat the Commander. I did not realise it then, but he hated and feared Secret Books. He knew that, sooner or later, a Secret Book would be lost and it would be his responsibility. With people like Christopher and myself handling them, he now knew it would be sooner rather than later.

On one wall of his office was an enormous Victorian mirror with a heavy gold frame, over a black carrara marble mantel-shelf, on which stood the Secret Book Orders and the tea-caddy. On the other wall were the principal key charts and a list of trains to Edinburgh. The middle of the room contained a long trestle table and Pat and Marjory. At our end of the room was a big plywood cupboard in which the Secret Books were locked up when the submarines were in harbour.

The muster was conducted as follows. In the cupboard was a large pile of books and documents which it had been, till now, Christopher's privilege to take care of, and opportunity to study, during the long weeks he had been at sea in the *Rubis*. (Naturally he had not opened one of them, except *Jane's Fighting Ships*, under a misapprehension about the identity of Jane.) In my hands was a long list of the books I was supposed to take over. They were identified not by names, which would have been easy, but by letters and numbers, like motor cars. I cleared my throat and called out a number. Christopher, making sure that the Wrens were looking, dived into the cupboard, pulled out an armful of books, and began shuffling them like an intoxicated conjuror, until he noticed that the Commander was coming up to the boil. He then called out 'here' and, with luck, produced the required book and put it on the table. I then put a tick against it on my list. The performance would then be repeated. At one point I got confused with the list and asked Christopher: 'Are these your ticks or my ticks?' 'Stop talking about your ticks' hissed Christopher with a fastidious leer, and dropped six books on to the floor by way of a change.

Christopher was very conscientious. He never repeated any item in his performance, and being very inventive, and an experienced entertainer, he kept it up till almost lunch time. In the ring with him, I watched spellbound. I was told that several officers came into the office during the morning on business and stayed an hour or so just to watch us. I never noticed them. A Wren officer who watched some of the performance saw in it an idea for a Christmas pantomime, 'The Babes in the Wood', with Christopher and myself as the babes, Pat and Marjory as the little birds, the Commander as the wicked uncle and herself as the Fairy Queen.

But at last it was all over. The list was covered with ticks, the books were covered with ticks, and Christopher swore he had my ticks inside his shirt. The list and muster were signed by myself and countersigned by the Commander. The books were all locked up again in the cupboard, like toys at bed-time, and Christopher and I strolled off to the bar, conscious of the admiring glances of Pat and Marjory, who had been prevented from doing a stroke of work all morning.

Christopher then went off on leave and was subsequently posted to a Dutch submarine.

The *Rubis* prepared to go to sea. Two days before we were due to sail, the Commander said casually to me 'You do understand your PQ444, don't you?' I gaped at him. 'My what, Sir?' I seemed to remember having heard that number before somewhere, but couldn't really place it. I pondered quickly. Then a cold feeling hit me in the pit of the stomach.

PQ444 was, at that moment, the most secret and confidential thing in the whole war. It was a signal detailing the emergency procedure to be adopted if the Naval Codes and Ciphers were compromised, to be used until new codes could be issued. It was so secret that it was not even supposed to be on paper. Just because it was so secret, it had been omitted from the list of Secret Books and Signals I had taken over from Christopher. But there was – or had been – a copy of that signal addressed to the British Naval Liaison Officer in *Rubis*.

It was so secret, and so rarely even mentioned (even by Admirals under their breaths) that we had all completely forgotten about it.

There was a chilly silence in the C.B. Room. Then the Commander swallowed hard and gave me three hours in which to find it. If it were still lost at the end of that time, he said, the Admiralty would have to be informed, the war would stop until it was found, and Christopher and I would be court-martialled and probably, he hinted, flogged round the fleet.

What I was looking for was a small piece of pink paper measuring about eight inches by six.

Christopher was, by then, well out into the Atlantic; I could not telephone him. I searched and searched. I had all my books out of the C.B. cupboard and all everybody else's. We had the C.B. cupboard out from the wall, and looked behind it. I searched what had been Christopher's cabin in the Officer's Hostel, and then went down to the submarine. I would have to search her, but I could not say what I was looking for; our allies were not supposed to know of PQ444's existence.

Rousselot, unaware of my quandary, was in his cabin. He was tidying it up preparatory to the next trip. There were two drawers underneath his bunk. 'Here,' he said, 'Christopher always used this drawer; you can have it too.' He pulled out a crumpled oilskin jacket and threw it on the deck. I picked it up and went through its pockets. The first contained chewing gum. The second contained two original typewritten poems by Christopher, a rubber contraceptive, and PQ444, on which the French officers off-watch had been playing noughts and crosses.

It would have been an interesting court-martial.

Christopher was eventually posted to a British boat, HMS P38; on patrol with her, he once left the bridge and went down onto the deck to help someone, and was washed overboard by a heavy sea and drowned, on 17 November 1941.

The Captain's cabin in Rubis.

12

ALL EXPERIENCE

We sailed two days later: but only as far as the mouth of the Tay, to make a film. The film was intended to help airmen to distinguish submarines from battleships, fishing-boats or whales – all of which look pretty much alike from a few hundred feet up, and all of which used to get bombed frequently by mistake.

Every morning for a week we ran out and sailed up and down the coast, diving and surfacing, while a Fleet Air Arm Swordfish filmed us from all angles and heights. It was good training for the crew and new Commanding Officer, and as for me, I had no work to do at all. I liked life in submarines.

When we were submerged, I lay on the Captain's bunk (by permission; I was more out of the way there) reading. One day I became aware of a slight commotion in the control room. Voices were raised. Rapid orders were given. When it was over I asked what had happened. We had dived with the diesel engine Air Trunk hatch open. This was a small hatch in the engine room used to supply air to the diesel engines when the main conning-tower hatch was shut. The error had been noticed instantaneously, before we had more than dipped below the surface; and the First Lieutenant had brought the boat back to the surface immediately. But in those seconds more than four tons of sea-water had poured into the engine-room. The book I happened to be reading at that precise moment was *Blow Main Ballast*: the account of the disaster to the U.S. Submarine *Squalus* in 1939, which was lost through exactly the same mistake.

At the enquiry, it was decided that no blame could be attached to anyone, but that it was due to the incalculable one-in-a-million human element; the men had been changing watch, and no-one could say exactly who had reported or failed to report the open hatch, whose state was clearly indicated on a panel of lights in the control-room.

I soon realised that I had been very lucky in being posted to *Rubis*. Of all the allied submarines in Dundee she had the best chef, and there was vin rouge every day; not as a luxury, but as a normal French ration. I do not know where it came from, or what genius of a victualling officer managed to secure a constant supply of it, but I do know that although we sometimes sailed without mines, we never sailed without vin rouge.

Only four officers could sit down to dine together in the tiny wardroom and we were six, so we ate in relays. During the week of filming we ate particularly well, because we had fresh provisions every day. I quite often ate alone with the Captain. Lieutenant de Vaisseau Henri Rousselot was then twenty-nine, tall, dark-haired, red-complexioned, with an aquiline nose, penetrating brown eyes and red lips. He was the son of a Judge in the Haute Savoie. He had already served six years in the *Rubis*, much longer than British Officers usually stay in one submarine: so he knew his ship down to her last rivet. He had been First Lieutenant when she came over from France; the Commanding Officer had been Capitaine de Corvette Cabanier, whom I had already heard spoken of as one of the best submarine officers in the British and French Navies, but his eyesight had begun to deteriorate, and Rousselot had just been promoted to his place.

Rousselot was a man of quick intuition. He nearly always knew what other people were getting at before they expressed it – whether they were dockyard officials, British officers, or his own men – because he looked for their motives of self-interest, and that was generally the key to the situation. I soon had a comfortable conviction that if we were ever hunted by a German destroyer, he would always be two jumps ahead and bring us clear.

The other French officers were Dubuisson, the First Lieutenant, a stocky man from the coast of Normandy; Brunet, the third hand, a fair-haired Parisian, destined for the diplomatic service, who spoke English with a faultless Oxford accent; and Hémar and Olry, the two junior officers, more or less my age. The former was broad-shouldered and tough, the latter was slight in build, and previously a cadet in the French Merchant Marine. Besides the officers, there were about forty French sailors and Bacchus the dog; and two English ratings, a Leading Signalman and a Leading Telegraphist. The Signalman, Tim Casey, had entered the Navy as a boy in 1919; then he had gone into submarines, served his time, left the Navy as a pensioner, and become a postman. When he was recalled in 1939 he had volunteered for submarines again, at the age of forty, because it was the life he knew. He had a rubicund face, and pale blue eyes, which seemed to have faded through much looking into the sun. He was idolised by the French crew, who regarded him almost as much their mascot as Bacchus: he often wore a French sailor's red pom-pom hat, and when more and more of the French sailors married Scots girls, it was said that soon he would be the only Frenchman left on board.

The telegraphist, Jimmy Green, was a much younger man, also popular with the Frenchmen.

My bed was the wardroom seat; but Casey and Green had no such comfort. A part of the control-room, behind the ladder up to the kiosk[*], had been designated

---

[*] The 'kiosk' was a compartment, not usually found in British submarines, above the control room and below the bridge, from which the periscopes could be used.

as 'Englishmen's Corner' and here they could curl up on a straw-filled palliasse. At least once every patrol they had to pick up their beds, and everything else they possessed, and move out quick, for they lay just below the mine-laying control panel.

My inexperience in everything that mattered was underlined as I gradually got to know Hémar and Olry. Hémar, for example, said to me the first time we met: 'McLean, savez-vous baiser?' My French being conventional, I thought he meant did I know how to kiss. He actually meant did I know how to make love. When I replied 'Er, yes, I suppose so,' we found ourselves at cross-purposes in several ensuing conversations.

He had just married an English girl; he was able to bring to her some ten years of vigorous pre-marital experience.

Having been brought up in Oxford, instead of Paris, I had virtually none. Just before the war, I had met a charming girl with large eyes and brown hair whose ignorance on these matters was even greater than mine: she also had a sense of humour and a small Fiat. It had seemed that we were about to hack out some basic information for each other, when a change of job moved me away, and her education was taken over by an R.A.F. officer, whom she married. Then there had been a girl in Brighton, but she refused to pass on what she knew unless I installed her in a flat. I suspected the information to be over-valued. There was another girl in Brighton who made no such demands: but one evening – having been tucked up on the sofa with her by her mother – before I could find out what she knew, her father came downstairs – there was an air raid in progress – and I found out that what he didn't know included my presence in his house.

Soon after I arrived in Dundee, as a brand-new Sub-Lieutenant, I found myself at a cocktail party, talking to a flaxen-haired, pink-cheeked young Wren with innocent looking blue eyes. When she told me that she had joined the Service only the day before, I gallantly offered to show her the ropes – to take her, if she liked, under my fin. She thanked me prettily and said 'Come and meet Daddy' – who turned out to be our host, a four-ring Captain and Naval-Officer-in-Charge, Dundee.

After avoiding her and her father for some days, I went to a dance hall, and made several circuits with a plump girl in green; I found that when I talked to her she put on a very dull expression, so that I could not tell if she had heard or understood. Later, she told me that she had developed this expression to cope with the bus drivers – she was a conductress – when they were telling black-out stories. She told me that they called her 'Dropsy' because she was always dropping things, including herself off a bus, by stepping off the wrong way, when the bus was going slowly. When I saw her home and asked if I would be shot at dawn if I went in with her, she replied, (I thought a trifle regretfully) 'sooner than that – right away'. My education was not being allowed to progress very fast.

I had been very fond of a girl at home, had proposed marriage to her before coming up to Dundee, and had been turned down. She had given me, as a sort of souvenir, a pair of socks. True, she had knitted them for me herself; but she was not a good knitter and they were now worn out. One of my favourite poems at that time was the Wandering Knight's song: (by John Gibson Lockhart, 1794–1854)

> *My ornaments are arms,*
> *My pastime is in war,*
> *My bed is cold upon the wold*
> *My lamp yon star:*
>
> *My journeyings are long,*
> *My slumbers short and broken;*
> *From hill to hill I wander still,*
> *Kissing thy token.*

Kissing the socks was not on, and as they were worn out, I now had no token to take to sea – whenever that might be.

Still, there was some consolation in not being in love; it gave one more time for reading. And although I imagined I was due for a period of discomfort soon, at the moment I was living a life of luxury and ease. I doubted if life was ever again going to offer me gin at twopence, practically no work or responsibility, and Wrens as servants whenever I rang the bell. (After that year, it didn't.) But my sea-time in a destroyer had taught me to appreciate whatever interludes of softness life might occasionally offer.

And this life had its moments. For example, the day before, the *Rubis* had been moved from one dock to another by a tug. An English sailor in the tug had produced a monkey out of his coat, which had caused great interest among the Frenchmen. 'Ha! 'E is *exactly* like you' said a French sailor seriously to the Englishman holding the monkey.

In the wardroom at Mayfield, I was slowly learning how to behave like a Naval Officer. There was a Mess Guest Night, at which I was hammered by the Mess President for producing a note-book at table. I was sitting next to a charming Wren Officer, and was making a date. The Mess President, being a kind man, fined Sub-Lieutenant McLean the second round of Port, knowing that there was only enough Port to go round once.

Later in the evening, when the ladies had left us, a free-for-all developed on the floor, in which one of the more human Commanders had his shirt ripped completely off his back, leaving his collar and tie round his neck, looking curiously surrealist.

I had another lesson when I suggested, in the Mess Suggestions Book, that the Wardroom should subscribe to *Vogue*. 'But it has no politics, or war pictures in it at all!' spluttered one of the Commanders, and they began to look at me sideways and suspect that I was odd, if not queer, and below par mentally.

Another and more memorable day was when a stranger appeared in the wardroom, wearing the khaki uniform of a Captain, Royal Marines. I asked someone who he was, and was told, vaguely, that they didn't know, but he had a German-sounding name.

That evening I found myself having coffee with him, and we fell into conversation. Suddenly, as sometimes happens, the conversation accelerated. We discovered that we had lots of things, and people, in common. I had to ask him his name. When he replied 'Ravilious', I nearly fell out of my chair; it was a name I revered, I possessed several of the books he had illustrated. Eric Ravilious, now a war artist, had come to draw the Walrus flying-boats then training on the Tay. He took me up to his room to show me all the paintings he had with him, and invited me to come as his guest to a Double Crown Club dinner in London.

We never met again; he was lost in a Hudson aircraft off Iceland a few weeks later. It had been, perhaps for both of us, a nostalgic sort of interlude.

Being an officer, I had to get used to being saluted in the street. I found it difficult, not only to acknowledge, but also to obtain, salutes from Wren ratings, especially Pat and Marjory. It's not me, I complained, it's the *uniform* you are supposed to salute, after I received a leer and a grin instead of the smart jerk they practised during their weekly drills.

And that reminded me. When I became an officer, I had to buy two new uniforms. I thought I would wear the second-best one at sea. But I now discovered that no one ever wore good clothes at sea in a submarine.

Submarine officers usually wore white jerseys and grey flannel trousers, with perhaps a very old reefer jacket stiff with grease and oil, when their top halves had to be seen on the bridge.

So I went into the town and found a little tailor who supplied uniforms for the merchant navy. I explained what I wanted, and he turned round and ferreted on the floor among a pile of rags and cuttings, and pulled up an ancient merchant navy reefer. It fitted me perfectly; he sewed on the right buttons and braid; and charged me fifteen shillings. I loved that coat dearly. It looked very experienced, and even before I took it on board it had the right smell.

The longer we were kept waiting, the more I found myself actually looking forward to my first patrol in a submarine. It was partly curiosity. It was mostly my rising mess bill.

Rubis' wardroom looking aft.

Opposite: Rubis' wardroom.

If you pull the ring beneath the cushion on which the First Lieutenant is sitting, out comes the coffer containing the officer's Ready Use Liquor Store. The post on which the table is supported is also a cupboard, holding our vin rouge.

The First Lieutenant is wearing a jersey he got in the Faroes, and airman's flying boots.

The seat on which he sits holds about two people, i.e. is about three-and-a-half to four feet long. The seat longways is my bed. By opening the Secret Books cupboard at right-hand side I get my feet in and get a full stretch.

The drawing was made from the doorway of the Captain's cabin, looking across the two-foot passage or corridor which runs the length of the boat.

wardroom

13

WAITING FOR IT

I was sitting at a green baize-topped table, making a new operational chart.

I had collected my pen, coloured inks and ruler from the C.B. Office, the secret QZ messages and a scowl from the Commander and some chocolate from my cabin. I proceeded to spread myself out in the downstairs ante-room, in front of an open window. It was a glorious summer's day outside, with a westerly breeze. Fleecy white clouds hung in the blue above; below, the river Tay lay shining between dockyard sheds. The air was full of a brisk hammering from riveters, a creaking of cranes and a clanking of railway trucks. From time to time a cloud of smoke or steam drifted across the window. Then, above the corrugated iron roofs I saw a hawk, motionless. There was a patch of grass between the Orphanage, in which we lived, and the Dockyard wall, which it must have been scanning for a mouse. I could check the hawk's position against the telegraph wires; it hung absolutely steady in a twenty-mile-an-hour wind. At last, it fell away and disappeared.

I lowered my eyes to my chart.

It showed the coast of England and Scotland on one side, and the long coast-line of Norway, Germany, Holland, Belgium and France on the other. A large expanse of innocuous-looking white paper in between represented the North Sea. It had been inscribed by me with notes and shadings in red and green ink to show minefields, our own or the enemy's. Some had been laid by the *Rubis*. A large strip shaded in black down the entire enemy coastline, and a similar one down ours, were the declared minefields. Our own, at certain positions, were marked 'Gap A', 'Gap B', and so on. The whole area looked too uninviting for words.

We did not know when we were sailing. Perhaps Captain (S) knew, and perhaps half the dockyard and town of Dundee knew – they usually did – but Rousselot and I did not know; all we knew was that we were still at twelve hours' notice, and had been, for a week. Suddenly the telephone rang.

I detected the voice of Marjory in the C.B. Office. 'Is Sub-Lieutenant McLean there?' 'Yes.' 'Will he come up to the O.B. Office now, we have something for him.' 'Rather,' I said, mystified, 'is it nice?' A smile floated down the line and I hung up. I gathered my charts (the Commander had stamped his foot in rage when I had left them unattended on a table the previous day) and went upstairs. The two Wrens, Pat and Marjory, were alone in their office and had a cup of coffee for me. It was strictly forbidden for anyone to enter the C.B. Office except on business; so I garaged my coffee behind a typewriter and held a copy of *Submarine War Memoranda* in my hand as an alibi.

Pat and Marjory hinted that I might, that evening, like to help them put in their pea-sticks, or even do some weeding for them, in their garden up at Mayfield. I regretfully explained to them that I was not to be trusted at weeding, as I didn't know which were weeds and which were flowers. Pat said the flowers and vegetables were planted in rows, and anything not in rows was a weed. I countered this by saying that I ... 'couldn't always see straight,' said Pat, taking the words out of my mouth.

However, I said, if they were so keen to teach me about nature, would they like to come for a picnic on the following Sunday. Two French officers had said that if I could provide girls, they would provide cooked chickens and wine.

At this point, the Commander scowled back into the office. Two fair heads bowed over typewriters and one junior officer thumbed through *Submarine War Memoranda*; then, catching the eyes of both the Commander and the Wrens simultaneously, he went hastily out; but plans for the picnic went forward.

On Saturday, one of the French officers fell sick, and on Sunday, the other; and, needless to say, no preparations had been made for chickens or anything else. But the day was fine. Pat and Marjory provided sandwiches and I provided Joseph Anchykowski, an extremely charming Lieutenant from the *Wilk*, the Polish submarine that had escaped from the Baltic, with the *Orzel*, without either charts or weapons.

We took a tram to Dundee's outskirts and walked until we found a wood on top of a hill on the edge of the Sidlaws, with a pleasant view. Here we parked ourselves and lay dozing in the sun, recovering from the effort of the hour's walk. Suddenly a harsh voice caused me to open my eyes: 'What are you doing here? You know perfectly well this is private property! Be off with you! Get out of it!' A stout gamekeeper with a telescope slung over his shoulder, and a dog, stood frowning at us. I got up and pleaded that we did not know it was private property, as there was no notice, and that we weren't doing any harm, and that we were naval officers (we were all in civilian clothes). At this, he showed some interest, and said 'Well, I'll report ye to Commander Studholme!' This shook me, but I thought I noticed a dim twinkle in his eye. It turned out that, of all the countryside round Dundee, we had chosen to picnic on the land regularly shot over by our senior officers. While the dog accepted a sandwich, the gamekeeper and I chatted about Commander Studholme, of whom, I gradually suspected, he was as terrified as I was. Then Pat said 'Did you know my grandfather, who owned the farm over the hill?' and the gamekeeper said 'Aye, but I knew Mr Whitton better' – and that was Pat's father. So we had a long exchange of family histories; and Josef said afterwards that he was on the point of asking the gamekeeper if he knew *his* father.

The gamekeeper and his dog stamped off, and we continued our picnic in peace.

14

A SUBMARINE SAILS

At last, in August 1941, we got our sailing orders. We were to lay mines off Stavanger, Norway. The day before sailing, I took a taxi down to the harbour, with my rucksack full of chocolate for the crew, two folios of charts, a pair of sea-boot stockings, three bags of assorted Confidential Books and novels, and an enamelled basin – not in case of rough weather, but because the Captain had asked me to procure one for the cook to wash lettuce in.

When I arrived at the jetty, everyone was in high spirits. A submarine embarking stores for patrol, and particularly a French submarine, is a sight worth seeing. The deck casing was piled high with buckets, mess tins, china dishes, loose cauliflowers and cabbages, baskets of tomatoes, sacks of potatoes, boxes of Verey lights, ammunition for the rifles, the machine guns and the .75 cannon, and a large barrel containing five hundred salted herring. Then there was the bread, which the baker had just delivered to the jetty in wooden trays. It was special 'submarine bread' supposed to remain eatable even at the end of three weeks. (This lot did but the next lot didn't.) A seagull swooped, but made off again, considerably shaken by the torrent of French abuse which greeted it. A chain of French sailors in blue-and-white striped vests were manhandling heavy boxes of tinned food down the steep and narrow plank from the jetty. It was low tide, and the plank was nearly vertical.

Up on the jetty, still to go down, were three crates of barley water, lime and orange juice, six crates of beer, a dozen mattresses and blankets, twenty bottles of H.P. sauce, which the Frenchmen, to my surprise, loved, several boxes of tinned soup, some Davis Escape sets in airtight cases, six jars of distilled water, two drums of oil, and a bevy of pretty girls labelled 'submarine comforts'. (At least, Creton the chef swore he had seen these, and the others hoped he was right.)

Also on the jetty, among the stores, stood Rousselot and Dubuisson, the First Lieutenant. They were making a last check of points with the British Engineer Officer of the base who had been responsible for the boat's overhaul since her last patrol. The submarine was French-built, but now, nearly two years after they had left France, they were having to accept a good deal of British-made equipment, of which they were naturally and deeply suspicious.

The *Rubis* had already used up all the French mines obtainable. She had just been converted to carry British mines, and this was the first patrol on which they would be used. At this moment, every single one of them, having been carefully put in, was being hoisted out again. The Admiralty had, at the last minute, ordered an additional adjustment to be made. The Captain thought the British mines were no good anyway, and said so.

Someone sat in some wet paint. Bacchus, the ship's dog, was chasing the harbour-master's cat. Seamen stared down from the stern rail of a steamer in the berth ahead and spat. Soldiers of the dockyard guard stood by and thought it was better than Ensa. Indeed, with the normal fairground noises of a dockyard in full swing all round, the scene of active confusion closely resembled an amateur dramatic society rehearsing a pantomime.

The ship's stores were not the only things to be thought about. Each man had his own personal preparations to make. Most of them wanted to get their hair cut on the last day to prevent its getting too shaggy and dirty after prolonged lack of attention. They had to collect sufficient literature: to run out of reading matter at sea is almost as bad as running out of food. Then, there were the odd, important things that each man took according to his idiosyncrasies: spare toothbrushes (keeping one's mouth fresh is more important, and easier, than washing) and pencils, and meat cubes, and scarves, balaclavas, gloves. And pieces of wood to carve, and mouth organs, and string and, of course, the lucky charm from one's best girl, not to mention her photograph to pin up.

Next day we were, in the official phrase, 'prepared for sea, and in all respects ready for war'. We were due to sail at 1900. In the afternoon I had my last briefing from the Staff Officers; my job, as British Naval Liaison Officer, included responsibility for all charts and information that the Captain might need for the operation.

I did my final packing, had tea in the wardroom, and tried to look nonchalant. At about 1800 I went down to the boat.

At 1940, we sailed before a full house: all the brass hats of the base were there, all the French officers and sailors from the *Minerve*, which had come in from patrol two days previously, and the British sailor friends of Casey and Green. Ribald cries in two languages flashed backwards and forwards between jetty and boat.

The Captain, who had been having a last word with Captain (S) stepped aboard. He looked round to see that all was ready, and gave the signal to hoist away the plank and cast off.

Silently, on her motors, the submarine nosed out into the Tay and made for the open sea. The men on the jetty saluted. On the submarine's bridge we gave a last wave, and settled down to sea routine.

'Supper is ready.' Those not on watch went below.

15

ON PASSAGE

At supper, the French officers were in excellent form, all talking hard and at the same time. Rousselot, Dubuisson and Hémar, with wives in Dundee, were used to going to sea and leaving women behind. Brunet and Olry lived in the officers' hostel, and were in high spirits at getting away from it. The only people they would miss were the Wren stewards. For everyone there was the novelty of a new Commanding Officer, a new First Lieutenant and a new British Liaison Officer. For Rousselot and Dubuisson there was the spur of their new responsibilities; and for me, the prospects of my first time to sea as an officer, my first patrol in a submarine, and my first real hope of learning to speak French without an Oxford accent.

Conversation that evening consisted chiefly of agreeing how dreadful the hostel was and how pitifully ignorant the English were of everything worth knowing, for example cooking potatoes, and how good the *Rubis'* cook was at preparing salad. (The cook's name was Gaston and he had liquid, pathetic eyes that went down particularly well with the women of Dundee: he was currently sleeping with both a mother and her daughter.)

The *Rubis'* wardroom, which was to be my home for some time to come, was minute, but possibly more homely than many English submarine wardrooms I had been in. It contained almost as many objects as a furnished sitting-room I had once had in Bradford, but they were mostly knobs, wheels and taps. At the back of the wardroom seat there was mahogany panelling, along the top of which ran a narrow shelf containing the usual wardroom debris: books, magazines, noughts-and-crosses pads, secret signals, cipher books, a tin of Oxo cubes and a naval cap. Above the shelf ran a continuous network of pipes, painted tastefully in eau-de-nil. For pure decoration there was an empty rehoboam of cognac, relic of some heroic party, and on one wall a small framed painting of an earlier *Rubis*, a three-masted vessel which, Rousselot explained to me apologetically, had fought and captured three English ships in the seventeenth century.

After supper I went up on the bridge for my last fresh air. We were diving at dawn. The east coast of Scotland – Arbroath, Kirriemuir, Montrose – lay somewhere, invisible, a few miles off to port. Our route took us north to the latitude of the Shetlands, where we would turn north-east for Norway, come round the top of the German-declared minefields and sail down inside them to Stavanger, where we were to lay some new minefields of our own. Then back the same way. We expected to be away about twenty days.

When I came below again to turn in, I found to my surprise that a bed had been made for me on the wardroom seat, complete with sheets and a pillow. Somehow I had not expected this, but had thought I would just be curling up in my duffel coat. I was alone in the wardroom, for the other officers all slept in two-berth cabins, except the Captain, who had a cabin to himself across the passage from the wardroom. In most English submarines at that time officers slept in let-down bunks in the wardroom.

I unlocked the Confidential Book cupboard at the end of the wardroom seat, inserted my feet, stretched out, and was very quickly asleep.

The voyage on passage was uneventful. It was summer, so the dives (they had to be in daylight) were long: we were generally submerged for about sixteen hours. At the end of this time, air in the submarine would be getting short, and we would be panting: but the *Rubis* had already executed successfully a thirty-six-hour dive, when they had gone to lay their mines eighteen miles up a Norwegian fjord. It was the limit of prudent endurance. Half the crew had been sick on surfacing.

We ate well, but progressively less well as fresh provisions were exhausted. We had red wine – *pinard* – on the table for every meal, and usually rum or brandy with our coffee at night.

My bed was made up each evening after dinner, and I turned in about midnight. At about 0500, when we dived, the captain came down from the bridge and had a cup of coffee beside my head, and made some toast on the electric toaster plugged into the light. A Frenchman drinking coffee and eating toast is not inaudible and, anyway, Rousselot never had any false modesty about waking me; he knew I had nothing else to do but sleep. He never did any tip-toeing. I woke and exchanged the time of day with him and heard about what was happening on top. Then he turned in to sleep and there was peace in the wardroom until the watch changed and the in-coming and out-going officers had their cups of coffee.

My only job was to decipher any wireless signals that came through at routine hours during the night, and make sure that they were comprehensible to the Captain. As he was an extremely intelligent and experienced naval officer and understood everything a great deal better than I did, there was no difficulty about that.

My chief obligation was to make myself an acceptable member of the Frenchmen's wardroom. I was a bit worried about this, since I had no piano-accordion, like my predecessor, could not sing or conjure, and had had practically no experience in any of the things that interested them most. My stock, I felt, was in the balance, when, one day, in pursuance of my self-appointed duty as comforts officer, I produced some French literature. This had come from one of my mother's sisters, a spinster aunt of well-maintained virtue and reliable generosity, who lived in New York, to whom I had written some time previously telling her of my new appointment and asking for any American magazines she might care to collect for me. In quick response had arrived four copies of *Life* and six French paper-backs with unfamiliar titles. I had put them into my bag of books and forgotten about them. When I found them, I laid them out on the wardroom table. Then the Captain came in. He picked up the top one idly, looked at its title, and immediately showed interest. He examined the rest with increasing eagerness. My aunt had, it appeared, sent me six celebrated erotic novels. What was more, Rousselot claimed he could smell perfume on them. Whether he believed in my aunt or not, my stock definitely rose from that moment. And where my aunt had acquired the books I never dared to ask.

So the days passed. We played mah-jong, we played noughts-and-crosses, we played a French version called 'morpions' ('crabs') in which you have to get five in a row, and we played chess. When we were still two days away from our patrol area, we got a signal from the Admiralty saying that we might meet two 4,000-ton ships, names supplied, and that if we did, we were to attack them. The day before we entered our patrol area, I played two games of chess with the Captain, and won both. He clearly was not concentrating. 'Tomorrow,' he said, 'I shall not need games of chess for my distraction.'

He was right.

16

ACTION OFF NORWAY

Early on Monday morning, 21 August 1941, I saw Norway for the first time in my life, through the periscope. We had made a perfect landfall and were exactly where we wanted to be. What I actually saw was a smudge of coast, with white-capped mountains rising behind, over a dirty grey-green waste of sea, with a long swell rolling shoreward. We were then about ten miles offshore. Rousselot said he had a scale of charges for Liaison Officers looking through his periscope, and Norway cost ten shillings a second. After that, various members of the crew were allowed up into the kiosk for quick looks, and I muttered (but not to the Captain) that it looked suspiciously like Scotland.

We had to lay our mines in three groups of ten, ten and twelve, in positions a few miles apart, in the shipping lane about two miles offshore. Our orders permitted us to lay them submerged or on the surface at night, or dived by day, and the Captain had decided to lay them submerged by day. After that, we were permitted about two days 'tourisme' (as the Captain said), in which to look for torpedo targets, before returning to Dundee.

Having dived at 0300 we went to action stations at 0745. At 0800 we began to lay our first group of mines. The Captain and Brunet were in the kiosk, the Captain at the periscope and Brunet plotting on the chart the exact position and time of each lay. The Captain shouted 'Mouillez un!'; a button was pressed in the control room; a slither and a 'ting' like a ticket-collector's punch, outside the pressure hull, indicated that the mine had gone; 'Première mine mouillée' was shouted up from the control room. 'Mouillez deux' 'Deuxième mine mouillée' 'Mouillez trois!' And so on. Casey, Green and I were sitting in the wardroom, out of everyone's way. The submarine was moving slowly forward at about two knots. Each mine, on being released, was supposed to go to the bottom, where, after six minutes or so, a soluble plug would dissolve and then the mine itself would rise on a cable to a pre-set depth, and become live, to be detonated by the breaking of one of its horns.

The first 'paquet' of ten mines was successfully laid. The Captain said the weather was perfect, and while we proceeded along the coast to our next position, hands went to breakfast.

Rubis had never yet, in all her war-time patrols, had a chance to fire her torpedoes; so there was a sensation when at ten minutes past twelve we heard the shout of 'Postes de Combat Torpilles' – 'Torpedo action stations'. Hémar came and whispered to me that we had met a large unescorted tanker. The attack was a short one; after only a few minutes of calling out range and bearings, the external tubes in the turntable at the stern were trained to 90°. Tube No. 3 (the large one) was brought to the ready. Then came the order from the Captain in the kiosk; 'Feu!' … 'Fire!'

Nothing happened.

'Has the torpedo left?' yelled the Captain into the voice pipe.

'Yes, Sir,' replied the Torpedo Coxswain.

Still nothing happened. If the torpedo had missed, it ought to run for about eight minutes and then hit the bottom and explode there. The Captain didn't believe the torpedo had ever been fired, and said so. The Torpedo Coxswain, almost in tears, swore that it had; the air pressure gauges had fallen, it must have left.

An argument followed, and the air bristled with French expletives. Meanwhile the tanker, empty, and steaming on an opposite course to us, at eight knots, was nearly hull down on the horizon. We could not overtake her, submerged. The *Rubis* had had her first torpedo chance, and missed it.

The torpedo tubes were then trained fore and aft again. Immediately an ominous throbbing was felt throughout the submarine. Torpedo No. 3 was now running, inside its tube, and was therefore live, and would explode on impact. There was nothing we could do about that.

We had lunch, and a furious argument took place in the wardroom. Of course, the British dockyard was blamed; the torpedo was defective. The fact that the air pressure gauges had fallen correctly indicated that, at the moment of firing, a great bubble of air must have been blown to the surface. As the sea was flat calm, our presence should have been disclosed if the tanker's look-outs were awake.

The whole boat was plunged in gloom. Disappointment was set in every man's face.

After lunch the crew went to action stations for the second lay. Casey, Green, Bacchus and I, the only ones with nothing to do, again sat in the wardroom, ostensibly wrapped up in a game of draughts, or a book, or a bone; all, privately, registering carefully the ting! of each departing mine. There was silence in the boat, except for the hum of the electric motors, and the succession of orders and tings as the mines fell down into the twenty-seven or twenty-eight fathoms of the sea beneath us. After about five minutes had gone, I was astonished to hear 'torpedo action stations after the lay!'

In six minutes, when the last mine of the second group had been laid, the bow torpedo men went through the wardroom to their posts for'ard, with broad winks to us as they passed. We had met, said Hémar, popping into the wardroom for a bar of chocolate, the two merchant ships mentioned in the signal. With them were two anti-submarine escort vessels.

This attack was even shorter. Within a very few minutes, I heard the Captain give the order to prepare to fire tubes 1 and 2, and then 'Feu un.' and then, 'Feu deux!' This time there were two unmistakable jerks as the torpedoes left the boat. I sat counting the seconds on my watch: one, two, three, four … then there was a terrific CRASH and then another CRASH. The torpedoes had certainly hit something, and at very short range. All our lights went out; there was the sound of breaking glass as the wardroom lamp smashed, and tumblers leaped. The boat took on a steep angle: were we diving or surfacing? Chaos.

'Tous le monde en avant! Tous le monde en avant!' 'Every one up for'ard' … Dimly, in the dark, I realised we must be up by the bows, and nearly, if not quite, breaking the surface; everyone was being ordered forward to bring the bows down. I found myself one of a crowd of excited Frenchmen trying to scramble up a greasy inclined deck; but in a minute it was level and we were being ordered back. Within a short space of time – my memory of those crowded seconds is not clear – the submarine was resting quietly on the bottom, in a depth of thirty fathoms, less than one mile from the coast of Norway. All machinery was switched off and complete silence ordered. The only illumination was from the blue emergency lamps in each compartment.

We settled down to wait for the inevitable counter-attack. Absolute silence was ordered, but it was not maintained. For one thing, every sailor on board had to come to the Captain, who was now in his cabin, and shake his hand in congratulations. Then they had to go and tell Casey and Green how pleased they were. They pulled them affectionately by the ear, or slapped their backs, and said with shining eyes, 'Two torpedo – boum! She sink!' They were ready for any number of depth-charges; they wanted to have something to boast about to *Minerve* (the other French submarine in Dundee) which had been depth-charged on her last patrol.

The Captain said 'The escort trawlers had great big Nazi flags. I could see the people on the bridge looking ahead with binoculars. They seemed to be wearing mackintoshes. I attacked the leading ship. She must have turned over, so, and sunk very quickly, with two hits.' As we dived, he said he had seen the shadow of the target ship darken the window in the kiosk, as we passed close to her.

Ten minutes after bottoming, there was an explosion, but not very near. Four minutes later, a second. Four minutes later, a third. '*Minerve* had 28 depth-charges' said one of the sailors cheerfully. 'The *Seal* had 61' said Tim Casey. They began recounting various depth-charge stories then current in the submarine world. After another four minutes came the fourth explosion, still not very near. A few minutes later, the fifth. After that, no more.

The rest of the day dragged itself on slowly in the semi-darkness. The men slept if they could; and the Captain made his plan of action. Once a motor-boat passed right overhead; we could clearly hear the chug-chug of its engine above us.

'Looking for survivors' guessed the Captain. Later, it passed overhead again; but there were no signs of an organised search for us. We heard no Asdic transmissions.

The Captain told me that in the middle of the lay, a convoy had appeared in the periscope, steering down the channel towards our mines. It consisted of the two ships we had been ordered to attack, escorted by two German naval trawlers. The Captain had to make a quick decision. Either he had to attack them before they entered our mine-field – which hardly gave him enough time to get into a good attacking position – or he had to wait till they had passed through our minefield, and, if they survived that, attack them afterwards. Obviously it was preferable to attack them before, and save the minefield for somebody else – if it was feasible. So he finished laying; but the range was by then – as we discovered – almost suicidally close. The six or seven seconds interval between the firing and the explosions indicated that in fact the range had been only about 400 yards. We had nearly blown ourselves out of the water, as well as the target.

We did not yet know exactly what damage we had suffered, but it was probable that our batteries were seriously damaged. It was unlikely that after surfacing (if indeed we could surface, but the Captain kindly kept that thought to himself) we would be able to dive again. That meant that we would have to go home straight across the North Sea. The Captain called for my operational chart, showing the minefields. It would be necessary to cross at least two declared German minefields. He remarked 'Both these minefields are very large, therefore I do not believe them. You cannot make a minefield 100 miles long and 40 miles wide.' We would send a signal to the Admiralty asking for air protection as soon as we had got a fair distance from the coast.

We wondered if any of the five explosions after our attack could have been the rest of the convoy blowing up on our mines; but that was too much to hope for.

The air got fouler and fouler. We sucked acid drops. I played a game of chess with the Captain; but his mind was not on the game, and I won too easily.

By 2100 the air in the submarine was very bad: we were all panting. We had been down for eighteen hours, and there had been an abnormal amount of exertion causing greater consumption of oxygen.

Bodies and brains were becoming lethargic: heads, which needed to be clear, were becoming sleepy. The Captain mentioned to me that it was possible, when we surfaced, that we would not be able to run the motors or the engines for very long, and we might have to drive the ship onto the Norwegian rocks, scramble ashore, and walk to Sweden. In such a contingency, I had to make sure that the Naval Codes and Ciphers and Secret Books were all destroyed or dropped in deep water. I made my preparations, including looking out a pair of shoes.

I longed for us to reach the surface. All hell might be waiting for us up there, but

I had a strong preference for dying in the fresh air. One piece of knowledge did not comfort me. I was the only officer on board who had had experience of the Davis Submarine Escape Apparatus. There was a set on board for every man, but the French had always refused to learn how to use it. I had been trained in its use, and had made practice escapes in the tank at Portsmouth; but I did not fancy supervising the escape of fifty French novices in it. If they decided to stay below, I could order Casey and Green to go up, but would have to stay myself.

At half past nine it was quite dark. The Captain decided to surface. Green and Casey came to sit with me in the wardroom, and Green thoughtfully brought along a half bottle of rum. We did not pretend to play draughts. We sat grinning idiotically at one another and listening intently to the orders in the control room.

A submarine surfaces by blowing air (which it carries compressed in steel bottles) into a series of tanks along its side, which, when it is submerged, are flooded with sea water.

When everyone was at his position ready for surfacing, the Captain gave the order to 'blow' such-and-such tanks, which should bring us up. The submarine seemed to lift a foot or two and relapsed again on to the rocks. We heard them scraping along our hull like a gigantic tin opener. I had never heard a sound I disliked so much.

The Captain ordered some more tanks to be blown. Again we rose a little, and again we went back on to the rasping rocks. I could hear them. I could almost feel them.

The Captain blew a third combination of tanks, and again we scraped along the bottom. Some of the tanks had been damaged and were leaking.

The situation did not look very hopeful.

I knew enough about submarines to know that there was not very much left that we could do.

The last thing to do (and if this had failed, the submarine would have stayed on the bottom) was to blow the emergency 'Q' tanks for'ard. This the Captain did; we lurched – and there was no scraping of rocks. In a few seconds we heard the most musical sound I have ever heard in my life; the lapping of water on the hull above our heads. We were on the surface. Since the air pressure in the boat was extremely high, the Captain relieved it by first opening the bridge voice pipes. Our eardrums popped and we swallowed hard. There was a gush of cold air, and a nauseating stench. The new air coming in showed us, for a second or two, what we had been breathing for eighteen hours. Then Rousselot opened the conning-tower hatch and climbed out onto the bridge, ready again for action.

17

HOME ON THE SURFACE

We came up, in pitch darkness, just below a lighthouse or coastguard station, which in a minute or two began to challenge us by lamp. While the engineers were trying to get the engines started, Casey was called up on to the bridge and told to answer. While he was wondering what to say, the diesel engines thundered into life. The submarine's bows turned slowly and we headed away. Casey told me afterwards that he relieved his pent-up feelings by flickering some very rude and short English words along the beams of his Aldis lamp to the cliff above. There was no reply.

Meanwhile I was composing and then coding a signal to the Admiralty. It had to be as short as possible, and yet we had to report our successful attack, our position, course and speed, and the fact that we were seriously damaged and could not dive.

At 0100 we were making ten knots. We were then about twenty miles from the Norwegian coast and the signal was transmitted.

At 0230 we received a signal from the Admiralty 'Expect fighter protection at dawn'.

At 0330 we received a signal 'Expect three Blenheims at 0630'.

At 0430 we received a signal 'Two destroyers and a cruiser are proceeding to your assistance with utmost despatch'.

At 0530 it was nearly dawn, and all our Hotchkiss, Bren and Tommy guns were brought up to the bridge, and manned. The guns' crews closed up on the .75 cannon forward and the twin Hotchkiss guns aft.

At the same time, the submarine's hull began to fill with blue smoke and fumes from the batteries, which were on fire. For another hour we crawled slowly into full daylight across a flat summer sea.

At 0631, a beautiful sunny morning, three aircraft were reported. All guns were brought to bear. They were the Blenheims; they seemed as glad to see us as we were to see them.

Four minutes later, we sighted several floating mines ahead. The Blenheims saw them too, and went into paroxysms of excitement. They dived on them, and circled, and flashed endless warning messages to us by Aldis lamp. At 0636 the engines of the *Rubis*, after stopping and starting again several times, coughed and

Rubis running on the surface in the North Sea, August 1941.

Rubis still under way …

broke down completely. We lay stopped, with a slight list to port. Nevertheless, the Blenheims continued to be interested only in the mines, which now that we were stopped were of even less interest to us; and it took them a long time to realise that we had seen them too, and that we had much more important messages to pass to them. We wished to report to them our damage, so far as we knew it, and the fact that we were now stopped; but Tim Casey, perched on the top of the periscope standard, following the aircraft round with his Aldis lamp, tried each one in turn, bringing down his speed to the slowest he could transmit; but they could only read the simplest words, and those only after endless repetitions.

The fumes in the hull, from the short-circuiting batteries, soon became so bad that we had to evacuate the interior of the submarine completely, except for the wireless cabin. The telegraphists maintained their radio watch, working in short spells with wet cloths over their mouths. Everyone else came up on top; and it was now that we felt the advantage of the flat wooden deck; a British submarine, with its narrow steel casing, would have been a much less attractive place for forty men to spend the day on.

At half past seven a signal was received. 'HMS *Lightning* and *Lively* left Scapa at 0430. HMS *Curaçoa* passed Bell Rock at 0630'. This was news indeed. *Lightning* and *Lively* were two new battle destroyers, and *Curaçoa* was an anti-aircraft cruiser. We calculated that they might arrive at any time from about half past four in the afternoon onwards; they definitely ought to have arrived by half past seven at the latest.

The Navy was on its way. We counted ourselves as fully rescued; and when the Blenheims signalled that their fuel was running out, and they would have to return, we waved our thanks to them, and did not mind. At 0920 they flashed 'Good Luck' and flew away, leaving us all by ourselves in the bright sunlight of a lovely summer's day. Visibility was at least fifteen miles. The German airfield at Stavanger was just below the horizon.

When a signal arrived, Casey and Green and I sat on the flat roof of the front of the conning-tower to decode it. As well as those addressed to us, there were others to other ships, which we deciphered, or started to decipher until we found that they did not interest us. Green put out a fishing line and then went to sleep, with the line round his finger. Four times he woke up with a start and hauled in his line furiously, before he realised that each Frenchman who went past was giving his line a little tug *en passant*.

Besides the telegraphist on watch, the electricians were also working below, wearing gas-masks. The submarine had two batteries, housed in the lower half of the circular pressure hull. Each battery had one hundred cells, and each cell was about the size of a man, so the physical aspect of their problem was no small one. They were still trying to find out how many of the cells were smashed; but even

Rubis lying stopped in the North Sea, August 1941. Photo by Brunet.

Rubis lying stopped in the North Sea, August 1941.

with torches the smoke and fumes made it impossible to see anything, or to spend more than a short time below. Later in the afternoon, they were able to start emptying the acid, which had spilt out of the smashed cells, by means of a chain of buckets up to the deck.

The rest of the crew lay on the flat wooden deck, sleeping, sunbathing, comparing domestic photographs, and outlining plans for celebrating in Dundee when we got back. The only question seemed to be: would we get back before closing time on Saturday? (we didn't). It was, during the middle half of the day, just an enjoyable picnic under a blazing sun and cloudless sky. Our puny guns were ready; but nothing flew out of Norway except seagulls, and Bacchus barked at any of them that came too close.

I asked the Captain about the rocks scraping along the hull, when we had been trying to surface. 'It would not have been long,' I asked, 'before they pierced the hull?' The Captain looked at me scornfully. 'Pouf!' he said, 'you have never heard the scraping of rocks before, no?' Months later, when the *Rubis* was in dry dock, I saw she had (like all submarines) an enormously heavy, wide false keel, built for grinding on rocks in perfect safety.

Green confessed that during the rock-scraping moments he had been so frightened that he had drunk the entire half-bottle of rum without us noticing, and with no effect on himself whatever.

The torpedoed ship was discussed. 'They must have been just having lunch.' 'Someone got his soup in his lap.'

Some time during the day someone found a fragment of torpedo embedded in the wooden planking of the deck. This started a treasure hunt and several handfuls were found. I have never, before or since, heard of a submarine carrying back fragments of its own torpedoes.

Then we found that the torpedo which had failed to run was sticking half out of its stern tube. We leaned over the stern curiously and could just see its dark shape down in the green water. It fell out later, and was lost.

The day wore on. The *Rubis* lay on the shining sea, drifting very slowly back towards Norway. Still no German aircraft appeared.

Neither did the cruiser and destroyers. From about four o'clock onwards we expected them to come up over the horizon every minute. At five, we smiled at each other and said 'any time now'.

It was getting a little cold, and blankets were brought up; the inside of the boat was still uninhabitable. Two electricians who had got acid splashed in their eyes and on their hands and feet were treated, bandaged, and lay wrapped up under the hood on the bridge. They became at times delirious.

At six, we frowned and said 'they're late', and at seven I felt that they were all looking at me and saying to themselves 'well, where *is* the Royal Navy?'

Just before dark, three more Beaufighters appeared (so much for our all-day fighter protection), but to our questions 'have you seen ships?' they replied 'no!' Then they too flashed 'Good Luck' and flew away home. We did not envy them, flying in land-planes hundreds of miles over the sea; and we heard later that one at least had stayed with us too long and, running out of fuel on the way home, had splashed.

Night fell and the reasons for the Navy's failure to turn up were discussed. It was decided to risk breaking wireless silence again (obviously, any wireless signal we made might be located by the Germans), but in order to get the power to transmit, it was necessary to run the diesels, and it was very doubtful if this would be possible. I concocted the shortest possible signal, giving only our position and the fact that we were stopped. The engines were started, and the signal sent.

But during those five minutes, a man was washed overboard, and no one saw him or heard him go. He was lying asleep on deck wrapped in a blanket. A wave must have just picked him off the deck and carried him away silently. The men lying beside him noticed nothing. His loss was discovered about three minutes later, by which time he must have been half a mile astern. It was too dark to offer much hope of finding him. We flashed torches and tried shouting; but the diesels could not now be restarted. We could not go back to look for him. He could not swim, anyway. He had been the Chief Gunner, a quiet, unmarried Breton called Leon, whose chief pleasure in life was his game of dominoes each evening. He had been particularly kind to me, and to Casey and Green.

At midnight, we received a signal saying that the ships were searching for us about sixty miles too far south, (the Beaufighters had reported our position based on their own navigational miscalculations) and had orders not to cross a certain longitude, i.e. enter the German declared minefields, unless we were attacked by surface ships. 'Ah, merde! ...' said the Captain. 'How can mines be sown thickly over an area 100 miles long and 40 miles wide? I have been over that minefield several times, me! Next time I want to be rescued, I will deal with a private firm of tugs in Dundee, not the Admiralty. Merde!'

At half past two we got a signal saying that three Catalina flying-boats were being despatched to the *Rubis*' position. If by 0900 we were still unable to move, they would alight, the Secret Books were to be destroyed, the crew embarked in the Catalinas, and we were to 'sink repeat sink' the *Rubis*.

When I took this signal to the bridge and read it out aloud, all the French officers burst out laughing, and the Captain shouted 'Mais c'est une manie! He is determined to sink us, the old man!' This referred to a previous patrol, when the *Rubis* had damaged her steering, and had spent two days going round in circles in the Atlantic. On that occasion, Admiral Horton had sent the submarine *Tuna* to *Rubis*' position, and signalled that if the steering could not be repaired by a certain time, they were all to embark in the *Tuna*, and then sink the *Rubis*. They had spent all night firing flares but praying that the *Tuna* would not see them, and she did not; then the seas had abated and an engineer had gone over the stern on a line and succeeded in repairing the rudder and they had come home.

On this occasion we realised that it was the Admiralty, not Admiral Horton, who would not allow the cruiser and destroyers to enter the minefields; but it seemed hard that, even if they would not risk a destroyer, they could not send something smaller. Of course, they did not know, because of the Beaufighters' inefficiency in reading morse, that apart from our batteries the *Rubis* was practically undamaged, and that all we wanted was a tow. The threat to sink the *Rubis* was perhaps a subtle stroke of psychology; it was certain that it would spur the Frenchmen on to row the boat home if necessary: and meantime it so filled them with indignation that they almost forgot their other worries. Sink the *Rubis*? Merde!

By dawn, the smoke and fumes in the battery chambers had abated enough for the electricians to examine every cell. As a result, they found that 140 out of 200 were smashed. By finding and coupling up the good ones, they hoped to provide enough power to run the blowers necessary for the diesels; and they set to work, still wearing gas-masks.

By about 1000 the electricians said they were ready. They hoped that with luck the *Rubis* might make about six knots for about forty-eight hours, but it would be touch and go.

The Captain did not want to move out of his position until the Catalinas arrived; he wished to tell them exactly what he was doing, and, of course, a flying-boat escort would be a help if we did hit a mine. By 1030, not only could we not send any more wireless messages, but we could no longer receive any.

A few minutes later, there was a shout, one of the look-outs saw the Catalinas. There they were, we could all see them, flying very low, on the horizon. Casey fired two flares and a signal rocket, but the aircraft disappeared. They were obviously sweeping; we assumed they would pick us up on the next leg of their search. We waited an hour but we never saw them again.

At about 1130 the Captain shrugged his shoulders, and gave the order to move. We set off at about seven-and-a-half knots. Everyone's spirits went up. The weather was perfect; a flat calm, brilliant sunshine, visibility about ten miles.

Five minutes later, a Blenheim arrived who was so good at signalling that we were able to pass a long message to him. He stayed with us about an hour, but could give us no news of the ships. But we did not greatly care. We would get home under our own power. We kept a strict look-out for mines, and saw several floating; and once we passed a buoy with a red flag; I exchanged glances with the Captain; it probably meant that we were entering an actual minefield. The Coxswain, who was on watch, had a photograph of his fiancée, a Dundee girl, in his trouser pocket, and during this somewhat anxious period, he would every now and then whip her out, take a good look at her, and pop her back in his pocket again.

We ran through an energetic school of porpoises; and fed on soused herrings, tomatoes, chocolate, dried apricots and tinned fruit salad. We were navigating by the sun, according to Lieutenant Brunet's calculations. The magnetic compass, intended for use when submerged, had been corrected with the conning-tower hatch shut, and was useless with it open.

At six o'clock in the evening, still no sign of the ships. At ten minutes past, three Blenheims arrived, and signalled rather ominously 'Your best chance is under your own power' – 'That means no hooking on to porpoises' said Casey, and raised a laugh. Then a fat-bellied Hudson arrived, and he was so good at receiving Morse that we were able to flash him a message of about forty words, including some quite difficult long ones. We asked him bluntly 'Where are ships?' to which he replied 'Not seen'. We had no sunglasses and I was becoming anxious lest Casey's eyes should break down; Morse from the aircraft was usually so dim and difficult that only he could read it.

At last, at twenty to eight, an aircraft made 'Ships seen' and we altered course slightly in the direction he indicated. In ten minutes, just as dusk was falling, we saw, near where the sun had set, three specks on the horizon.

By that time we had long ago exhausted all our emotions about the ships, and had nothing left to register. I can remember seeing the ships, and not feeling any relief at all.

When we got into communication by lamp with HMS *Curaçoa*, Casey was at last able to show us how the Navy signals; the Aldis rattled like a machine gun, and his beaming smile made everyone on the bridge laugh.

At half past ten we stopped, close to the destroyer *Lively*. We had signalled for a doctor, and they sent one over in a motor boat, and he examined our men with acid burns and took them away to be looked after in the destroyer's sick bay. Next day they signalled us that their eyes were safe, and they would be taken to hospital in Scapa. In the smoky half-light of summer dusk, we could just make out the men crowding the *Lively*'s decks to look at us.

They asked us if we wanted a tow. Having done the difficult bit alone we did not want a tow now, but signalled that our steering was undependable, so a destroyer led us.

That night some of the officers had their first sleep for about eighty hours; and the next morning a fire was lit in the deck-galley (the interior was still uninhabitable) and we had some hot coffee; the first hot drink for eighty hours.

The scene was quite impressive. We were in the centre of a small fleet: ahead of us was the *Lively*, on the port wing was the *Lightning* and a fleet trawler, on the starboard wing was the destroyer *Wolfhound* and another fleet trawler, there was a fleet tug just astern and the *Curaçoa* hovering round like a sheepdog with a brood of chickens. And what seemed like the greater part of Coastal Command was in the sky above. We could afford to relax a little.

About nine-thirty the *Curaçoa* suddenly started drawing alongside of us, to starboard. Men emerged to line her sides and stare down at us; and the entire crew of the *Rubis*, filthy, bearded, sunburned and grinning, lined our rails to stare up at the cruiser. When she was abreast and about twenty yards off, her loud hailer began booming out in courteous Public School French, saying how glad they had been to see us the previous night, how sorry the Captain was not to have been able to say so then, but he had been too busy; how he hoped some day to make the acquaintance of our Captain over a 'bonne bouteille'. The message ended 'Bravo, *Rubis*! Bravo!' The faces of my Frenchmen, and especially of the Captain, were a picture. They were deeply gratified.

As the *Curaçoa* drew slowly away, Casey leaped up on to the conning tower and semaphored a brief thanks from the submarine.

That 'bonne bouteille' was never split. Only a few months later, HMS *Curaçoa* was cut in half by the Cunarder *Queen Mary*, whom she was escorting, travelling at full speed at night in the Irish Sea. The cruiser sank with only two survivors.

About mid-day we had a hot dinner, our first since before the torpedoing. It was a picnic meal, taken lying on the deck; the officers had theirs aft of the conning tower, the men for'ard. We had soup, with port or sherry; then cold ham, with cucumber and salad on silver dishes, anchovies, spring onions, hard boiled eggs, hot French tinned peas and new potatoes, fruit salad and dried apricots; and gracing the table were, besides the ration of red wine, two bottles of white burgundy, the last remaining on board of what they had brought from France. And, to finish, coffee and cognac. The sun shone down, the glassy blue sea lapped past at our elbows, and the binoculars of every Ship in the Fleet were turned on us. The Captain, jerking his thumb at the *Curaçoa*, laughed and said 'They are jealous – aboard there, mashed potatoes'. Then he lay back, stretched out, and had his first sleep for four days.

We chugged steadily on and reached home waters. During the night our escorts went their ways, except for one destroyer. In the morning (Monday, 25 August) we were off Bell Rock, but our adventures were not quite over. Instead of being able to steam straight up the Tay estuary, we found the port closed owing to German mines, and were ordered to wait until the channel was swept. This did not suit us at all, for apart from our eagerness to get home, the leaking ballast tanks were now so full that we were practically sinking, and no power was available to pump them out. The Captain fumed and swore, and the men employed the time in decorating the sides of the conning tower with chalk drawings: a gigantic V was put on each side, with a grinning French sailor on the starboard side and on the port side a bold representation of a German ship blowing up (with Germans in the air) and fishes with their mouths open.

Eventually, having crossed the North Sea under our own power, we had to be towed up the Tay.

There was a big gathering on the quay to welcome us. The crew of the *Minerve* gave us three cheers as we came alongside. Captain Roper (in command of the Flotilla) was the first to come on board. He heard the story and saw the mess the boat was in; and he was presented with a plate bearing two of the *Rubis'* pickled herrings (which before we sailed he had seen and said he envied us) artistically arranged to form a V, with pickled onions forming dot dot dot dash.

I was taken in a Staff Car, with my codes and ciphers and secret charts, to the Staff Office, before I could begin to bath and change. I had to make a short pre-liminary report, because an immediate message had to be sent to the Admiralty, reporting our return, our damage, and what we had done. I stepped up cheerfully to the Staff Officer (a wiry, white-bearded R N R Lieutenant-Commander) and saw him flinch, with his nose twitching. He kindly but firmly asked me not to stand too close. I did not smell very good.

It took two razor blades to hack off my beard, which I did in my bath. I then went to the bar in the wardroom, to be stood gins in a rather dazed condition by my envious equals. Christopher, now B.N.L.O. in a Dutch submarine, told me that they had been on patrol just north of us, and that when on their way home they had been sent back one hundred miles to look for us, with orders, again, if we were still unable to move, to take us all on board, and sink the *Rubis*. We did not know about this because of our wireless breakdown. The Dutchmen had spent a day wondering how they could accommodate an extra forty-seven men; the only ones looking forward to it were Christopher and his signalman and telegraphist. Dutch submarines are non-alcoholic on patrol, and Christopher and his two men had decided to stand at the hatch as we came on board, and send back every French-man who was not carrying a bottle.

After a session in the wardroom, I was taken to a cocktail party in a private house in Broughty Ferry. I found the drawing-room and all the nice, noisy people in it, utterly unreal; I was still out in the North Sea. I was only too glad to find an early way to my cabin, and to sleep.

The French submarine *Minerve* was due to go on patrol the next day. At the last moment her Third Officer fell ill, and could not sail. Brunet, our third hand, when he heard of it, immediately volunteered to take his place, and did so. He had a bath and a few hours sleep and went off for another twenty days on the Norwegian Coast. He got a special three cheers for himself from the crew of the *Rubis* when we turned out to give *Minerve* her send-off. I thought it breath-taking: but he was an exceptional young man.

During the next few days, many detailed reports and track charts had to be made out by the Captain and myself, to describe our patrol; and both shore and submarine officers learned many interesting things about each others' problems during the days when we were 'lost'. The first Beaufighters had taken photographs of us, and these had been rushed to Edinburgh for a conference, attended by Home Fleet Staff Officers and French and British submarine Officers from Dundee[*]. They had no idea of what had happened (our first signal had not been received correctly) and thought we had been depth-charged; but their deductions from the photographs about our damage had in essentials been correct.

Before we went on leave, a small party was held in the Rousselots' house, presided over by a bottle of champagne which had been kept especially to celebrate *Rubis*' first successful torpedo attack. We also drank the health of a young Free Frenchman, born to the wife of one of the crew at the approximate time of the firing of our first torpedo.

For this patrol, Rousselot and Dubuisson were awarded bars to their DSCs and Brunet a Mention in Despatches; and several of the French crew were awarded DSMs and Mentions. Tim Casey, who already had a DSM, was awarded a Mention and so was I. The Free French Admiralty had just thought up a new decoration called the *Croix de la Liberation* and made the *Rubis*, as a ship, the first recipient of it. General de Gaulle and Admiral Muselier came up to Dundee and pinned it on our flag; and at the subsequent handing out of Croix de Guerres, I was honoured with one *avec palme de bronze*. Regulations at that time prohibited the wearing of French decorations by British officers. Rousselot advised me to wear mine on my pyjamas.

Bacchus, newly decorated, is toasted by the officers of Rubis, *in their Dundee mess.*

[*]   These photographs are shown on p. 83.

Two photographs of the crew of Rubis *in Dundee, September 1941.*
The author is identifiable by his Royal Naval cap.

The Captain, with Bacchus decorated.

18

LOOKING FOR THE *TIRPITZ*

The sailing of any ship is an emotional occasion. I have nearly cried when watching a dirty old tramp steamer dropping down London river on a summer's evening. I had a lump in my throat – I could not show tears – when on board a battleship leaving Algiers harbour with her Royal Marine Band playing 'Hearts of Oak' on top of a gun turret and her battle ensign flying. When any ship is leaving a wharf, when the last cable is slipped from the shore and splashes in the water, when she slowly moves away, (in David Bone's phrase, 'ground-free at last') whether she is a fair craft or an ugly one, it is a stirring event. When the world is at war, and the ship is a submarine sailing to the enemy coast, there cannot help being drama in the scene, however much it is played down.

When a submarine sailed from Dundee, there was no official ceremony. But the senior officers of the base always came down informally to see a boat off on patrol; and as she moved away, the men on her casing stood to attention, the officer on the casing and those upon the bridge saluted, the officers on shore returned the salute, and that made a ceremony.

When we sailed for our next patrol, we were a rather famous submarine, and our departure was expected to be well attended.

It was an afternoon in late November.

I came on board about half an hour before we were due to sail. I saw Green, and asked him if Casey was on board; he said he was. Having stowed my gear in the wardroom earlier, I did not need to go below; it was a pleasant, sunny afternoon, astonishingly warm for the time of year, so I leaned over the rail of the bridge and surveyed the scene.

The jetty was a long one, with tall cranes on wheels bestriding railway trucks, and backed by warehouses and sheds. Astern of our berth was a recently-launched small aircraft carrier; ahead lay a merchant ship, with merchant seamen sunning themselves comfortably on her gun platform. The jetty, after stretching in a straight line for a quarter of a mile, ended in a gate leading to the Royal Naval quarters, containing the seamen's mess-decks.

All the senior officers of the base had come down. Some had come out of courtesy, some out of curiosity, some as a matter of duty. Some were, no doubt, savouring the emotion of submarine departures seen from the shore. Some, like the Electrical Officer, had been working hard in *Rubis* up to the last minute, and had come to take pride in their handiwork; the Padre had come because Commander (S) had told him to; Commander (S) himself, who had commanded *Seawolf* all through the deadly Norwegian campaign the previous summer, had come because we were one of his boats.

Rousselot was on the jetty talking to the Commanding officer of the *Minerve*, and some other French officers. French naval officers' uniform is much lighter blue than ours (which is really black). In cut and cloth, in the placing of the buttons, and the useless little gold strap on the shoulder, it is all just wrong; perhaps it reflects the fact that in France the Navy is of less account than the Army. The French Army is glamorous, and has what is probably the most handsome military uniform of any service in the world.

I was deep in a reminiscence with a sub-lieutenant on the jetty about a dance we had both been to the previous night, when I saw Rousselot throw away his cigarette stub, look at his watch, shake hands with the three or four French officers on the jetty, and walk across the plank into the ship. He waved a hand to the crane-man up above. The plank had to be lifted on to the jetty, and the crane-man, who was asleep, was roused by a series of French whistles and halloos. Down came the hook. But then, up came Green, looking rather pale, and whispered to me 'I'm afraid Casey's not on board, sir'. I glared at Green. I looked round feebly to see if Casey were perhaps at my feet, or underneath the chart table. Rousselot was now on the bridge. Hastily I told him the bad news. I cross-examined Green, and it appeared that he had thought Casey was on board and had only just found that he was not; he supposed Casey was still on the mess-decks, at the end of the jetty. This meant that he would be drunk. Green was sent post-haste to get him. Captain Rousselot shrugged his shoulders and lit a cigarette. For him, the consolation, as he said, was that for once it was an Englishman, not a Frenchman, who was going to disgrace a naval occasion. We waited.

After a long five minutes, three tiny figures appeared at the end of the jetty. From the moment they came into view, it was quite easy to see that an argument was taking place. Casey was completely drunk, but he could walk; and he was walking with dignity, haughtily brushing away the arms put out to steady him. His shining red face – it shone at any time, but when drunk it shone like an aircraft beacon – was beaming with happiness, alternating with horrible frowns when they tried to hold his arms. He flung aside their childish offers, and marched breast-forward – oops, mind those bollards …

To reach *Rubis*, Casey would have to pass close in front of all the gathering of officers. His grin was obviously partly due to seeing so many friends awaiting him. What sort of greeting he would give them paralysed the imagination. The Frenchmen waited, hushed.

As one man, the assembled British naval officers turned their backs. With heads down, they found urgent matters to discuss gazing at the ground, like a lot of cricket captains examining the pitch.

So Casey, who could never refuse a drink with friends and who was so easily made drunk, continued his career with a beatific grin, unhindered and unsaluting, the superb embodiment of the eternal and gloriously drunken sailor.

How they got him across the plank I do not know – no amount of practice will help a drunk man to cross a plank, it is always sheer luck – but once on board he was in affectionate hands, and he was hustled tenderly out of sight. The officers on the jetty turned round with relief in their faces, Rousselot raised his hand again to the crane-man, the plank was swung up into the air and deposited on the jetty, the springs were cast off, the other ropes hauled inboard, and we manoeuvred away from the side. We saluted; the officers on shore saluted, and then waved us luck; we slid down the river.

This time we were not being used to lay mines. It was believed that the *Tirpitz* was about to go to sea: every available submarine was being rushed out to Norway to watch every possible fjord from which she might emerge. The Captain was furious; he hated being used as an ordinary submarine.

It turned out to be a typical North Sea winter patrol: short, dark, dirty, beastly and uneventful.

There are two great facts of life for submariners on patrol. The first is whether it is night or day. The second is whether you are on watch or off watch. Snorkels and atomic power have changed life in submarines now, but in the *Rubis*, the difference between night and day was that at night we were on the surface, running noisily on the diesels, and by day we were submerged, running quietly on the electric motors.

At night, the boat was throbbing with noise, a sort of subdued and rhythmic crashing that quickly stamped a pattern on one's brain that would remain there for years: to be recalled, suddenly and unexpectedly, long afterwards, perhaps by just a whiff of diesel oil in a bus.

The noise of the diesels did not signify only that we were moving from A to B, it signified that the batteries were being re-charged. In those pre-snorkel days, a submarine could remain dived only as long as her batteries and her air lasted, and every submarine officer had to know, at any given moment, just what remained of both. While the boat was on the surface, air was constantly being sucked down through the open conning-tower by the diesels; if, as sometimes happened, a wave or other accident knocked the conning-tower hatch shut, a sudden vacuum would be created, pulling on everyone's eardrums, before the diesels coughed to a standstill.

A submarine on patrol in enemy water always (if it wished to survive) dived well before dawn. Many a submarine had been lost by a rash commander's weakness in remaining on the surface too long (to get the sun-sight or to get an extra half hour of run at ten knots, instead of the two knots or so that was the normal submerged speed) and being seen by an enemy aircraft or another submarine.

As soon as the sky showed the first signs of lightening into day, and the submarine was beginning to become a darker spot against a paling sea, the order would be given for the bridge to be cleared. The look-outs and finally the officer of the watch would clatter down the steel ladder. As the last man closed the hatch and clipped it above his head, the klaxon was sounded three times, the diesels stopped, the 'planes were turned out for diving, the vents in the saddle tanks opened and the sea rushed in and took us down. In twenty or thirty seconds, the surface of the sea was empty of our presence; our splinter of steel, displacing nearly a thousand tons and carrying fifty men, had sunk, and was proceeding slowly on her course at sixty or eighty feet below the waves.

Immediately there was peace in the boat. The electric motors ran quietly, and there was no movement from the sea – unless, perhaps, if it were very rough up above, a swell would be felt down to even a hundred feet, which would sway us gently and evenly.

This peace continued all day. At least once in every watch, and if there was another special reason, we came up to periscope depth (thirty feet) and had a look round; otherwise we continued quietly on our course. Those who were not on watch in the control room or the motor room spent most of the day sleeping.

We had a meal at mid-day, and then slept again. About tea-time we began waking up, and talked or read or played games until it was time to surface. Soon after surfacing, the cook would be allowed up on the bridge to throw overboard the two or three buckets of the day's accumulated garbage, (in English this is called to 'ditch the gash', in French 'vider les moques') and then supper would be served.

The other main interest of life, besides night and day, was watch and off-watch. This did not affect me, because I was not a watch-keeping officer. The normal watches were four hours on and eight hours off, a relentless, steadying rhythm, one from which men could build up reserves of energy for the periods when they might be at action stations for unlimited hours.

*   *   *

We ran into the dirty weather that characterised this patrol the first night. When I went up on the bridge after supper, about eight-thirty in the evening, it was blowing hard and pitch dark. As one's eyes got accustomed to the darkness, one could see the white of the wake astern and the jumping-wires silhouetted against a slightly less dark part of the sky above. Geoffray, the young Coxswain, was on watch. We had no escort, and there were supposed to be no British ships on our route, so that if we met anyone we would have to dive immediately. Ahead of us, Norway; astern, Dundee. I asked Geoffray how Casey was, and Geoffray, with a broad grin, said he was now asleep. He had come aboard in his best suit, without a stitch of winter clothing, or any change. however, they had found him some spare jerseys and a fleece-lined jacket (called a 'Canadien') and a duffelcoat. 'I think he will be in trouble when he gets back, yes?' said Geoffray. I thought so too and meanwhile they all had it in for Green for not looking after his shipmate better. Then Geoffray asked: 'Did you have a nice leave, sir?' and we were off on the ever-congenial topic. Geoffray and I were both still bachelors but Geoffray at least had a Dundee girl whose photograph he carried about.

Soon I had to go below and decode wireless signals. Wedged in the corner of the wardroom seat, with the signal and the code-book on my lap and the signal pad on the table beside me, I pencilled down word after word, while the sea got worse and the movement of the submarine more violent. From time to time there was a great clatter and splash of water in the control room as a sea came down the hatch. Now and then a sailor passed through the wardroom, removing his cap and grinning at me as he passed. The Captain came yawning from his cabin, looked over my shoulder and then went up on the bridge. His wife was expecting a baby in Dundee, and if it happened while we were on patrol, we would probably have a signal about it. On this night there were no signals directly for us, but all movements on the coast of Norway were interesting. Eventually I finished, and pushed the code books back into my locker; took off my jacket and shoes, opened the Secret Books Cupboard door at the end of the wardroom seat, put my feet inside the cupboard, and turned out the light.

The next morning we dived at seven, and settled into our patrol routine. It was routine that the mornings and afternoons should be quiet and that around tea-time there should be a furious argument. We had our first argument about abstract art. It started because the Captain found two paintings by Ben Nicolson reproduced in the copy of *Horizon* that I was reading. I tried to defend them. Isn't a Persian carpet abstract art, I muttered. It can't be compared, they said, lashing themselves into ecstasies of derision. 'It is either snobbism or interest' said the Captain 'that makes people praise these things.' (He always looked for the worst motives in everybody's actions.) 'Just look at these rectangles and circles. They are a disease of the post-war world.' *Impasse*, while we each pitied the other. The argument would normally have then proceeded from art to religion and then, in easy stages, to sex, but we were due to surface at 6.30 p.m.

The procedure for surfacing was for the Captain and Casey, or a French signal-man, to go up into the kiosk. The First Lieutenant brought the boat to periscope depth, the Captain had a look round for surface ships and aircraft, and if all was clear, gave the order to surface. (The word 'surface' sounds much more dramatic and decisive in French than in English.) This night the sea was so rough that it was impossible to hold the boat at periscope depth, so we went to the surface quickly. The Captain stood with his hand on the hatch above his head, waiting for the First Lieutenant, watching the depth gauges, to shout out 'Surface!' and Casey had to follow him up immediately with an Aldis Lamp in case we came up near another ship and were challenged.

When Dubuisson, the First Lieutenant, called out 'Surface!' the Captain opened the lid, and the sea poured in. Down in the control-room, we were alarmed to see a sheet of water pour down, with Casey in the middle of it, like a great black fish. Dubuisson rushed half-way up the ladder and heard the Captain shouting 'Chassez partout!' 'Blow all tanks!' – which we did, and surfaced fully.

Surfacing in a heavy sea is dangerous. Submarines with negative buoyancy, coming up beam on to the sea, have been rolled over and lost. And more than once, a Captain has got out on to the bridge, and the submarine has had to dive again, and lost its Captain.

For supper that evening the chef had laid cold chicken-and-ham roll. As each officer entered the wardroom and saw it on the table, he cried; 'Mon dieu, qu'est-ce-que c'est que ça?' or 'Merde, quelle connerie est ça?' or 'Bacchus ne le mangerait pas – il pisserait au-dessus, certainement pisserait au-dessus'. So we had bread-and-butter and anchovies and tinned *singe**[*]** and macaroni and red wine and bread-and-butter-and-marmalade and rum and coffee, and Bacchus was very grateful for some chicken-and-ham roll.

I went up on the bridge at 8 p.m., wearing my Ursula[**] suit and not caring how wet I got. Olry was on watch. The wind howled and shrieked in the jumping wires, the grey seas rose above our heads and swarmed away to port, streaked in white; dimly one could see waves breaking white ahead of us, to starboard and to port. There was no universe and no stars, no England or Scotland or Norway; just a tiny wet bridge, like the cab of a railway engine, with a hood under which one could cower when seas came over, hurled by the shrieking wind. Down one would go for a minute, and then force one's head up again into the storm. One could not see more than about two waves' crests away from the ship, about fifteen yards. The *Tirpitz* herself might pass close without our ever seeing her; and if we did see her, we would be able to do nothing. We peered into the murk, and waves whipped over and caught us unawares, and pints of sea-water slashed us in the eyes and mouth, and trickled down our necks, and we lowered our heads like cattle, and let it drip off, and looked out again.

[*]   Generic nickname for French tinned meat.
[**] Two-piece waterproof suit, named after HM Submarine *Ursula*.

Not being a watch-keeper, I did not have to stay on the bridge, and after an hour or so I weakened and went below. But the *Rubis'* bridge, with its cab, was a great deal better protected than the bridges of most British submarines; and with her wide mine-carrying saddle tanks, she did not roll so much as an ordinary boat would have done. To have an officer washed off the bridge seems an unnecessary way to lose a life in a submarine, but it happened to two of my friends from Dundee.

Day followed night, and night followed day. Bacchus developed some internal disorder and began misbehaving all over the boat. When this happened in the wardroom, the little pile was not noticed for some time, and the smell was so bad that I had to get out a green bottle of German lavender water (with sentimental connections) and scent my handkerchief. Olry poured some of it on my hair, and the Captain, next time he came into the wardroom, complained bitterly about it and said it was worse than Bacchus. He said he even noticed it on the bridge, six hours later.

The next night so much water came down the conning-tower hatch that we ran with it closed (with two men on the bridge) and the small waterproofed engine-room hatch open; and then, since visibility was nil, we ran blind, with nobody on the bridge at all. For two consecutive nights we were hove-to, just keeping our bows into the gale. The Captain remarked that we ought to get the *Rubis* photographed when we returned, just to record the damage the seas had done: already some of the decking was stove in, and heavy seas had wrenched away two of the mine chamber lids, tearing one in half, and had torn away the doors to the navigation lights in the conning-tower.

On the fifth day out, which was a Sunday, the tea-time argument was on religion. The Captain started it by asking me why there were so many bigamists in England, and motorists who did not stop after an accident; Dubuisson took him up on the latter point and soon he and Rousselot and Hémar were at it hammer and tongs, arguing Roman Catholicism versus Protestantism. It was pleasant to watch. My French was not, unfortunately, equal to a lot of the most interesting bits but at least I could watch their eyes, their faces and their hands.

A signal that evening told us that *Minerve* was coming out to join us. We were supposed to be already in a position adjoining *Tuna* and *Trident*, but the gale had made us late.

The next night it was rougher than ever. When I went up on the bridge, waves were washing over all the time; mountains of grey streaked with white, rearing up and sliding away into the night, in procession. The air was white with blown spray. We could not have seen the *Tirpitz* fifty yards away, nor cared; nor would they. Again we were hove to, with the conning-tower hatch shut.

The next day we surfaced after lunch to take sun sights – our first sun that patrol and the first time I had seen daylight for nine days.

Rubis *control room, with Bacchus.*

That night we surfaced early, about five. During dinner, about seven, I was called up on to the bridge to see the Northern Lights. A great curtain hung across the sky, changing its tints as if by a switch; it was mostly pale green, overlaid on the blue of the night.

I went up on the bridge again from about ten to eleven-thirty, and watched the Northern Lights, and discussed the storm with the Captain. If it was hampering us it was certainly hampering the U-boats and helping our convoys. Then a 96-group signal arrived addressed to *Tuna* and *Rubis*, which caused great excitement because we thought it might be our recall. I had many volunteers to help me decode it. However, it turned out to be only *Tuna*'s recall. It looked as if we would have at least two days in our patrol position, if better weather had come at last.

That night I dreamed there was political street-fighting in Dundee, and that I was cantering in a cavalry charge (that must have been the movement of the boat) then I was driving a curious motor car along a road, with the steering wheel as far above my head as I could reach; then I was steering the *Rubis* into a cathedral, then sitting in the congregation next to a pretty girl (unidentified); then I woke up as the klaxon went and we dived. The Captain came and had a cup of cocoa beside me before turning in, and explained to me the difference between the French and the British routines for diving. He preferred the French system, because he said it was safer, although it might take two seconds longer.

That morning we fixed our position by land sights, and I looked through the periscope at snowy mountains and a very distinctive and characteristic vertical cliff, somewhere near Statlandet.

At night we surfaced about seven-thirty in brilliant moonlight. The coast of Norway was a shadow along the horizon: we were about twelve miles off shore. This was a night we would have seen the *Tirpitz*, if she had come our way. I kept watch with Olry until 11 p.m., and then we made some Bovril. Still no recall.

The next day, when we dived, the Captain and the First Lieutenant broke precedent by having an argument at breakfast. It was on what we should do to Hitler if we captured him. Put him in a submarine and depth-charge him? The Captain (and I agreed with him) was for putting him in a cage and exhibiting him all through the countries he had invaded. The First Lieutenant rather wanted also to permit everyone to commit abuses on him, on a rising scale of charges, thereby raising much money for refugees. They were afraid Hitler would escape to Sweden.

At supper we were offered beans, or 'haricots musicales'. Hurrah, said the Captain, now we can bombard the *Tirpitz*. That night our recall came at last: we were to leave patrol after dark two days later, and be at the edge of Gap A (in our own minefields) at 0200 on the following Saturday. This meant we would probably be in Dundee for Christmas. My imagination immediately concentrated on every detail of returning – the displaying of my beard to the Wrens, the collecting of mail, the luxurious bath and shave, the shampoo down town, the telephone calls.

The thirteenth day of the patrol was marked by an argument on parasites. The First Lieutenant very kindly drew a picture of a 'crab' ('morpion') in the back of *Anna Karenina* which I was reading. (It was a Free French crab, with a Cross of Lorraine on its back.) At one time, he said, every officer and man on board his ship had had them for four months, and they had bred them. He himself had started a very fine strain, South American X Martinique. He took them home and gave them to his sister (how?). He explained that you can cure them in a night with a black paste; but if you fail, they reappear when the eggs hatch out. Then they discussed what the Captain said was called in English the itch (the tick?), a parasite that grows under the skin. It is treated with sulphur ointment. Later, in India, I met some interesting tropical bugs and leeches, but at this time I was inexperienced.

The Frenchmen's attitude to dirt and parasites was almost affectionate. One of their great quarrels with America was the American 'cellophane mentality', based, according to them, on hypocrisy. American packaged food was, they said, put in the cellophane by hand; and it had no taste anyway.

Sailor at depth gauge with Bacchus.

19

RETURN OF A SUBMARINE

The last days of a patrol contain as many minutes and hours as all the others, but they seem much longer. One plays such games as noughts-and-crosses with desperation but is disinclined to read. The bread is probably no longer eatable; on this patrol I think we were on to biscuits by about the fourteenth day. There are certainly no more vegetables (except dehydrated ones) and no fresh food of any kind – there may even be a shortage of food altogether. One has read all one's books and magazines, and the only thing that thrives, by this time, is one's beard.

The one incident worth recording, of the homeward run, was the night when Green woke the Captain urgently to tell him there must be a submarine close to us because of the strength of the radio signals he was receiving. When we decoded the signals, it was from P.551 somewhere west of Ireland, five hundred miles away. The Captain was a sarcastic man.

At last, at last we were nearing Dundee.

The Captain peered ahead through his glasses. It was just after dawn, but still confoundedly dark. This morning we did not have to dive. We should be sighting the buoy very soon. It was the first buoy of the swept channel on the way in, as it were the first street lamp of Dundee: and we always held a sweepstake on the time we passed it. Everyone in the submarine had, grumblingly, handed in threepence the night before. A few hours after passing it, we would be tying up alongside.

It was now eight years since Rousselot had gone into submarines, and two since he and his men had declared for Free France. He had never so longed to be back from sea. It had not been a pleasing patrol: it had been boring, and unrewarding, and exhausting; he had hardly slept (he had done all the navigation himself) for a whole fortnight; and he had had no message about his expectant wife. He would certainly be glad to be back.

Rousselot was thinking of the hot bath and the meal that would be waiting for him, when he saw the buoy. It was riding in the stream about a cable's length off the port bow. Its red ring was the only spot of colour in the grey morning. He had the stop-watch ready: the others on the bridge sucked their cigarettes and watched the buoy come nearer, speculating. The sweepstake was held on the number of minutes past the hour at which the buoy was dead abeam. Every man therefore chose a number under 60 and had to have a reason for his choice. The Captain had chosen 13, because this had been his thirteenth patrol. Dubuisson had chosen 22 because that was the age of his wife, thereby depriving Hémar of the same number for more or less the same reason; Geoffray, the Coxswain, chose 52 because that was the number of his mother's house in a street in Nice; and Bacchus was allotted 57 because – well, because he was that sort of a dog. Olry took 49 because that was the course on which we had fired our successful torpedoes on the last patrol; and Creton, the cook, chose 48 because that was the number of the policeman whose helmet he had knocked off in a slight tiff with the Law.

The buoy came abeam. The Captain shouted 'top' and pressed the stop-watch. Three had won. The list was hastily consulted. Three was an engineer. The news was shouted down the voice pipe. And when would three be paying for drinks all round?

Later in the morning, as we were actually coming alongside, the sun shone. Except for those on duty below, the entire crew was up on deck. They were a strange, piratical-looking crew, these Frenchmen; a great deal more picturesque, with a greater variety of costume, than any British ship's company I had seen. All of them wore the caps with the little red pom-poms on top, though few still had the ones with which they had left France; they had a high value with girl-friends. There were some fine black beards among them, but quite a few, to the disgust of the others, had shaved that morning and looked offensively clean. All, as they watched the houses and buildings on shore come closer and closer, had a warm feeling in-side: it was good to enter harbour safely after three weeks in the North Sea.

Men in other ships in the harbour watched us curiously and half-enviously as we passed; the Aldis Lamp on a friendly destroyer was seen to wink; and seagulls in the air murmured 'Ah, I prefer scraps from French cooking, don't you?' Finally we came to our berth. Rousselot, standing on a step in the conning-tower from which he could survey the whole length of the ship, gave his orders quietly, almost in a whisper. The first heaving lines snaked out and fell short, as usual; the second attempts were caught, the heavy mooring cables were led ashore and made fast, the Captain climbed down from his perch and lit a cigarette.

The men on the jetty (no array of officers this time, but Commander (S) and a few casuals) ran their eyes over the submarine, noticing the damage: they thought we must have been depth-charged. As soon as the plank was lowered to the deck of the *Rubis*, Rousselot climbed ashore and shook hands with Commander (S) and the senior French Officers who had come down. A crowd of French and British sailors now swarmed down to the submarine's deck to hear all about our trip. The base Engineer Officer was already making a list of the repairs we needed, and arranging for our refuelling. Bacchus, the only member of the crew who had actually been born in a submarine, was already on the jetty, running wild with excitement. The rest of the crew began climbing up the plank with their belongings in battered old suitcases, eager to be off, and telephone their girls and have baths and get into clean clothes and begin celebrating. Casey saw the Master-at-Arms waiting for him, and was told he had to appear before Captain (S) the following day. Rousselot and I were driven off in a Staff Car to the Staff Office to make a preliminary report: Admiral (Submarines) in London would be clamouring for it over the telephone, negative as it was, if he didn't get it immediately. The others, officers and men, walked the short distance to their quarters rather unsteadily. They had not yet got their land legs.

The celebrations that evening followed their normal course. The French sailors were popular in the town, where they had been stationed for over two years now. They had never thrown in their hands and their gaiety was as infectious as ever. Many had married or become engaged to local girls; these left the bars early with smug expressions on their faces. The rest continued drinking and singing and en-larging on their exploits until if half of what they said was true, the war was as good as won.

Rousselot, as I ascertained by telephone, was at his own fireside, with his wife in excellent health, still waiting; he was glad to be on land again, even if it was not France.

As for Casey, I found him in the Anchor Tavern at half-past eight that evening. We all got drunk together – him, me, and the Master-at-Arms.

Leading Telegraphist Green and Leading Signalman Tim Casey.

Rubis' five officers: l. to r., Dubuisson, Hémar, Rousselot, McLean, Olry.

McLean and Rousselot on Rubis, *Dundee, September 1941.*

20

DOWN TO BISCAY

We left Dundee on a January morning which opened slowly in pink and gold, as the sun rose above the hills on the far side of the Tay. Mist lay on the river until the sun was high enough to disperse it, just a few minutes before our departure. There were delicate icy clouds in shreds and streaks tinged with gold, above the hills of Fife.

Two days later, it was again a glorious morning, and we were sailing through some of the most magnificent scenery in the world. Barra lay astern on one side, and the mountains of Skye on the other. The sea was glassy calm, and the sun blazed in a blue sky; along the horizon the blue was flecked with lambs' tails of white cloud, centred with deep lavender shadows. It was difficult to believe that it was January – except for the wind, blowing off snow-capped hills, which went through one's duffel coat, and jerseys, and vests.

This time, we were going to lay mines off the Atlantic coast of France, and were being escorted as far as Land's End by the trawler *Loch Monteith*. If it had only been a little warmer, I would have lain on deck reading a book. It was not likely that we would have to dive suddenly here …

After they had breakfast, Rousselot and Dubuisson came up on the bridge. I assumed a proprietorial air, for this was my country, and courteously invited them to make themselves at home, and admire the place as much as they wanted. They glanced critically at the snow-covered mountains of Skye and said that Norway was better. Rousselot then expatiated at length on the virtues of the Haute Savoie, where he had been born. When they went below again, I hunched my duffel coat more tightly round myself, for the wind was almost unbearable, and continued to be content with Scotland.

Ahead of us, the *Loch Monteith* (known to us as the Loch Ness Monster) was contriving to roll through ninety degrees even in this calm sea. About one and a half miles out to westward, an ex-U.S. destroyer slowly overhauled and passed us, a curl of foam at her bows, her four stacks making a little smoke. Between her and us I watched the breath-taking vertical dive of a gannet; and, later, we were surrounded by a school of porpoises.

In the afternoon we saw Ireland. The last time I had seen that country it really was the colour of an emerald, but this time it was only a faint blue smudge. When I told Green I could see it, he replied 'Well, don't touch it, sir, leave it where it is, we might need it when we come back.' This was stock Naval repartee. The next day, no land was in sight at all, except (very faintly) Anglesey.

And then, suddenly, the next day, the skies became leaden, the sea turned a horrible blue-grey, and we were in the Atlantic. The wind started whipping the wave-tops into foam. Seagulls came flying close to us; one made a glide along beneath the conning-tower, and I tried to spit on its back, but my spit was torn sideways by the wind.

The *Loch Monteith* was due to leave us at dusk, at a certain point off Wolf Rock, out in the Atlantic south-west of Land's End. But the wind and sea were rising, and made us late, so that it became dark while we were still in an area where we should be escorted. We signalled to the trawler that we would have to heave-to for the night, and she agreed; but we soon lost touch with each other, and although we used our Aldis lamp like a searchlight, every second or third wave was like a high wall. The *Loch Monteith* was nowhere to be seen in the morning, and so we parted without the customary courtesies – merely with a mental prayer that they would not drink all the beer in Dundee before we got back.

The Bay of Biscay had always looked (to me) quite a small place on the map. It is in fact a vast extent of sea. We were crossing the main U-boat route to the Atlantic and there was a heavy traffic in those days: the Admiralty gave us the numbers of twelve U-boats we might meet. In theory, it seemed like crossing a much-used series of railway-lines; in practice, we had only a little more chance of finding a U-boat than two stars have of colliding in space.

This was the patrol on which we began playing bridge in the wardroom.

Bridge had formerly meant for me a green baize-topped card-table in my mother's Oxford drawing-room, a folding wooden cake-stand with three tiers (bread-and-butter, scones, and sponge cake), the heavy silver tea-pot, and new packs of cards. They never played with a pack unless it was brand new, those serious, silent North Oxford, afternoon friends.

In the *Rubis*, things were slightly different. 'On joue un bridge?' asked Rousselot after lunch one day. 'Père McLean, vous savez jouer?' I explained that I knew the rules but had never played regularly. 'Vous jouez Culbertson, ou non?' asked Dubuisson. 'I, er, well, that is to say …' Well, at least I knew who Culbertson was. It appeared that Dubuisson was a Culbertson fan, the Captain not. A green cloth was fetched from the Captain's cabin and thrown over the wardroom table, two extremely greasy old packs of cards produced from a locker, and half-a-dozen bottles of Whitbread's Light Ale ordered up from the 'cellar'. Rousselot, Dubuisson, Hémar and I sat down. The submarine, steady at sixty feet below the surface, slowly puttered on towards the enemy coast at two knots. The gyro-repeater in the adjacent control room produced a constant but erratic click-click in the otherwise silent boat.

I was told the names of the suits in French (tréfles, diamants, coeurs, piques, and atout for trumps) and had the current conventions explained. Then we started.

Yes, bridge in the *Rubis* was very different from the bridge I had watched in North Oxford. My mother's friends were tight-lipped during play. They never criticised their partners openly, let alone cursed them. They never shouted, roared with laughter or tore their hair. The officers of *Rubis* did all that, and told me that I played like a child, like a dead body, like ordure, like filth, and like many other things that I have never yet succeeded in finding in any dictionary. After every game, they turned on me, venting their sarcasm and wit, only about half of which, perhaps luckily, I understood. If I wasn't learning bridge very quickly, I was certainly adding to my French vocabulary.

We played for a penny a hundred, and the Captain wrote down the results after each session in a little green note-book. My debts rose twice as fast as anybody else's, but gradually the curve flattened: I began to notice that I was not always on the losing side. I also noticed that although Dubuisson played by Culbertson (and constantly referred to Culbertson's *Golden Book*) the Captain ignored Culbertson, and much to Dubuisson's disgust, nearly always won – because he read his opponent's minds and faces like pages of large type.

By the end of the patrol, it was less certainly a catastrophe to be partnered with me; and occasionally they would even say: 'Il sait apprécier un jeu maintenant, ce McLean' or 'Le perfide Albion'; and once, after, the Captain and I had won a rubber, he rubbed his hands and said in a surprised tone: 'Il joue vachement bien, le père McLean'.

We played bridge every day on this patrol, and I would have expected it to replace our tea-time arguments. But they loved talking, and not a day passed without a passionate controversy. Once we got in a great bother because we could only remember the names of six of the Seven Dwarfs (Walt Disney's *Snow White* had been in Dundee over Christmas).

This was followed by a long domestic discussion about the scandals of Bizerte, the French naval base in North Africa. I could not join in that one; but the next day the subject was English table manners. They loved jeering at all English habits and I had the difficult task of having to defend something of which I did not always approve. Why do you eat from the back of your forks? Why do you eat soup from the side of your spoons when the spoon is obviously designed to enter the mouth straight? Why do you cut everything in half before you put it to your mouth, however small it is? Why are you horrified when we dip our toast in our tea, or our bread in our boiled eggs, or eat chicken legs with our fingers? You do not allow yourselves to enjoy yourselves! When we eat Langouste à l'Americaine, properly done, what a mess we get into, but how we enjoy ourselves!

When he had finished with our table manners, the Captain turned to English cooking, and having demolished that, proceeded to attack English fashion (in particular English women's hats), English trains, English driving manners, and English shops, all with his characteristic gestures of scorn and impatience and fiery conviction.

Finally, running short of subjects, he started to criticise English printing. At that point, I sat up and, trying to copy his own fierceness, demanded 'tell me *one* series of French books that is one *half* as well printed as our Penguins?' He thought hard for a few seconds, and then said (very intelligently) 'Editions Nelson!' – which, as I then happily explained to him, were printed in Edinburgh.

Another discussion was on the so-called 'intelligence angle'; the Captain said that the intelligence of all men (and animals) can be judged by how near the angle from ear to nose to brow is to 90°. Whose theory this was, and what arguments there were to support it, I cannot remember, but it served to pass an animated hour. It led to a general discussion on the intelligence of animals. Elephants are the most intelligent said the Captain. No, rats, said Dubuisson. When Casey came into the wardroom with a signal, he could not understand why we all stared at his face so closely. His intelligence angle seemed to me to be pretty nearly 90°.

Our second day out in the Bay was Casey's 42nd birthday. I drew him a birth-day card with a cake and 42 candles on it, and the legend 'Many happy returns to the surface' and an I.O.U. from all the Officers (payable at the Opera Bar in Dundee). We presented it to him at lunch, and the Captain led a chorus of 'Happy Birthday, dear Casey, happy birthday to you' and we gave him a glass of rum. Unfortunately by tea-time he was utterly drunk. As Green said, when he put him to bed, birthdays come but once a year, and birthdays in submarines less often than that. As I discovered myself, later.

The night before we reached our mine-laying area, the sea was full of fishing boats, some with lights and some without. Although most would have been friend-ly, it was probable that some would contain German stool-pigeons, and we had to proceed cautiously. As far as we knew, we were not seen. Some lights were visible on shore, and the wind brought the scent of pine trees from the land.

Avoiding fishing-boats made us late, and the Captain was afraid we would not reach our position in time to finish the laying by daylight. He preferred to make his lay submerged by day, for greater accuracy in fixing his position. At 1530 we went to action stations. It was at first said 'Postes de Combat torpilles' and I said to my-self 'Off again – they are devils for going to torpedo action stations before laying the mines' – but it was in fact mines only. Green and Casey came and sat in the wardroom with me.

The first two batches were laid successfully, and we got out the tin of shortbread (our Christmas present from the Wrens) and opened it.

The third batch was situated in the hull just outside where we were sitting, and the mines went away with such a clatter and clang that we felt sure the horns were being broken off as they went down.

Then the Captain came down to his cabin for a few minutes in great form, which cheered us; and he took me up to the kiosk and let me look through the periscope 'to prove that we were where we should be, not in the middle of the Atlantic'. I had to say that it looked just like Broughty Ferry, but the Captain said it was Biarritz.

The French officers drank beer during the mine-laying which took three long hours. At last the mines were all away, and there had been no hitches: none of the mines had stuck or failed to leave. After laying the last group, when the men had fallen out from action stations, Hémar flopped down to the wardroom beside me and cried for a game of morpions (a variety of noughts-and-crosses, in which you have to get five in a row).

In the middle of playing this, we hit the bottom, quite gently, at eighteen fathoms or so. The First Lieutenant ordered everyone aft, but it was unnecessary: the bottom was sandy and we did not stick. That was the last excitement. We moved away and turned for home as quickly as we could, without further event.

On the bridge that night, at about eleven, we could see two lights astern of us, one in France and one in Spain, winking away blindly: it was good to have them behind us. A terrific hailstorm came on (there was already a swell which every now and then broke over the bridge) and I was standing in my waterproof suit getting the salt nicely washed out of my beard by the fresh rain, until it began coming down with such force as to be painful. Then I noticed blue lights sparkling on the jumping wires and aerials, on the top of the telescopic aerial, on the end of my gloves and on other points. This was the first time I had seen St Elmo's Fire, the sailor's name for the electrical discharge which flickers with a blue light. Eventually it became too wet and miserable and I went below for a cup of Oxo with Dubuisson, who had just come off watch.

The run home was uneventful.

We were again crossing 'U-boat Alley', and again they were reported all round us, but we saw nothing. It would not be true to say that we heard nothing, for there were always noises in the sea: sometimes faint enough to be picked up only on our hydrophones, sometimes loud enough to be heard by all in the boat; sometimes the queer sounds of the sea itself and the creatures in it, sometimes the abrupter noises of war. The sound of underwater explosions travels far, and it is not always possible to say from what bearing it comes. Some noises would be attacks made by our destroyers and aircraft on U-Boats; others, heard by the men in one of our submarines, might turn out later to provide the only evidence for the moment of death of a sister ship.

A submarine, when it is sent on patrol, has orders to go to a certain area, perform certain duties (which may be to lay mines, or attack certain ships only, or
note enemy movements without attacking) and, usually, to stay in the same area
until ordered to return. At a certain pre-arranged hour, perhaps twenty or more
days after the submarine left its base, a wireless signal is sent out telling it to return
by a given route, and to rendezvous with a surface vessel at a given place and time.
During the whole period of its patrol, the submarine may not have communicated
once with its base, since any wireless signal may be detected and disclose the
intruder's presence and even its exact position. A submarine normally breaks wireless silence on patrol only if it is *in extremis* (as we were on my first patrol) or to
report sighting a major unit of the enemy fleet.

So until the submarine kept its rendezvous in home waters, no-one on shore
knew if it was afloat or not: it might have been sunk days or weeks previously.

There was, therefore, whether those who took part were aware of it or not, a certain drama in this rendezvous between a small trawler and a submarine twenty-
five days from base, in a piece of flat and featureless ocean. Rousselot could always
find it with as much precision as if it had been under the clock at Euston Station,
and it was a point of honour with him to arrive at exactly the right time, to see the
escort before it saw him, and to surface astern of it, hoping to watch, through his
binoculars, the scene on the escort's deck as they suddenly noticed him.

The escort then set course for whichever port she had been directed to take us
to, and we followed; and the escort wirelessed to our base that we had been met.
When we arrived in port it was our duty (and, particularly, mine) to make an
immediate report by teleprinter upon the results of our mission.

The direction of the submarine war was in the hands of the Flag Officer, Submarines (F.O.S. for short, and at that time Sir Max Horton) in conformity with the
general strategy of the war; but we were operated, tactically, by the Captain and
Staff Officers of our own Flotilla at Dundee. It was curious to reflect that sentiment
would enter into the Staff Officers' reaction to the news that we had returned – or
had not returned – no less inevitably than it would affect our friends and relatives.
There were some on the staff, just as there were some at home, who could not care
less; but in the main, the men who now sat at desks had done everything we were
doing, and more, and were bound by ties of intimacy and affection to the officers
and crews of the boats they were directing. The presence of women among these
officers was an additional complication. Our relationship with our escort vessels
contained this human element too. It was in our interest to be as friendly with them
as possible, because in a crisis our lives might depend on their efforts, and it was
not too cynical to suppose that they might make just that extra effort for their
actual friends than for an unknown crew of Frenchmen.

At the end of this patrol we were due to rendezvous with a new escort, the *White*

Bear. She was a steam yacht, now painted Admiralty grey, and commanded by her peace-time owner, a white-haired retired Commander RN. She operated from Falmouth, which was where we were now going before returning to Dundee.

We made the rendezvous with Rousselot's usual accuracy and followed the *White Bear* to Falmouth, where no Senior Officer greeted us, but we were confused by a series of contradictory orders from the elderly Captain of *White Bear*. Then he very kindly invited all our officers to have baths and drinks on board his ship, and in addition he asked Rousselot to stay and dine with him. This embarrassed my Captain, who said to me: 'On board *Rubis* I have my own cook and a fine French dinner awaiting me, but on board there (jerking his thumb contemptuously) will be mashed potatoes. However, perhaps I had better go, it will be polite to the old man.' And with great resignation he went.

We had two fried eggs each on board the *Rubis*, with our red wine, which was extremely good, with fresh salad, followed by cognac with our coffee. Late in the evening a message came from the Staff Officer at Falmouth to say that F.O.S. was asking urgently for *Rubis'* short report – which I had forgotten. So I had to go across the dockyard to where *White Bear* was lying, to collect Rousselot to write the signal. I shall never forget the expression on his face when I found him. The two Captains were then well into their third Benedictines, and were puffing long Havana cigars. As we returned, I heard the full story: a superb dinner of six courses with oysters, and a different wine with each course; the best meal he had had since leaving France. 'Ah, je lui pardonne tout pour ses huitres' murmured Rousselot, and then said I was drunk. I said he was; and indeed he was as nearly drunk as I ever saw him. It was a testing walk back, for we had to pick our way by moonlight over railway lines and among stacks of coal, timber, rope, buoys and all the paraphernalia of a dockyard, and finally negotiate a narrow, unroped plank from the quay to the conning tower of the submarine, now dropped on the ebb-tide. But I think no sign of our cheerfulness, not even a wrong group, got into the signal to F.O.S.

The next morning the British submarine *Tuna* came in, which was exciting for me, as I had never seen a big submarine (she was twice *Rubis'* size) so close before. We exchanged visits with their officers, and learned they had been on a short agent-dropping patrol to France; and the men of the *Tuna*, and some of our Frenchmen, had a vociferous game of football on the jetty with a bundle of rags.

At 1330 we sailed for the Clyde: *White Bear* leading, then *Tuna*, then us, with an escort of Spitfires overhead. It was a grey day of rain squalls and low cloud. About 1930, when it was getting dark, and we were sitting down to dinner, there were four loud explosions outside, lifting the boat. A Junkers 88 had dodged out of a cloud, after the Spitfires had gone home, and bombed us, and disappeared before any gunner in our ships had woken up. *Tuna*, who had a young Captain, followed text-book procedure and dived; but Rousselot decided that it would be dark in a few minutes and that the attack was over anyway, and stayed on the surface. When *Tuna* surfaced an hour later (having probably had dinner in the calmer water below, in the meantime) she signalled to us; 'How are you?' Rousselot roared with laughter and signalled back 'Very well, thank you'.

The trip to the Clyde was accomplished in continuous dirty weather. We waited there, tasting the pseudo-comforts of a submarine depot-ship, for two days, and then sailed north again, in company with a Polish and a Norwegian submarine and still led by *White Bear*.

This time we were to pass through the Sound of Mull. I asked the Officer of the Watch, to let me know when we were passing Duart Castle, the ancient home of the McLeans, which stands on the water's edge, at the mouth of the Sound, looking across to Oban. I was fast asleep after lunch when a French sailor shook me and said deferentially, like a butler, 'Your castle, sir'. I rushed up to the bridge and watched the gaunt tower go past against a background of snowy mountains, mist-shrouded. The Captain and Dubuisson, who were on the bridge, were impressed and jealous, and the next castle that came up Rousselot claimed as his, and the one after that was Dubuisson's.

The day was improving, although there were still squalls; and Tobermory looked a pleasant little harbour, as we passed it, with sunlight shining on its roofs and chimney-smoke. I counted eight trawlers and a destroyer lying inside. But the wind was rising. I watched it whipping up the surface of the sea, causing waves to spread out in little pieces, like the fan-tails of birds, or the scales of a fish. The surface of the dark water was ribbed and veined with white, like snow on a wind-swept rock face. Gusts traced their way over the surface as across a rabbit's fur. This was more like January.

In the evening, I went up on the bridge filled with romantic ideas (after reading a novel called *Frenchman's Creek*) and found a scene of intense beauty. The sea was dark; it could hardly be said to be any colour, but it suggested the deep green of a bottle. About three miles away on our beam lay Skye, looking exactly as I imagined Homer's Ithaca: a pale violet silhouette on a still paler blue sky; which became a deeper and deeper blue the higher one looked; right in the middle rode the half-moon, and below her was Orion, pricked out faintly. Fleecy puffs of cloud sailed everywhere, quite white near the moon but carrying dark shadows in the middle as they got nearer the horizon. And, to remind me where I was, the strong scent of French cigarettes floated from the Officer of the Watch and the look-outs, while they conversed about the coming attractions of Dundee.

21

THE BANK OFF JUTLAND

We had about a month in harbour, and then prepared to sail again. Just before we sailed, I had to appear in the police court to testify to the saintly character of one of the men in *Rubis*, who had unwisely hit a policeman when drunk. As a matter of fact, the French were by far the best-behaved of the allied seamen then stationed in Dundee. They had nearly all settled down and married Scots girls.

There was one change in the crew. Our English telegraphist Green had been appointed elsewhere, and in exchange we got another pensioner like Casey, Leading Telegraphist Whitbread, who had grey hair, a leathery face, a DSM and a Cross of Orange Nassau, awarded for service in a Dutch submarine. He and Casey were old cronies. Naturally they were both abominably drunk when we sailed, but I had taken the precaution of getting the Master-at-Arms of the base to promise me faithfully that he would see that they were aboard, drunk or sober.

When they sobered up we found that they had both come on board without any of their submarine winter clothing. They had only what they were wearing; and we were going rather close to the Arctic Circle, in March. Now Casey and Whitbread were old campaigners: yet this improvidence was somehow typical, not only of them, but, I felt, of a type of amiable sailor right back through every cruise in history, to the Ark. What surprised me was not their being drunk every time they sailed, but that it never occurred to them to provide for the fact that they might be, and carry their things on board beforehand. Here were two men, good seamen of long experience, forgetting their clothes, like two small boys without their mothers.

But Casey and Whitbread did not forget their rum. They drew their rum ration for the estimated number of days of the patrol, plus a few days extra, from the Coxswain of the base, and carried it on board the *Rubis* the day before, in a wicker-covered yellow earthenware jar. It was in their own keeping (not, I am glad to say, in mine or the French Coxswain's) and they could use it up as they liked; and it did not greatly matter if they used it up too quickly, for they had only to ask the French Coxswain for some more from his store and he would have regarded it as a privilege to be able to do them that favour. This was a loophole in the Navy's rum system which the Navy could do nothing about. In British warships, the serving up of spirits after the morning's work was an ancient and hallowed ceremony, seething with regulations and taboos, official and unofficial. In what other country is it possible, for example, for a sailor (as I have seen) to wear a ribbon on his right breast (where the only other ribbons that may be worn are those for life-saving) earned by signing a pledge of seven years abstinence from alcohol?

That was a ribbon Casey could never have won.

During our previous leave, Casey had received a 'draft chit', which meant that he must return to barracks and be drafted to another ship. This was not surprising: Leading Signalmen with Casey's experience and skills were rare birds and becoming more so as casualties rose.

When he went to say goodbye to his French ship-mates, they were appalled. Lose Casey? That was impossible, he was the ship's mascot. Words were passed round and reached Captain (S). Casey was quietly sent on leave, without an address, and returned the day before we were to sail. Nothing more was heard of his draft.

So we sailed. Our assignment for this patrol was a more interesting one than last time's. We had to lay our mines off Jutland, close to all the most heavily defended German naval bases; and to fix our position for the lay, we had to find a certain underwater sandbank, since the coastline was too flat and featureless to identify. The curious thing was that this position was only two hundred miles in a straight line from Dundee. We could have reached it in twenty-four hours if we could have gone direct. But our route, planned to avoid the declared and suspected German minefields, took us a long way north, and then down the German shipping lane along the coast of Norway. As we had crossed all the minefields quite safely once already, the French officers wanted to do it again. They argued that the danger from mines on the direct route was completely offset by the danger of floating mines and other hazards on the fourteen-day passage; and they proposed that, after the lay, we should return by the direct route across the North Sea, put in at St Andrews, spend a week there in peace, and then go round to Dundee at the proper time, looking tired and sea-worn. It was a strangely feasible idea.

The fourth day out, we dived at 0500, with such a sharp list that I was thrown out of my bunk and only prevented by the wardroom table from shooting across the floor into the Captain's cabin opposite. I picked myself up and went to sleep again, and thought I had dreamed it; but at breakfast-time the Captain asked me if I had heard the news? I said no, what? He told me that our list when diving had caused the bread in the food locker to shift and it had knocked open a cock on the wine jars, and a hundred and fifty litres of wine had gone into the bilges before any one discovered it. He was marking it in the log as a day of mourning, he said. However, as we carried between eight and nine hundred litres, it did not seem likely that we would go short. (English submarine officers used to say, with some jealousy, that while English submarines were designed round their torpedo tubes, French ones were designed round their wine tanks and American ones round their ice-cream plants).

After tea we played bridge, and I distinguished myself by going four down on my own call of four spades, after my partner had called four hearts. It would not have been so bad if our opponents had not doubled, and I had not redoubled … The only possible thing to say was what the Captain of the US battleship said after he had run it aground at Palm Beach 'It's just one of those things'.

After supper, I could not be tempted to play bridge again, so instead we had an argument. Hémar led by saying that the King of Belgium was a Boche, which succeeded so well in its purpose of infuriating Olry that the Captain intervened and challenged Hémar to say that the King of England was a Jew. This started a prolonged, and at times profound, discussion on monarchy, the Papacy, Communism, the priesthood, celibacy and what expedients (e.g. cactus plants) the French Foreign Legion use when they have no women. From this we went on to how to furnish a bedside table for a honeymoon. This led to a discussion of detail between Hémar and the Captain which outstripped what I knew both of French and marriage, and left me panting for information but too shy to insist on having it explained to me – an omission I have been regretting ever since.

When I next agreed to play bridge, which was the following afternoon, they all said to me 'Joue bien, McLean, tu m'étonneras'; but I suffered no debacle, and my luck improved, for Hémar and I won two shillings. We stopped for tea, and then went on playing till half-past seven, and there was even some discussion as to whether we should stop for supper. That day's patrol report included the statement '… did not surface until 2100 hours owing to having to finish rubber of bridge'.

The following morning, about eleven, our peaceful routine was broken by the sudden order: 'Postes de combat torpilles'. I fortified myself with a raisin or two and waited, with Casey and Whitbread, in the wardroom. Nothing seemed to be happening, and after a quarter of an hour I went into the control room and the Captain invited me up into the kiosk. The attack, such as it had been, was by then all over. The alarm had been given for two destroyers going north: probably the reliefs for the two going south about which we had had a signal. The Captain said that, of course, no-one had been on the hydrophones, and he had heard the noise of their screws in the ear-phones hanging up in the control room on his way to have a look through the periscope. When sighted they had been at a range of 1200 yards; just right for an attack, but our orders were to attack only cruisers and above. The destroyers had been well camouflaged, and he had been able to see their hulls, between the waves, for only a few seconds at a time, and had not been able to identify their class.

But he had been able to identify the coast exactly; we were, as usual, just where our dead reckoning put us. We might be able to mine the next day, probably on the surface at night. It depended on our having a clear run in favourable conditions of sea and wind to find our bank.

We played bridge again in the evening, followed by a long discussion on the officers' hostel in Dundee. It was agreed unanimously that the messing was robbery (because you had to pay for all meals whether you were in to eat them or not), that the only distraction was drinking (drinks were duty free, it being a seagoing' officers' wardroom) and that if you changed the position of furniture to suit yourself, it would be changed back by the stewards up to five times. And anything you left lying about, added the French officers, would be borrowed or stolen. 'In a French mess,' they said, 'we drink much less and amuse ourselves much more.' The Captain turned on Olry (the youngest and most innocent-looking of all the Free French officers in the base) and tried very hard to get him to say how many of the Wrens he had made love with – he wanted to know, he said, purely out of a love of statistics.

It was noticeable that the French officers did not often use the officers' hostel in Dundee: they were nearly all married, or had girl friends. They did occasionally turn up for the monthly Mess Dinner, and I remember one evening when, after the dinner, Rousselot succumbed to requests to give one of his 'recitations', of which someone had heard tell. He asked for a soda-water siphon, a bucket or pail, and a waste-paper basket, and sat down in an armchair in front of the fire and had the lights turned out. Subject of his act: a French peasant's evening in bed with his wife. Rousselot's foot on the waste paper basket gave an amazingly lifelike sound of a cheap mattress in nocturnal use. The details can be imagined, supported by Rousselot's gruff voice whispering both love and grumbling to the wife. The British officers had never heard anything like it, and Rousselot's fame was enhanced.

That night the weather deteriorated. It was soon so bad that we had to put off our dead-reckoning run to find the submarine bank, and stay wallowing in heavy seas off the southern tip of Norway. When I went on the bridge, it was not cold, but stupendously, utterly dark; the sea was coming from dead ahead, breaking in cascades of water over the bridge, drenching the officer of the watch and the look-out, and sweeping in white breakers along the hull on both sides of us, gleaming in the darkness. The wind was rising and howling into a full gale, and it was a most uncomfortable night: we dived early, to get out of it.

After lunch the next day, Olry and I lost so much money at bridge that the Captain said we were making him feel embarrassed and conscious of his social position; it was not at all *comme il faut* for him to fleece his junior officers.

After supper, the air inside the boat was worse than usual, for we had been dived for fifteen hours; and the First Lieutenant said he was feeling old, and another year in submarines would probably be all he could manage. The Captain said *he* was afflicted with nervous depression; his worst time was always between 6 and 9 p.m. We were all depressed by the continuing foul weather, and if it did not improve soon the Captain said we would go and drop our mines in an approximate position. This was said not out of impatience but because it might be better to lay them somewhere in the area now, rather than exactly in the right place, too late. We were taking part in a big operation whose purpose we did not know; but we knew that twelve other of our submarines were already in, or approaching, positions off the Norwegian coast; three French, two Dutch, two Norwegian and six British; upwards of six hundred and fifty men, at least seventy-two torpedoes, and thirteen ambitious commanding officers with their fingers on firing buttons.

When we surfaced that night, I put on my waterproof clothing and spent two hours on the bridge. It was very dark, but less so than the previous night; one could occasionally see ragged clouds and a star or two. But the wind and sea were at their shrieking worst; half the sea, it seemed, was constantly flying past in the air. I stood with my back to the periscope standard, looking aft, and watched the stars and clouds swing backwards and forwards in our aerials. I thought about the faces of the men in *Rubis*, whom I had grown to like so much; particularly the lean-greyhound-like face of the man who had escaped from the Vichy French forces through the New Zealanders in Syria, who wore a red scarf inside his blue jersey.

> *What thoughts at heart have you and I*
> *We cannot stop to tell;*
> *But dead or living, drunk or dry*
> *Soldier, I wish you well.*

The storm did not abate that night. Next day, we started playing bridge early; but the game was interrupted by the arrival of an 'Immediate' signal addressed to ourselves, which I had to decipher. It ordered us to go to a position 260 miles (i.e. at least 26 hours running on the surface) north of where we had to lay. The Admiralty thought, of course, that we had laid our mines two days previously and were now patrolling in zone K.3. The Captain laughed and described the Board of Admiralty (which to me, anyway, always conjured up a particular picture I had once seen of six elderly and very hard-bitten Admirals sitting on a bench) moving little flags about on their charts and rubbing their hands and saying 'Ah! *Rubis* is there and *Uredd* is there and *Junon* is there …' while actually *Rubis* was waiting a hundred miles away to go to her lay, and *Uredd* was hove-to in the middle of the North Sea, etc. etc.

For all he knew it might now be a matter of great urgency, if something big was coming south. They should have told him about the plan, and put him in the general picture; but they hadn't, and so he decided to proceed from our fix that afternoon and run out all night, and if he could not find the bank, he would lay in an approximate position, which should not be more than five miles away; and if the Admiralty didn't like it, he said, he would tell them to go and shift the mines themselves.

In an argument about the Germans that evening, after we had shaped our course for the coast of Jutland, Rousselot said 'I don't care whether they are good or bad; they've no right in France – enfin – c'est fini' – with a shrug of his shoulders – 'that's my only reason for wanting to drive them out; they're foreigners'. He looked round at our faces, and then put a finger on his lips to enjoin silence, and inclined his ear to catch the murmur of conversation coming to us from the Poste des Maitres (Petty Officers' Mess) next door. Although lost on me, the wardroom always enjoyed the endless stream of political argument that floated along from the Chief Petty Officers.

The next morning we were somewhere near the bank; we began a slow, precise search for it with our echo-sounder, like a bat looking for a mouse in a cathedral.

The Captain had his navigational chart in his cabin; and as the day wore on, he became more and more restless. Out to the echo-sounder, to gaze reproachfully at its face; into the wardroom for a cup of coffee; back to his cabin to pore over the chart again, as if to learn every sounding on it by heart, and then to detect our position by will-power. Had he allowed enough, or too much, for the set of the current? Was the bank still where the chart said it was, or might it have shifted? Was the echo-sounder working properly? Where *was* the bank?

The day wore on, and up and down we went, quartering the sea-bed. The echo-sounder ticked away and scratched its trace on the gridded reel of paper; the men at the 'planes chewed their quods of tobacco and spat accurately into their bucket; those off watch slept or played dominoes; and the Captain almost swallowed the chart in his efforts to absorb it. Still we could not find the bank.

At last the Captain decided to surface and take a sun-sight. We were at that time within a stone's throw – or at least a gun-shot – of the enemy coast, so this decision, although popular with the French officers, was not applauded by me. Luckily, however, there was no sun. As a last effort, he turned ninety degrees to port – and found the bank. It was a great relief.

Once we had found the bank, it took us some time to run to our correct laying position, and it was dusk when we began to lay.

Everything appeared to me to go well, until the sixteenth mine was laid. Then to my alarm and despondency I heard the order to surface. I sat still, but my eyebrows must have been raised to their fullest extent. Hémar, coming into the wardroom, explained that it was feared that the eighth mine had not left us. It was thought that the dashpot had gone; that was to say, the weight anchoring the mine to the bottom had gone, but the mine itself was still in its chamber. If that was so, then in fifteen minutes or so the mine would become live, and if, in joggling about, one of the horns had broken, it would blow us up.

So we surfaced, and everyone was ordered up on deck. It was now dark, and fortunately it was also utterly calm, after eight days of storm. If we blew up, with sixteen mines still on board, it might be quite a bang; but on the surface, there just might be some survivors; while submerged, there couldn't be. So forty-nine men and a dog huddled on deck and looked at the cloudy sky and their watches.

Being the only person on board (except Casey and Whitbread) who had been taught how to use Davis Escape apparatus, I asked the Captain if I might put it on and go down beneath the submarine to try to free the mine, if it were stuck. The Captain thought, probably wisely, that he was safer without me fiddling with his mines beneath him, and politely declined my offer.

It was a really pleasant evening, and good to be in the fresh air again. Eventually it was decided that the eighth mine had probably left after all, although it had not given the proper signs. We finished our lay on the surface, and when all our mines were laid, the boat itself gave a sigh of relief, and we headed north again for Norway.

The next day was the Captain's birthday: he became thirty. When your age begins with a three, he said, it's a pity, although you still feel young here – and he patted his heart. His present arrived in the form of a signal from the Admiralty recalling us from patrol and ordering us to rendezvous off Lerwick in the Shetlands. Other signals indicated that we might coincide there with the British submarine *Sealion*, in which my friend Edward Young was then serving.

I drew a birthday card for the Captain, with thirty mines rising on their cables from a birthday-cake, instead of candles, and we played bridge. I made a few gaffes, but not expensive ones; and, to clear up a point of doubt in my mind, I invented a test hand which started a life-and-death argument between Hémar and the First Lieutenant.

That night it was foggy, and still dead calm; useful for the Germans to move their ships about, in freedom from everything except – we hoped – the *Rubis'* mines.

Our passage home took four days. The Captain, who did all the navigation himself, was the man in the boat with the most work. The First Lieutenant had to maintain the trim of the boat, making daily adjustments in the water ballast to compensate for the fuel and food we consumed. Apart from that, the other officers and men, keeping watches, had little or nothing beyond routine duties to attend to; to keep awake when on watch, to have one or more political or moral arguments a day over their meals, and to sleep. I had no duties to perform, and slept and ate and dreamed and read.

Life in a submarine when on passage submerged, for passengers, has a curious negative, peaceful quality which reminded me of Sundays in London. There were three or four men on watch in the control room (and some of them sometimes went to sleep); the Captain padded in slippers to look through the periscope every now and then; there was occasionally a game of bridge in the wardroom or dominoes in the Poste des Maitres, and everyone else was sleeping. But one couldn't, when one felt at length like some sort of action, get up and stroll out to the pub round the corner.

I was happy with these Frenchmen, but I used to long to be in a British boat. My French was improving all the time, but it was still a stumbling-block, hindering complete communication. Their friendship, or at least their toleration of me, was offered without reserve: but I was continually finding that I was missing something; that a promising path, in exploring another human being, could no longer be found, after one had stopped to translate a word or phrase; that a lesson, in humour, or wit, or morals, or savoir-faire, was lost because I was about three nuances behind; and when I tried to talk in French my inadequacy was even greater than when I was listening.

However, I did enjoy intensely those days that I knew would never come again in my life: and I steadily wrote down in my diary the words and phrases I learned every day, about three-quarters of which would be no use to me anywhere except in a submarine. Among the politer ones I learned on this patrol were 'le fin du haricot' – 'the last straw' and 'defendre son bifteck' – 'to stick up for one's self'; also a parody on our National Anthem, which is most impressive when sung to the correct tune. It runs:

> *Le bon pouding Anglais*
> *Est un excellent met*
> *   Apprecié des gourmets;*
> *Il se fabrique avec*
> *Un quart des raisins secs*
> *   Un livre de suif*
> *   Et puis un oeuf.*

At last we came to our rendezvous, at 0730 in the morning. The last time we had seen land had been five days previously; we had, since then, come five hundred miles on a devious course and in bad weather, and we arrived half an hour early. The Captain had reason to congratulate himself.

The Shetlands appeared as tawny, low-lying craggy islands, covered in snow. The approach to Lerwick was past several interesting-looking caves lapped by a grey-green sea. Until the houses came in sight there was nothing to give the land locality: one half of my mind insisted that it was either Terra del Fuego, or Aeaea.

Captain in his cabin navigating.

When the town came in sight it was a funny packed little collection of grey houses half up a hill, surmounted by a church. Some smoke rose from the chimneys. Casey's beer-famished eyes were quick to notice lettering painted on the sides of two houses which read 'Imperial Hotel' and 'Queen's Hotel'. Against the grey background, there were two houses washed in yellow, two fishing steamers with red funnels and white paintwork, a Norwegian flag on a grey submarine and the white, crying gulls.

Sealion had just left, so I missed my pre-war friend Edward Young and Commander Ben Bryant, her famous Captain; but the *Seawolf* was in, and so was the French submarine *Minerve*, and the Norwegian *Uredd*. We had parties in each others' wardrooms, lolling at ease, talking shop, exchanging news of mutual friends and acquaintances; and in the evening the *Minerve, Rubis* and *Uredd* sailed for Dundee, escorted by the *Loch Monteith*. I was due to have some leave immediately we got back to Dundee, and, remembering what had happened just before we sailed, I decided to make a proclamation to the crew. The Captain helped me to translate it into French, and so this is what went up on the notice-board, with a drawing of Punch (dressed as a French matelot) hitting the policeman on the head with his big stick, while Judy (as the Liaison Officer) looks on in horror:

> *CITOYENS!*
> *Au cours de ces libations copieuses dont le Comman-*
> *dant a déja fait mention en vous rappelant*
> *de ne pas parler de vos exploits, je vous prie*
> *de ne pas vous battre contre les Policemen, car*
> *je voudrais bientôt aller en permission et*
> *n'aimerais pas perdre du temps à dégager mes*
> *camerades du Rubis des mains de la Loi.*
>
> (signed): Officier de Liaison Britannique

COMRADES!

In the course of those copious libations which the Captain has already mentioned, and reminded you not to talk about your exploits, I beg you not to get in a fight with policemen, as I want to go on leave rather quickly, and do not want to spend time in freeing my *Rubis*-shipmates from the hands of the law.

(signed): British Naval Liaison Officer.

French sailor and policeman.

When a naval officer is informed that he has "incurred their Lordships' grave displeasure"

He imagines this.

But ...

The C.O. steps ashore.

22

IN DISGRACE AT LERWICK

The lights of Dundee behind the black-out were as bright as ever, when we returned from patrol; but no one got himself arrested on our first night ashore and I was able to go on leave the next day.

When I came back we were due to sail again in a few days, and I had to busy myself with my usual preparations for patrol. These included checking all amendments or additions to minefields shown on the operational chart and other secret documents; and visiting the padre, the most valued of whose functions was to hand out sweets, chocolate and reading matter for the comfort of submarine crews on patrol.

On this occasion I had also, for some reason which I now forget, to visit the French seamen's mess-deck, down in the docks. They had exactly the same accommodation as the British seamen, but had contrived to give their quarters a much more homely and individual atmosphere. Perhaps this was because their room was much more 'home' to them than to the British seaman (although by now most of the French had married Scottish girls or been adopted by Dundee households) or perhaps it was just that Frenchmen are better at making themselves comfortable than Englishmen.

You realised you were in French territory immediately you entered the room, because of the smell of French tobacco, together with an *arrière-pensée* of garlic. In the middle of the room a stove, its draught open, was in parts red hot, and in front of it, his paws nearly in it, slept Bacchus, the over-fed, over-pampered, submarine dog hero. Round the chimney-pipe hung drying socks, shirts and underclothes. On top of the stove, directly on the Victorian decorative cast-iron lid, two sailors were roasting kippers, one of which I was immediately offered. In the same second, a glass of red wine was put in my hand. A gauloise was proffered. My rank, as a Sub-Lieutenant, was so junior that it could be ignored, except that they addressed me flatteringly as 'Mon Lieutenant'. Round the room the crews of the *Rubis* and the other French submarines in harbour were washing clothes, playing dominoes or bezique, reading, writing letters to girls in Portsmouth, and arguing.

I forget into what group I was drawn, but I think it was the one which was examining photographs of its girl friends in France. I also forget exactly how many glasses of wine I accepted, but I remember suddenly noticing that Rousselot was in the room, sitting at a table, and that the men of the *Rubis* were getting paid. I immediately joined the queue, and when my turn came to step up before him, I had borrowed a French sailor's cap in which to receive my pay. There was such a howl of laughter when I did this that Rousselot looked up and, seeing me, grinned. I pulled my pockets inside out to show I was penniless, but I got no pay.

When I soared out of the over-heated French mess-decks into the crisp, frosty March air of Dundee, the world had never been more beautiful. But my bicycle had become strangely erratic.

We sailed two days later. On this occasion, Tim and Whitbread, for no known reason, were dead sober. This departure from protocol made everyone uneasy, and was regarded as a bad omen.

We were on a short and quick mine-laying patrol off Norway. There was to be no 'tourisme' after the lay, but an immediate return home.

The only events on the way out were the arrival of a small brown bird, probably a knot, which flew on to the bridge when we were on the surface the second day and the sea seemed very lonely, and had a rest for an hour, and the sudden addiction of the Captain to a jigsaw puzzle of Anne Hathaway's cottage, which he did and re-did for hours on the wardroom table, preventing me from getting my full twelve hours sleep.

We found our laying position on the fourth day. I was duly shown the mountains of Norway in the periscope; and we laid between nine and ten o'clock in the evening, on the surface. Immediately afterwards we set course for home; and the Captain and the First Lieutenant made up for their lost sleep; for, as always before a lay, they had not slept, and had been actively busy and anxious, for two nights and a day.

The next night there was a mediocre display of Northern Lights: yellow only, flashing and flickering on the northern sky-line like an immense bonfire in a wind. Planes flew over us during the night, sending the watch on the bridge hurtling below, but we did not dive. Later, we heard two submarine explosions seeming very close.

After that we played almost continuous bridge, except for one argument between Hémar and Olry. The only thing that they were arguing about, as far as I can remember, was whether, during a certain air raid on Portsmouth at which they had both been present, the British night-fighters had been above the town or not. Olry, slim and girlish in build and temperament, was often tormented by the extremely masculine, broad-shouldered Hémar, and on this occasion they nearly came to blows. The argument stopped at the Captain's request, but it left a bad taste. Olry had, before now, threatened suicide, and once had only just been prevented from committing it. I wished that they would wait for their sinisterly dramatic scenes until they got ashore.

We had been ordered to Lerwick, and we made our landfall in the early morning according to schedule. At about 9 a.m. three aircraft appeared and the Captain cleared the bridge. They were three-seater, single-engined aircraft with U.S. markings. They circled round us, and then came in low from astern, the first one firing his guns, for what looked suspiciously like the kill. Casey hastily pulled off one of our recognition flares and the aircraft immediately became friendly. They waved to us, formed up again, waggled their wings, and flew away.

We were a couple of hours early on our rendezvous time, and so proceeded straight to Lerwick, meeting the little escorting smack *Lord Dunwich* just rounding Noss Head. We followed her in at six knots, everyone up on deck, including Bacchus, very excited at smelling the land. It was a day of beautiful sunshine, and the sun was still climbing. Every crack and crevice of the cliffs was clear, licked by sunlight or bitten by shadow; their stereoscopic roughness seemed to grate on one's hands, as one passed, a mile away.

We anchored out in the harbour, as there were no berths alongside. The *Rubis'* rowing boat was immediately launched and a party of five, almost enough to sink her, went away to look for mussels, periwinkles and other delicacies.

Then a drifter came out to take the Captain and myself on shore. I was sorry to go, as everyone was settling down to sunbathe on deck, and Hémar had just ordered up some beer; but it was interesting to glide off and see *Rubis* from sea level, lying on the glassy water. I had never, since joining her, seen her afloat in calm water, and been able really to look at her as a craft, and memorise her lines. One doesn't, in any case, often see one's own ship at sea. R.H. Dana in *Two Years before the Mast* describes his ship the *Alert*, seen from the end of its own flying-jib boom, and wrote: 'Notwithstanding all that has been said about the beauty of a ship under full sail, there are very few who have ever seen a ship, literally, under all her sail.'

A ship coming in or going out of port, with her ordinary sails, and perhaps two or three shedding-sails, is commonly said to be under full sail; but a ship never has all her sail upon her, except when she has a light, steady breeze, very nearly, but not quite, dead aft, and so regular that it can be trusted, and is likely to last for some time. Then, with all her sails, light and heavy, and shedding-sails, on each side, alow and aloft, she is the most glorious moving object in the world. Such a sight very few, even some who have been to sea a good deal, have ever beheld; for from the deck of your own vessel you cannot see her, as you would a separate object

The Staff Officer (Operations) to whom we had to report, was a genial Lieutenant-Commander RNR We made our preliminary signal to Admiral Horton in London, reporting that the mines had been correctly laid; and we were told that the explosions we had heard on our way back had been torpedoes fired by a British submarine at a U-Boat when both had been submerged; unfortunately the time interval indicated that the torpedoes had probably exploded on the bottom.

'Vas-y, Bacchus!' In harbour at Lerwick, 1942.

Captain at the periscope.

We were told we could go alongside the *Loch Monteith* when she came in with the *Minerve* in about an hour; which meant that Casey and Whitbread could go ashore to the canteen for a beer and I need not feel guilty drinking it on board when they couldn't.

So Rousselot and I were taken off to the *Rubis* again, And we spent a pleasant hour sitting on the deck, basking in sunshine, watching the gulls, and the smoke curling out of Lerwick chimneys, and the squares and angles of light and shade on the houses crowding down to the water's edge. At last, a plume of black smoke over the headland announced the entry of the 'Monster', and in a few minutes she came in sight with *Minerve*.

We were soon tied up between the two new arrivals. The trawler's skipper had brought our mail from Dundee, and after collecting it I returned to their ward-room for a drink and some English conversation. That started a very alcoholic evening.

I was back on board *Rubis* for supper, and I ate periwinkles, limpets, and dandelion salad, all for the first time in my life. The winkles were a bit sandy. Then Sonneville, Captain of the *Minerve*, dropped in for rum and coffee; he got into a terrific argument with Dubuisson about whether the *Tirpitz* could be bombed in the Norwegian fjords, and kept saying 'When I saw the *Scharnhorst* in my periscope …' Rousselot and I went up to smoke a cigarette on deck, and that led to our being inveigled down into the *Loch Monteith* to drink again; as a result, we later found ourselves going ashore to a dance at the Queen's Hotel.

We would never have gone ashore to a dance in our sea-going clothes if we had been sober. Hémar was actually wearing his great black leather sea-boots. The others, all unshaven, were at least wearing naval jackets and trousers, although not collars and ties. I was wearing grey flannel trousers and my oily-smelling reefer. We were a repulsive group. Rousselot, I was glad to notice, was drunker than I had ever seen him before. He rarely drank now, he said, because his constitution could no longer stand it: he had an extremely strong head, and claimed that however much he drank he would always be capable of taking his ship to sea (which is easier than bringing it in to harbour). I was certainly drunker than I had ever been in public. There was an auction going on for the Red Cross, and Sonneville, also drunk, bought a sailing-ship in a bottle for £10. Hémar and I then sat on the edge of the dance floor, watching the waltzing Army Officers, with shining buttons, and pink, carefully-shaven chins, and occasionally put our feet out to trip them. We were not in the least ashamed of ourselves. Then, somehow, some of the pots in the hall containing aspidistras got broken. I claimed one, Dubuisson another, with a third possible. They broke quite easily and left neat little piles of earth on the red carpet. The police were called. They arrived, two very nice Lerwick War Reserves, with whom I soon got on most friendly terms. They did not want trouble, and had no desire to throw us out. Rousselot talked for one and a half hours solidly with the Manageress of the Hotel, trying to explain how willing we were to pay for the aspidistras, which he claimed were dying anyway; but even all his persuasive charm could not make her friendly.

The party went on, when the dance was over, on board the *Loch Monteith*. The *Loch Monteith*'s bar was open, and her officers were determined to keep it open, and would not take no for an answer. About 4 a.m., after a long discussion on marriage, Rousselot being the only one who had any experience of the subject, we crawled back to *Rubis*.

At ten o'clock next morning someone remembered that we had invited some women (including the Manageress of the Queen's Hotel, but it was doubted if she would come) to drinks on board at eleven. The Captain shaved and put on a collar and tie. I was just able to notice that it was a beautiful morning.

Later, I sneaked away from our party, which was too crowded, went ashore, and walked up through the town to the hills, and climbed a fence and lay down among some interested sheep. I was looking south over blue sea and islands which receded into misty blue distances, and decided to come back to that place after the war.

In the afternoon, we lazed about on the decks of our ships. The cooks of the two French submarines had bought some fish from a trawler and were busy gutting them. A heated argument developed over the name of a certain fish. The fish was carried repeatedly from one submarine's deck to the other for each expert's verdict – delivered vehemently and with withering scorn for all other opinions. The fishes' heads were chopped off and kept carefully for making soup. One of the *Minerve*'s seamen, a consciously good-looking young athlete in striped vest and sea-boots, practised vaulting over *Minerve*'s guns. Our own periscopes were both raised, and a seagull perched on top of each, beadily watching the fish-gutting. A mongrel bitch appeared on the jetty and Bacchus rushed up to greet her, egged on by cheers of 'vas-y, Bacchus!' from the delighted sailors. A knot of soldiers, elderly fishermen and small boys stood watching us from the jetty all day; and a few admiring soldiers and airmen were conducted round the interiors of the boats.

During the afternoon, the *Loch Monteith*, now anchored out in the harbour, began playing jazz on her loud-speaker, which was delightful. Later, the British submarine we had been waiting for arrived; so leaving *Minerve* (who was going out on patrol the next day) the rest of us sailed for Dundee in company, Rousselot being this time Senior Officer.

That night, after a wonderful supper including crab, we came on deck in poetic mood and watched a coppery sun sink into a sea of mauve and green glass; the following night we were back in Dundee.

23

BIRTHDAY UNDER THE SEA

Two days out from Dundee, while coming down the West coast of Scotland, we passed through a school of porpoises, who were leaping clean out of the water, in pairs. The First Lieutenant, who was on the bridge, called frantically for a 'mousqueton et balles' and the Hotchkiss machine-gun. The latter, when fetched up, wouldn't load, and by the time it was ready the porpoises were gone. 'C'est toujours pareil' he remarked bitterly, 'quand vous avez un mousqueton il n'y a pas de marsouins, et quand il y a des marsouins, vous n'avez pas de mousqueton.'

* * *

Two days later, we were off Cornwall. It had been a cloudless sunny day and the land looked very peaceful. Sitting beside the Captain, on deck, after tea, I remarked: 'Must have been a lovely week-end ashore. Think of all the picnics.' Rousselot sat up and said, in a horrified tone, 'What???? Is it Sunday?' I said 'Have you forgotten your Mass?' 'No, I've forgotten to wash.'

* * *

We were going down again to the Biscay coast of France, to lay mines for the ore-carrying ships from Spain. It got hotter and hotter. We saw no ships, nothing but a glassy sea and a hazy horizon. The heat sapped everyone's energy, so that no one felt like playing bridge or any other game. On the ninth day from Dundee, we laid our mines in the prescribed spot, submerged by daylight. As we left the area, the Captain, saw, or thought he saw, one of our mines on the surface. The next day he saw, in the periscope, what he decided were three minesweepers going to sweep up our mines. 'C'est écoeurant, ça me fait pisser' were among the things he said. We had come 2500 miles for absolutely nothing.

We patrolled up to Arcachon. The coast was featureless but on the surface at night we could smell the pine-woods.

* * *

The klaxon sounded the signal to dive.

I woke up and listened warily to hear if this was routine or emergency. The diesels stopped throbbing. I could hear the look-outs clattering down from the bridge, the First Lieutenant's voice shouting 'Pareil à plonger' and the Captain's order 'Dix-huit métres'. Levers were pulled and wheels turned. There was a hissing and bubbling as the ballast tanks flooded. With a barely perceptible angle the submarine slid down. In less than a minute from the klaxon, the sea had closed over us. The Captain came into the wardroom for his coffee. It was only the dawn dive. I made a mental note to make another complaint about being woken by the klaxon in the small hours, and turned over to sleep again, completely forgetting that it was my twenty-fifth birthday.

The coast was crawling with Germans, the sky probably lousy with Germans, but there were no German ships at sea. Undisturbed, and disturbing only fishes, the *Rubis* proceeded slowly on her motors all day, on the sleepiest and most boring patrol we had had so far.

> *Are there sounds in the sea*
> *Fifty fathoms deep?*
> *No, there is not a sigh*
> *There, but like sheep*
> *Valley-wandering on the mountain-side*
> *Soft as the wool of sheep collide*
> *Sister-sounding streams*
> *In dumb clash of dreams.*

Later, during the morning, I was sitting in the wardroom, when suddenly a sailor put his head round the door and said I was wanted in the kiosk. In a second I was up the ladder and in the kiosk. The Captain was tense, examining something through the periscope. There were expectant grins on the faces of Hémar and the seaman beside him. The Captain moved aside, motioned me to look through the periscope and said 'Is it worth a torpedo?'

I put my eye to the eye-piece. At first I could see nothing. Then I saw the green sea. Then in the distance I saw a ship, small, with one funnel, but a ship. She was alone.

'Of course she's worth a torpedo,' I said. 'She's small but she must be carrying something for the Germans. Anyway, it's my birthday.'

'She's very small' said Rousselot, 'and she's nearly past us. I don't know if we can catch her. Perhaps the gun? Déscendez le periscope.'

The periscope was lowered.

'Seize mètres! Moteurs en avant quatre!'

Our electric motors were increased to full speed. The submarine vibrated. Could we catch her? Our top speed submerged was low; and we could not afford to run for too long at top speed and exhaust our batteries.

I looked round the kiosk. Hémar, the torpedo officer, was sharpening his pencil. Bacchus was wagging his tail. The Captain was smiling grimly. After twenty minutes: 'Moteurs en avant deux. Douze mètres! Montez le periscope!' But our target was still too far off. We increased speed again for another burst.

Slow down again – to prevent the periscope making too much of a wave when raised – and another look. The Captain frowned. 'Now what do you think? I will put it in low power – no magnification.' And he pulled a lever in the periscope.

I had not realised that we had been looking in high power – in other words, through a very powerful magnifying glass. And now that we were close enough to see her clearly she was revealed as a miserable little fishing trawler: three hundred tons perhaps, but not a cargo carrier. We had to let her go.

At lunch, Rousselot said: 'Perhaps that is why the German U-Boat Commanders always magnify their claims? Perhaps their periscopes are always in high power? May I pass you a grain of salt, mon vieux?' And then they drank my health, and asked me how I had enjoyed my birthday. It would have been discourteous to say that I hoped I would never have another one like it: so I said I'd enjoyed every minute of it. As a matter of fact, it was not over yet. After tea, Casey invited me to have a drink with him in 'Englishman's Corner' and we discussed life in general, and our own in particular, sitting on a blanket beneath one of the mine-laying panels. While we talked he kept on filling up my cup unobtrusively with rum: and what with half-thinking that it was tea, and not realising how much I was drinking, I had had much too much by supper-time. I remember joining the other officers round the wardroom table, and perhaps I was giggling a bit. I stretched out my hand to pass someone – probably myself – the wine, and I knocked over the bottle. I can remember to this day, very clearly, the look which the Captain exchanged with the other officers round the table. I was then helped into one of the officer's bunks and passed out, thereby missing the arrival of the present we were all waiting for – the signal ordering our return.

24

THE *QUATORZE JUILLET*

We returned to Portsmouth, not Dundee, and were quartered in HMS *Dolphin*, otherwise Fort Blockbouse. My French officers were made very welcome, but it was a bit like St Paul's Cathedral, not the sort of place in which they could ever feel at home. After fourteen days (most of which they spent on leave in Dundee) we prepared for another patrol in the Bay of Biscay. We were due to sail from Blockhouse at 1900.

At the last moment there was a hitch, which looked like developing into a crisis. The red wine had not arrived. It had been promised from London, and signals had flashed to and fro between victualling yards, but at 1800 we still had no wine. We had never yet sailed without it. The crew were looking very glum.

At 1830 there was still no wine. At 1845, a look-out came running to report that three barrels had been sighted on the jetty at HMS *Vernon*, about a mile away across the harbour. He thought they were being lowered into a boat. We dashed to the walls of the fort, and saw a motor-boat actually under way, labouring towards us, with the barrels visible. I had to go to Captain (S) and request permission for our sailing time to be postponed by half an hour to enable us to take the wine on board. It had to be siphoned out of the barrels into our tanks. Permission was granted – the first time, perhaps, that a submarine's sailing had ever been postponed in *Dolphin* in order to take on wine.

Finally at 1930, with all French faces beaming, we sailed. 'Look at the dress of the men' sighed Rousselot. It was far from being the rig of the day. They made a barely visible attempt to stand to attention as we were piped past the white ensign on the flag-mast.

When we got into the Solent, the Isle of Wight was bathed in soft evening sunlight and looked very like a Birket Foster water-colour. 'Look at it well, McLean,' said Rousselot, 'you will not see it again for a fortnight.'

*   *   *

Once again we passed right across 'U-Boat Alley' in calm weather and good visibility and saw no U-Boats. One night, towards dawn, we dived early because the officer on the bridge thought we were being challenged by a signal lamp, but it

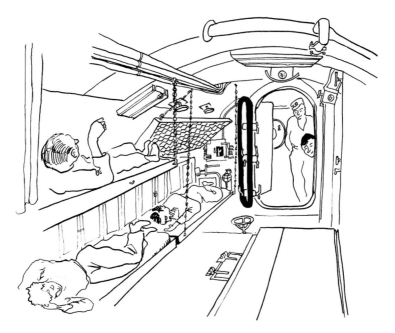

Poste des Maîtres (Petty Officers' mess).

Poste Arrière.

Poste Avant.

was probably only a fishing boat. The sea was burning with phosphorescence; long streamers of white-green bow-wave ran down our sides and looked, from the conning-tower, just like tubes of neon lighting.

*   *   *

The day of our lay arrived. We were submerged for eighteen hours, and the activity in the boat meant that our oxygen was used up much quicker than usual. We were in the neighbourhood of Arcachon and had to lay six groups, two at 1100, two at 1600 and two at 2100, all submerged in daylight. I spent half an hour in the kiosk during the second lay, and the Captain showed me an aircraft in the periscope, a large one flying low down and well astern. 'Patrouillez, mon ami, vous verrez rien,' said Rousselot.

None of our mines reappeared on the surface this time, and we left the area contented. That night, on the surface, the porpoises put on a spectacular display of phosphorescent swimming. Their tracks ran straight like torpedo tracks, and then suddenly curved off like spent rockets. Two or three would come tearing up and past us, and then suddenly criss-cross each other, and then all three would weave round towards us and pass underneath and re-appear on the other side. The night was filled with their sighs.

*   *   *

Our signal of recall came in good time and we turned for home. The great anxiety was whether we would arrive in time for the *Quatorze Juillet*. It was known that on that day there would be free drinks for all, ordered by General de Gaulle; but my cynical ship-mates doubted if there would be any left for those who had unfortunately been at sea and arrived back a day late.

Rousselot and his officers despised the Free French Navy, at least the administration of it. It appeared to them that it was being run purely for the political benefit of those in London. No one in London, they alleged, was primarily concerned with trying to get on with the war. We pressed on, but the short nights gave us only five or six hours run on the surface. We were hot and sticky.

The pattern of the foetid hours below was always the same. We tried to sleep as much as possible; but after tea we played bridge until seven, had supper, and then played again till it was time to surface.

We were due to pick up our surface escort at 0800 on 14 July, at a rendezvous off Land's End. For the first time, we were being met by a French ship, one of the *Chasseurs*. We made a perfect landfall, as usual, and reached the rendezvous at 0630. We waited for *Chasseur 8*; surely she would be early. At 0800 she was not in sight; at 0845 she had still not arrived. Rousselot was furious. He checked and re-checked our position; then he wondered if we were a day out in our calendar; but we had made no mistake. Then he began cursing the F.N.F.L. (Forces Nationales Francais Libres), and said this was typical of them. They must all be drunk on board *Chasseur 8*, because it was the fourteenth of July. I could only be thankful that it was a French and not a British ship that had missed the rendezvous.

It was a grey morning and flat calm. Rousselot decided to wait no longer, but to proceed on the surface to Falmouth. We were in sight of the Lizard Signal Station and tried to call them by Aldis lamp to inform them of this decision, but no one was looking; at least, no-one answered. Two Sunderland flying-boats flew over, dropped identification flares, and flashed to us 'O.K.'. So we made for Falmouth. Just outside Falmouth an M.L. came out to meet us, and signalled us to stop. We conversed through megaphones. 'Can we enter Falmouth?' I shouted. 'We are your escort to Portsmouth' replied the M.L.'s Captain (a Sub-Lieutenant RNVR.). 'Where is *Chasseur 8*?' Rousselot told me to ask. 'Never heard of her' was the reply. 'What is your speed?' we asked. 'We can do twenty knots, what can you?' replied the M.L. Captain briskly. Rousselot roared with laughter. 'Our speed is 10½ knots. Do you think we can make Yarmouth tonight?' I asked. 'Doubt it, but we can always stop at Dartmouth or Weymouth' replied the M.L. 'Have you the swept channels?' 'Yes,' I replied, and the M.L. shouted back 'Thank God for that – we came out at ten minutes notice, without anything.'

So off we went, wondering what had happened to *Chasseur 8*.

Presently a wireless signal came from C-in-C Plymouth, ordering us into Dart-mouth for the night.

We arrived off Dartmouth about 1730. The entrance to the harbour is difficult to distinguish until you are close to it. Then you can see a gap between two forts; the entrance is so narrow that chains used to be hung across to prevent Spaniards or Frenchmen sailing in. A few soldiers on the walls of the West Fort waved to us as we passed, and then we were looking at the houses and the gardens full of roses coming down to the water's edge. Most of the crew were up on the deck absorbing the new scene. Hémar was snapping his fingers and saying 'C'est vachement joli'. Dartmouth in summer must be one of the most beautiful small harbours in the world. Only the Captain could not gaze around: he was too busy looking ahead through the binoculars and attending to the navigation. Going up the Dart is like sailing up a street. Old men and children sitting on benches, girls, Wrens and sailors watching us, all seemed only an arm's length away. We saw several other vessels wearing the tricolour: we passed a French tug very close, whose crew waved at us, grinning. Most of the ships in the harbour were motor gun boats or motor torpedo boats or trawlers and small patrol craft. We had orders to go alongside *Bertha*, a Fleet oiler some way up the harbour, below the Naval College beyond the town. Above the *Bertha* were shoals of small sailing dinghies, manned by the cadets; and then the river Dart curled round beneath trees and out of sight.

As we came alongside the *Bertha*, a nondescript dog came out on deck and Bacchus nearly went mad, jumping up and down and whining excitedly. The Captain and I had immediately to get a boat over to N.O.I.C. Dartmouth to report to the Staff Office. There we learned why *Chasseur 8* had not kept the rendezvous. She had been bombed and sunk during the night in Portland Bay, and no one knew about it until 0900, when two bodies had been picked out of the water. They were the British Liaison Officer, alive, supporting the body of his French Captain, dead.

When we got back on board, the sun was shining warmly. I had a quick bathe in the sea and half the crew followed me. The thing to do was to dive off the conning-tower. A rope was put out for us to climb back on board over the ballast-tanks. Then I joined the party in the wardroom. It turned out that, in the skipper of the oiler, Rousselot and Dubuisson had found an Englishman who knew the coasts of North Africa and Mediterranean France as intimately as they did. They were having a wonderful time, going right along the coast brothel by brothel. There can be few pleasures in life greater than that of sitting in a submarine wardroom after a patrol, with the hatch open so that you can see the blue sky above, yarning and drinking. We carried on with these pursuits until we had drunk two bottles of sherry, one of rum and one of gin, and had started on the brandy, when we were electrified to see a female leg come through the hatch above our heads.

Rousselot's and Dubuisson's eyes nearly came out of their heads. Two real live Frenchwomen had come on board. They were French Wrens down from London for the *Quatorze Juillet* celebrations, and had been brought on board by Geoffray, the Coxswain, who had been ashore collecting fresh meat and vegetables. They were rather plain, and one was elderly, but no matter. The skipper of the oiler and I retired on board the *Bertha* and left Rousselot and Dubuisson to it. Rousselot tackled the elder one, who was a friend of De Gaulle's, and put in some useful propaganda on our behalf with her; Dubuisson offered to sleep with the younger one, and then remembered we were sailing at 5 in the morning. They left at midnight, and Rousselot and Dubuisson came and had tea with us in one of the *Bertha*'s cabins. When we finally returned on board the *Rubis*, Rousselot was clutching a magnificent framed picture of a girl (a double-spread from *Esquire*) in pyjamas with an 'I'm ready' expression on her face, which had been pressed on him as a farewell present from the skipper of the oiler. He was probably the first Englishman the Frenchmen had ever met with whom they could talk, on certain subjects, absolutely as an equal.

Our escort the next day included Spitfires: that part of the coast had been getting dangerous. We reached Portsmouth at 7 p.m. Bacchus was down on the ballast tanks as we closed in to the catamaran, whining and wagging his tail, and as soon as the gap was narrow enough to jump, off he went up the ladder and onto the jetty at full speed, pausing only to anoint a bollard. Standing beside Commander (S) watching us come in was a young Sub-Lieutenant RNVR with the same sort of vacant expression that I had worn a year before: my relief, the new Liaison Officer of the *Rubis*. I pressed my charts into his hands and explained that I would have loved to muster the Secret Books with him, but unfortunately … At that moment the Staff Commander came up …

We spent an amusing evening together, laughing about the coming muster, which I was able to assure him was always a complete farce. When I mentioned Christopher's ticks, he said that although he didn't know much about ticks, he did in fact possess a performing flea, called Miss Blanche. Would I care to see her? He produced a small circular box from his pocket and laid Miss Blanche (I could not actually see her, but he convinced me that he could) on his left hand. 'Miss Blanche will now jump from my left hand to my right, and do a double somersault on the way. Miss Blanche – allez hoop!'

This was repeated, with some embellishments, several times, by which time we had an interested audience of other naval officers. Then Miss Blanche got lost. A search took place. She was retrieved from a member of our audience. 'Miss Blanche will now do a straight jump from my right hand to my left. Miss Blanche – allez hoop! Miss Blanche! Good God, it's not Miss Blanche!'

When I went next morning to say goodbye to Rousselot, and settle my bridge debts, which I thought must now be considerable, the Captain very apologetically said he couldn't find the little green note-book anywhere.

Postscript

Rubis survived the war. When Rousselot took her back to France in June 1945, he had served the entire war in one operational submarine without missing a single operation, an unusual and possibly unique achievement. *Rubis* was credited with having laid 683 mines on 28 operations, and having done more damage to the enemy than the rest of the Free French Navy put together. Rousselot retired as an Admiral, after being Commander-in-Chief Atlantic and Prefét Maritime, Brest. In 1984 we had a reunion in Brest. All the surviving sailors and their wives, some of them still living in Dundee, attended a ceremony at which the Croix de la Liberation awarded to our *Rubis* was handed on to the new nuclear attack submarine *Rubis*, after which the 'anciens' were entertained inside the new *Rubis* – and found there was much less room in her than in our older boat. Admiral Rousselot died in August 1994.

The *Rubis* was later retired and deliberately sunk in the Mediterranean close to the coast of France, where she now lies as an honoured memorial, and can (with permission) be visited by divers.

BACCHUS

I know a dog whom I wish I could teach to write, so that he could write his autobiography. It would make fascinating reading. The dog is Bacchus, who was recently awarded a medal for his courage and continued good behaviour. Bacchus has been the mascot of the French submarine *Rubis* for nearly five years. Five years in a submarine – including two and a half years of war – and when I saw him last Thursday he was chasing the harbour master's cat down the road like a young greyhound.

He is always the last to come on board, and the first off, but he's never missed the boat yet. Some of the crew say he's getting old, but I've not noticed it. His coat is as glossy, his short legs and long tail are as active as you could wish.

I wonder how many people in France remember seeing him in the days before the war? For the *Rubis* was one of the show submarines of the French fleet, and during the summer she used to visit resorts along the coast of France, especially those of Brittany and Normandy. Thousands of citizens came on board her, and they must all have seen Bacchus. Do you remember a black and white smooth-haired mongrel with short legs and a longish black tail; a mongrel with the wisest, the most intelligent head and eyes you have ever seen, and a quite pathetic weakness for sugar?

Yes, I wish he could write his autobiography. He's seen the world, has Bacchus, and only he knows what frolics he's had in the various Mediterranean, North Sea, and Atlantic ports he's visited. He enjoys himself ashore like any sailor.

As for our adventures at sea, well, he conducts himself just like the 40 other Frenchmen on board – with complete sang-froid. Once when we were being hunted with depth-charges, his nonchalance was a perfect example – if example were needed – of how a Frenchman behaves under fire. He seemed to realise that his duty was to keep as quiet as possible – for the slightest noise might be picked up by the enemy's hydrophones – and Bacchus lay down and very sensibly went to sleep.

Bacchus has not yet got, as some ship's dogs have, a hammock of his own. He usually sleeps in the bunk of a certain Petty Officer Electrician. This man, who belongs to the *midi* and has a beautiful long beard, has taken particular care of Bacchus since he came aboard as a puppy. Bacchus recognises him, more than anybody else, as his real master; although of course the chef, who gives him his food, comes a close second in his affections.

If we are on the surface, and rolling about in a rough sea, it is amusing to watch Bacchus, quite unperturbed, adjusting himself on his sea legs to the boat's motion. Sometimes he stands with his fore-paws on the bottom rungs of the conning-tower ladder, asking to be carried up; but he is allowed on deck only when we are in British coastal waters. As for looking through the periscope, Bacchus is not over-ambitious, and leaves that to the Captain.

People often ask: Doesn't the lack of air when we are submerged affect Bacchus? The answer is: not more than the rest of us. And it is because he always puts up with it so well, and never shows a sign of objecting, or does anything but wag his tail, that he so well deserves the medal with which he has been decorated. Of course, he is very much petted on board. He always comes along to the wardroom after lunch and after dinner, when the officers are drinking coffee, to beg for sugar. He lets himself be ragged, be made to sit up, stand up, shake hands, be tormented and tantalised and laughed at, for he knows, at the end, he'll eat sugar out of the hands of every one of us.

I suppose Bacchus is in a way better off than the other Frenchmen who are here. He doesn't smoke or drink, so doesn't miss his Gaulois, his Pernod and Dubonnet. Whether his thoughts ever turn to a Mrs Bacchus in Brest, or Cherbourg, or Bizerte, I cannot say. But, when, after the victory, the *Rubis* returns to a liberated and a once more proud France, Bacchus will be the first to rush ashore, the most demonstrative in his delight.

Until that day, my congratulations on your decoration, Bacchus, and my respects. Bravo, Bacchus!

1940s' article by RMcL; illustration from colour strip in Eagle *19 February 1954.*

Part 3

CANOEIST

Indian riverside camp, March 1944..

25

LEARNING AGAIN

After a year in *Rubis*, I needed to do something more difficult. It was not open to me to become a proper submarine officer, since my one defective eye prevented me from watch-keeping. The Frenchmen were so good that they didn't need a liaison officer; a rating could have performed the technical part of my job, looking after the Confidential Books and signals. Or even a girl, which the Frenchmen would have greatly preferred.

Robert Harling, a pre-war friend who had been at sea and was now in Naval Intelligence, offered me a job in that area called ISTD – The Inter Service Topographical Department – which I accepted. ISTD, recruited from sailors, soldiers, airmen and civilian experts, prepared highly detailed reports on parts of the world that the planners asked for, of future strategic rather than present tactical importance. I found myself sitting in an Oxford College, working along the coast of France, preparing extremely detailed descriptions of every port and harbour, from the tiniest fishing village to, in due course, Brest and Toulon – of which, I was astonished to find, the Navy's intelligence and charts were extremely inadequate. We worked from every available printed source, from all ground and air photographs available, and from interviews which we conducted with anyone who could be found who knew the place – for instance, the British Consul in Toulon, a Frenchman who had lived there all his life; he had come to England, was located, and provided invaluable help. We developed techniques for cross-checking verbal information and grew to suspect instantly the people who claimed that they knew any place 'like the back of my hand'. The details we wanted included the exact location of dockside ladders, ring bolts, and whether rails on jetties were flush or raised.

The job was fascinating, but having taken a lot of trouble to get to sea, it was embarrassing to be now working in Oxford, my home town, wearing civilian clothes. One day I met a pre-war friend, Geoffrey Galwey, in the Admiralty in London. He had an interesting history: he had been invalided out of the Royal Navy, as a Midshipman, with rheumatic fever, some years before the war; had worked in Fleet Street, eventually joining Rupert Curtis and becoming a Director of his advertising agency, and had then contrived to rejoin the Navy at the time of Dunkirk when medical inspection of volunteers who had some rudiments of seamanship was a bit perfunctory. When he was eventually sent to the *King Alfred* to get a commission, he found that one of the Divisional Officers had been in the same 'term' at Dartmouth and the Chief Gunner's Mate, Vass, was an old shipmate from the *Nelson*. The Divisional Officer, standing in turn in front of each candidate and inspecting him, had not batted an eyelid when he came to Geoffrey, but at the end of the inspection he had turned to the Chief Gunner's Mate. 'Did you see what I saw, Vass?' They agreed over a drink ashore with Geoff that his medical record was none of their business, but when the Admiralty discovered that the same man was being paid a Sub-Lieutenant RNVR's salary and receiving the Disability Allowance of a Midshipman RN, he was very nearly thrown out again. He was allowed to stay, on condition roughly speaking that he never got wet or did anything dangerous, in case he died and his family sued the Admiralty.

It must have been an oversight of somebody's that around midnight on New Year's Eve, 1943-44, in a Force 8 wind, Geoffrey was engaged in the reconnaissance of a beach in Normandy, and that at H-hour on 6 June 1944, he revisited the scene of the crime in the special navigational motor launch that homed on the midget submarine (x-craft) with whose crew he had been training. He didn't put in for his special diving pay till a long time afterwards in case of awkward questions.

When I met Geoffrey in London, I knew that he had been editing a magazine for the Combined Operations Command, and disliked the job, but now he looked happy. He had been roped into a much more interesting assignment; 'it's all done at night,' he explained, 'and no one can see in the dark, so eyesight doesn't matter. Won't you join us?' So I did.

It was called COPP – the acronym of Combined Operations Pilotage Parties and also of Combined Operations Police Patrol which was the cover for some of its furtive midnight training activities.

When, after the fall of France and Greece, Britain was pushed out of Europe, a young Navigating Officer, Lieutenant-Commander Nigel Willmott RN who had taken part in the evacuation from Greece, realised that (1) some day, the Navy was going to have to land our armies back on the Continent; (2) that it would have to land them on beaches, as all the harbours were enemy-held; and (3) the Navy's entire training being to keep clear of the shore, it did not know much about finding, and landing on, enemy-held beaches. He devised and carried out a reconnaissance of Rhodes beaches but the operation for which it was intended was called off.

When he suggested to the Admiralty that someone should look further into this matter, he was told politely to go away, they were busy. But he was appointed to train landing craft crews in pilotage early in 1942. And, very late in the day, he was summoned to study the approach to some of the beaches and to mark them during the assault on North Africa, with a hastily trained team of navigators, sailors and commando soldiers, using folbot canoes, launched from submarines, and swimming, as he had done at Rhodes. When the North African landings took place they were fortunately unopposed. Few landing craft flotillas touched down on the right beach at the right time. Some were not even released from their carriers at the right place. The exceptions were where Willmott's teams reconnoitred the approach and marked the beaches. It was realised how infinitely worse the shambles would have been if there had been enemies shooting at them. Admiral Cunningham demanded more Willmott reconnaissances and marking for future operations in the Med. Admiral Somerville demanded them for Burma and Malaya. And there was the longer term requirement for Normandy. Admiral Mountbatten as Chief of Combined Operations told Willmott to go ahead and put in hand the organisation he needed – but urgently and with very high priority.*

Lieutenant-Commander Willmott luckily knew and appreciated Geoffrey Galwey and appointed him as his adjutant, to find and organise a base where training could start, as soon as he had some chaps to train.

Willmott's concept was that he had to train people to (a) find, reconnoitre, and survey proposed landing beaches, and (b) mark them during actual landings.

Reconnoitring and surveying would have to be done at night. It meant finding the right beaches, and then surveying them, their approaches, their gradients, their textures and bearing capacities, their underwater and above-water defences, and their exits. Marking meant merely finding them again with complete accuracy and remaining there, signalling the way in to our forces, without being observed.

The best way to land on an enemy-held beach at night without being observed, he decided (with the help and experience of some friends with whom he had already been practising it) was for two men to be carried to the area by a submarine, motor boat or even aircraft, be launched in a two-man canoe which would paddle to the outward edge of the surf, and for one man then to leave the canoe and swim into the shore. The most difficult part would probably be for the swimmer to find the canoe again, and for the canoe to find its carrier. For this, most rigorous training was required.

The parties that Willmott planned to carry out this work, and which he was now recruiting, were generally composed of five officers and six or seven men; the Commanding Officer was a trained Naval Hydrographic Officer (or later, a Navigator); the First Lieutenant, or Second-in Command, was a non-specialist Naval Officer; to reconnoitre the landward aspects of beaches and their defences and exits, there was a Royal Engineer Commando Captain; in addition there was a Naval Officer in charge of all equipment, on which everyone's lives depended, and a Midshipman as general reserve.

The men usually consisted of three Seamen (as senior as could be found) an

---

* For a full account of how COPP was evolved by Willmott, see Strutton & Pearson's *The Secret Invaders*, Hodder & Stoughton, 1958 and *Stealthily by Night*, by Ian Trenowden, Crecy Books, 1995.

Electrical Mechanic, and two Royal Engineer Commandos.

By the time I was interviewed by Willmott, accepted, and released from ISTD, he had six parties under training; I was appointed as 'A' COPP, i.e. First Lieutenant, or second-in-command, of the seventh party.

*   *   *

'Here's your bed. But of course you won't be in it very much.'

The room contained three two-tiered wooden bunks, hung with khaki uniforms, webbing and weapons, and looked rather like a trench dug-out.

On one bed sat a man in khaki battle-dress, with two straight naval stripes instead of pips, oiling the parts of a dismantled revolver with a very grim expression. (It was grim, I discovered later, because he could not remember how to put the revolver together again.) On the beds lay cartridges, commando knives, binoculars, compasses, charts, pencils, drawing blocks, note-books, and barley sugar. On the floor lay boots, gym shoes, balaclavas, a hand-grenade, tommy-guns, socks, and, out of sight, a screw from the revolver. I was very impressed indeed.

In the wardroom I was introduced to another naval officer in khaki, poring over a chart with a gin in his hand. He was Geoffrey Hall, my new C.O. Besides being a Lieutenant, Royal Navy, he was a hydrographer, had come from being navigating officer to a flotilla of minesweepers, and had twice been engaged to girls in Iceland, although he hated the cold and considered himself spiritually at home in the South of France. The Naval Party which I had joined also included Captain Bill Lucas R.E.; we found him sitting in a water-filled bath, wearing a new pair of brown boots, no doubt for some good army reason. He was large, green-eyed and on intimate terms with nearly every kind of explosive.

Our Maintenance Officer was, like myself, a Lieutenant RNVR, Norman Jennings, who had been a London West End tailor; and our Midshipman was Peter Gimson, aged nineteen, with a mature man's broad shoulders. We also had a Petty Officer, two Leading Seamen, one Mechanic, and two Royal Engineer Commando Lance-Corporals.

We did not have much time – a few months only – to make ourselves operational; and there was a lot to learn; more for me than for most, because I was so inexperienced in seamanship. It was easy to learn how to handle our canoes, and how to get in and out of them in the water, and to become fit enough to paddle them long distances; it was also fairly easy to learn how to write soundings on a xylonite pad strapped to one's wrist, while treading water in a choppy sea at night. But basic seamanship cannot be picked up so quickly.

The longer we practised, the clearer became the central problem; how to ensure that the canoes homed to the carrier submarine, and the swimmers to the canoes.

COPP 7 (Naval Party 735). l. to r. Lieut Norman Jennings, RNVR,
Lieut Ruari McLean, RNVR, Lieut Geoffrey Hall, RN, Captain Bill Lucas, RE.
Missing: Midshipman Peter Gimson, RNVR.

It needed the strictest training, the utmost adherence to rules and timetables, perpetual use of common-sense, and good luck. Failure meant death by drowning or capture by the enemy: and to be captured or leave the enemy any trace at all of our existence would prejudice the success of the subsequent operations involving thousands of lives.

Experience taught us early that the danger of detection by the enemy was negligible compared with danger from the weather; the initiative always rested with us, as intruders, and we would be poor at our job if we ever allowed ourselves to be detected. But wind, sea and tide could be enemies with whom we had to reckon more seriously. The first COPP parties, anxious to justify themselves and at last do the job for which they had been training, launched their canoes in weather which made success impossible; and four valuable officers were drowned.

I had my first lesson about weather quickly. We had, one night, the simplest of all night exercises: eight canoes were to paddle to a point about three miles from the depot and then, steering visually and by compass, home to a point on the beach where someone was showing an intermittent light. When we set out, the wind was rising; what we did not know, and what the officer of the watch at the depot only discovered after we had left, was that there had been a gale warning. The area of sea in front of the depot was sheltered so that the sea there was deceptively smooth. I had with me, as my paddler, the beefier of our two commando corporals, an amiable heavyweight called Thompson.

We wore water-tight rubber suits which took one hour to put on, and one hour to take off; and inflatable life jackets. Our canoes carried full operational equipment, including a light anchor, a Tommy gun, grenades, emergency rations, water, a compass, binoculars and beach-measuring gear. All canoes paddled out for a pre-arranged time and turned towards the depot. We could see the light at the right moment. Our compasses were in order. We looked at our watches. It then slowly dawned on me that the wind was blowing up. I guessed it was already about Force 5. It was also raining. We could not see the other canoes. I instantly made the wrong decision: to put our heads down and paddle all out, on a compass course. I reckoned that if we could keep it up for long enough – about two hours perhaps – we would just make it. But there would be no time to stop paddling, we would be blown backwards.

So we put our heads down and paddled. I was sitting in front, with the luminous compass on a board across my knees. I could just see it when rain and spray were not blinding me. It was hard work, but it was exhilarating. The thing that worried me was that there was absolutely no means of telling our progress. It was pitch dark, there were no lights and no stars. I could not even tell if we were going forwards at all. I put a lead line over the side, missing a stroke to do so, to see which way it hung, but the water was so disturbed round the canoe that I could tell nothing. After about an hour I was wondering if we could afford a rest. It is very demoralising to paddle at night and have no idea at all how far you have got. Suddenly, out of the darkness, a shape loomed up – a ship! 'Look out, sir' shouted Thompson, 'she's going to run us down!' She hung over us, I saw the water foaming at her bows. I paddled furiously to get away from under her. As she went past, I saw that she was anchored – it was we who were being blown backwards past her. At last I knew where we were. She was one of a group of small coastal steamers anchored in the channel down which we looked from the club house; the fact that we were there meant that we had been blown backwards fast. We were in fact going backwards so fast that we could not even catch hold of her stern mooring chain, although we nearly capsized in trying to do so. The ship whizzed away into the night, and I said to Thompson: 'In a minute, we'll be among the landing craft off Northney: we must grab one of them. Be ready to ship your paddle.' And very soon we came among the landing craft. They were about a cable apart from each other and in that wind and in the darkness, we were nearly carried past them all. However we managed to catch the mooring of the second one; and securing the canoe by her painter, we climbed on board. She was an empty steel barge, but we were out of the wind, and there was a sort of bench to sit on. I had a flask of rum which we shared, and we had some sweets to suck. We huddled together for warmth and I remember falling asleep while talking and waking up to find myself still talking. At last the dawn arrived. When we looked at our canoe, it was floating upside down and we had lost our paddles. Another lesson in elementary seamanship. We had to wait till we saw a boat going to another of the landing craft, and we fired a burst with our tommy gun (which we had brought out of the canoe) to attract its attention. It was manned by Wrens.

When we reached the shore, I telephoned our depot to report ourselves, and sent Thompson back to get a hot bath and a change; as a penance, I set out to look for our paddles, by swimming if necessary. Luckily I found them washed ashore.

The final humiliation was when I found that the only canoe to arrive back at the depot that night was the one manned by two soldiers. (No RN officer had taken part in the exercise). They had paddled for the land which I had forgotten was only half a mile away on our starboard hand, and having reached it had paddled back quite comfortably all the way in shallow water.

We continued training in this way for some months; and it was eventually decided that we were ready for action. We thought that our first operational experience would be in the Mediterranean, and practised swimming and canoeing there for a few weeks; We were then ordered to India. We were, in fact, the first COPP Party to go to the Far East, and would operate in warm, not cold, water. We were able to discard our rubber suits and could now operate in thin overalls, with naval or army badges.

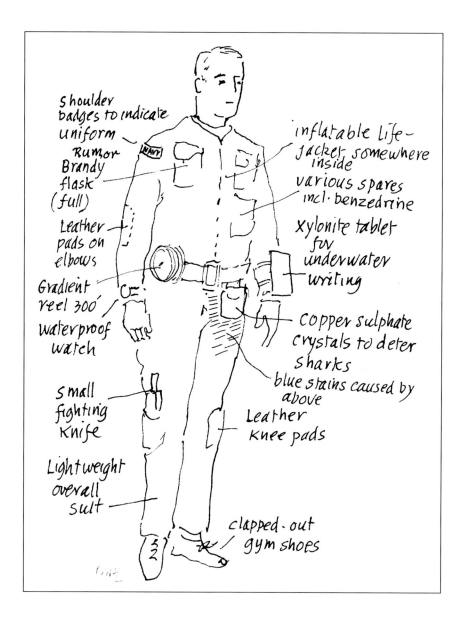

Shoulder badges to indicate uniform

Rumor Brandy flask (full)

Leather pads on elbows

Gradient reel 300'

Waterproof watch

Small fighting knife

Lightweight overall suit

inflatable life-jacket somewhere inside

various spares incl. benzedrine

Xylonite tablet for underwater writing

copper sulphate crystals to deter sharks

blue stains caused by above

Leather knee pads

clapped-out gym shoes

COPP Canoeist in warm water gear.

26

CHRISTMAS AT COCANADA

'I think she's beautiful,' said Geoffrey, looking critically at the photograph of the girl to whom I had just become engaged. I had asked him to be my Best Man, thinking it might be easier to get leave when I needed it to get married.

'No, not her, you idiot, her,' I said, seeing where his eyes were fixed. 'That's her younger sister. She'll be chief bridesmaid.' 'Oh, she will, will she?' said Geoffrey. 'Well, I'd better write to her and introduce myself, hadn't I?' And despite the fact that we were embarked in a troopship, about to leave England for an indefinite period, and that I told him I personally thought such behaviour distinctly forward, he sat down and did so.

He found a letter waiting for him at Gibraltar, and wrote again from Algiers. Then we were sent on to Alexandria. At Alex, he met a popsie on the bathing beach and temporarily forgot all about writing to anybody. But down on the Bitter Lakes, where we found ourselves sent to wait for a ship to India, there was plenty of time for writing, and the correspondence thrived. When we reached India, it lapsed while we prepared ourselves furiously for operations; and then it lapsed again when Geoffrey met the daughter of an English sugar factory manager a few miles outside the town. She was called Honey, and was only sixteen; but girls ripen early in the East, or so Geoffrey said.

The town was Cocanada, on the coast of Coromandel, about 300 miles north of Madras and 600 south of Calcutta. It was a small, undistinguished, dusty little town typical of many in Southern India, but had two advantages for us: there was no military authority nearby to give us orders, and it was situated on a vast sweeping bay of shelving sand on to which the surf pounded unceasingly from the Bay of Bengal. It was ideal for our training.

We installed ourselves in a bungalow lately vacated by an Englishman who had joined the Army, hired our own Indian cooks and bearers, and set about getting to know the local fauna and flora. These included crabs and frogs who climbed walls, crabs who waved one large pink claw above their heads while eating with a smaller one, biting ants as big as bees, scorpions who nestled in our shoes, mosquitoes with malaria, twenty-pound fish who leaped out of the sea in parabolas above our motor launch, lethal water snakes who swam beside us, but could not bite while swimming (we believed), and the sinister triangular fins of rays, cruising in greater depths than we usually swam in. To ward off sharks, we carried little bags of copper sulphate crystals, which dissolved slowly as we swam, and stained our clothes blue. India, on shore and at sea, teemed with life.

Most of our training was done at night, which prevented our attending what few parties were given by the limited society of Cocanada. We got to some, however, and two were memorable. The first was the one at which Geoffrey met Honey, and her parents; the second was the one at which Honey, and her parents, said goodbye to Geoffrey,

The first party was given by an Indian contractor to celebrate the fourth birthday of the war. There were very few white people in the area, and they were all at the party. Honey, with pink cheeks and fair hair, was the only girl, and Geoffrey was instantly at her side, leaving me discussing whether the Chinese invented lithography with an Indian schoolmaster and a Canadian Baptist missionary.

Eventually I walked home by myself through the streets, under the bright stars. Every house, however poor, had a little stone verandah on which the owner and his family and friends reclined, or sat cross-legged, meditating, observing, cooking, eating, sleeping, knitting, talking or spitting on to the red dust of the street.

A bullock cart passed by, its driver asleep, with a lantern slung underneath, between its wheels, casting the gigantic shadow of a wheel rolling slowly along the white walls of the houses. I accepted the offer of a rickshaw, and was trundled the rest of the way gently home, pausing only to buy twelve bananas for about a penny-halfpenny. Geoffrey and the others came home much later, with an invitation to visit the sugar factory.

The second party was the one we gave at Christmas. I have been associated in the giving of several parties which got out of hand, but this one got out of hand in a way which has remained, in my experience, exceptional.

The earlier part of Christmas Day was devoted to celebrating with our troops; but in the evening we gave a party to repay the hospitality we had received from all the white inhabitants in our 'neighbourhood' – an area which extended, as it often does in India, for a hundred miles or so. Our guests included a Brigadier-General, two Colonels, a Second Lieutenant, the Bank Manager, the Port Officer, the Missionary and his wife, and the Manager of the Sugar Factory with his wife, and Honey.

It was a good party. We had a buffet and plenty of drinks but no drunks. Lucas had offered to fix up the house with booby traps, but this had been firmly declined by the rest of us. ('It's lucky we didn't,' he said afterwards, 'every time I've put booby traps before, someone has been hurt – usually me.') Lucas was also longing, if the party seemed to be tending that way, to introduce cock-fighting, armchair polo, and other rough army games; but luckily it didn't.

We played charades; and then the carol singers and mummers arrived. The carol singers consisted of about twenty children, mostly tiny, from the Sharon Poor House India Bible Mission, and a band which included two long native drums, pipes, and percussion instruments including spoons. The mummers had painted faces, powdered white, and wore vaguely Mephistophelian costumes. They sang and performed, by the light of a lantern, on our verandah, framed in the large archway of our drawing-room, with the tropical greenery of the garden behind and the stars above. They yelled their way through 'O Come All Ye Faithful', and when they had exhausted their English repertoire, they continued non-stop in Telegu; they were obviously enjoying themselves so greatly that we could not bear to interrupt them.

After they had been congratulated, paid and fed, we decided to play paper games. It should be mentioned here that the previous owner of the house had clearly been a great reader. His collection of books was normal except for one shelf, which contained items ranging from perfectly harmless picture books, such as *Sunbathing in France* and *Fifty Studies of the Nude*, to volumes of fairly advanced pornography. When paper games were agreed on, someone handed out sheets of paper and pencils, and the soldier Second Lieutenant, who did not know the house, went straight to the bookshelves, and before we could stop him, gathered in strong arms the cream of the pornographic section and distributed them with a pleased smile to our guests. In frozen horror six pairs of naval eyes watched Honey idly glance at the spine of her book and then (since the title on the spine was deliberately illegible) glance inside. The book was called *Female Sex Perversions* and was illustrated. It was such a pity; of course, her parents thought it was deliberate.

There were two sequels to that party. One was that Geoffrey found time hanging on his hands again, resumed writing to England and eventually became my brother-in-law, which I am glad to say he still is; the other was that, almost six months later, we were visited by a Flotilla of Motor Torpedo Boats from a Naval Base over two hundred miles away. They had come, they said, to inspect a certain Confidential Book they had heard we possessed. It was some time before the penny dropped.

27

NIGHT SWIMS OFF BURMA

Our first operation was to reconnoitre the beaches of Akyab, on the coast of Burma, some 100 miles within the Japanese lines. The sea off that part of the coast was considered too shallow for submarines, so we were to operate from our own 40-foot L.C.P., (Landing Craft Personnel, a wooden boat designed for beaching) which had a fairly silent engine and was just big enough to carry two canoes on its deck. We were to be towed to the area (to save fuel) by an M.L. (Motor Launch, 120ft) of the Royal Indian Navy, which would remain off-shore as our escort, and bring us home.

We had proposed paddling right into Akyab harbour; we could have gone in on the flood, and out on the ebb. But the authorities in New Delhi would not allow this. It was the first operation of its kind ever to be carried out in the Far East, and they insisted that Security, not Daring, was to be our keynote. They did say, however, that if all our investigations of the beaches were completed successfully, with no Japanese interference, we could reconnoitre Oyster Island 'in force', and use force if we found any Japanese. That would look like an ordinary commando raid. Oyster Island lay about twelve miles off Akyab and contained a lighthouse; but no one knew if it was occupied.

What we had to do was find out whether the beaches were suitable for landing craft to land troops on, whether troops, vehicles and tanks could cross the beaches safely and get off them at the back, whether the beaches were defended, and whether the sea approaches to the beaches were clear of rocks or other dangers. In particular, had a long sandbar running out from the mouth of the Mayu river changed its position?

At the moment of sailing, Lucas fell ill with jaundice, so we had to leave him behind, furious, sitting up in bed reading a manual on Bailey bridges.

Nothing went seriously wrong during the preliminary part of the operation, which was getting to Akyab, but we did not form a high opinion of the navigating abilities of the Commanding Officer of the M.L., a young English Sub-Lieutenant RNVR attached to the Indian Navy.

At Chittagong, we picked up the results of an R.A.F. reconnaissance of Oyster Island; the Intelligence Officer was actually bathing, but the results of the flight, which were negative (a Spitfire had flown over 'at 0 feet' and seen no sign of life) were found in his trousers pocket on the beach.

We sailed from Chittagong in the morning and kept out of sight of the coast till dark. We fixed our position by Oyster Island lighthouse (unlit, but conspicuous) at 1740. At 2000, at a pre-arranged position about two miles from the shore, we embarked in our L.C.P. with one canoe, slipped the tow, and set off towards the beaches. The M.L. retired to seaward, to patrol 6 miles offshore; she had to be ready to pick us up by 0300 the next morning (or earlier, if we signalled her, or if she heard firing) and take us away to rest during the day. We were to operate again the next night, and the M.L. would then have to return to Chittagong to refuel. We would then return to the beaches, if necessary, and Oyster Island itself, for a further two nights.

The sea was calm, the wind light – about Force 2. When we were close in to the shore, and could recognise high ground shown on the chart, Geoff and I embarked in the canoe, and our L.C.P., now commanded by the Midshipman, retired to anchor a little further out – again at a pre-arranged position fixed by bearings on recognisable objects.

We ran two lines of soundings from the canoe to find if the spits had changed position. The second was straight inshore till a depth of 9 feet was reached, where we found ourselves in heavy surf. We paddled out of that, and then went to the position, about the middle of the beach, where we had to take soundings by swimming. At 2230 Geoff put his legs over the side of the canoe, as we had done so many times in practice, steadied himself so as not to make a splash, slid into the water, and swam into the darkness. From that point, the trees and bushes at the back of the beach could be seen silhouetted against the starlight; the moon had not yet risen. My job was now to paddle away clear of the surf, climb from the back seat, where I had been sitting, into the front seat, anchor the canoe, and wait for him. I had to make absolutely certain that the anchor was not dragging, by fixing my position with cross-bearings taken on the hand-bearing compass; I had a clump of trees at one end of the beach and a low hill at the other, and having fixed on these, I settled down to wait. I chewed some barley sugar, and kept a close watch on the beach through binoculars to see if I could see any movements, lights, or other evidences of the enemy. I saw nothing. From time to time, I felt the tension on the anchor cable (about the thickness of picture-hanging cord) and checked the bearings. I did not think we were dragging, but there seemed to be a current of about two knots setting down the beach.

It was with great relief that we could now wear light overall suits, not for warmth, but for protection when crawling over rocks or sand, with naval badges to make it uniform; anyone captured not wearing uniform could be shot as a spy. We also needed pockets and belts to carry our large amount of gear; a fighting knife, two waterproofed torches on lanyards, a compass on a lanyard, sheets of plastic strapped to our wrists on which to write underwater, a waterproof watch, emergency rations and flask, the little bag of copper sulphate crystals which was supposed to keep off sharks, and various other items, including waterproofed and silenced pistols, which we later discarded, as our job would have been a failure if we had to use them.

In the canoe, we had hand-grenades, drinking water, rations, a spare torch, and signalling equipment.

Meanwhile Geoff was doing his stuff, considerably hampered, he told me afterwards, by a strong undertow: he was not a very strong swimmer and was glad to reach the beach. On his belt he carried a reel on which was wound 150 yards of line with a lead pellet fixed every yard. At the end was a brass stake. He had to drive this in to the sand at the water's edge, then paddle out, keeping it taut, but not pulling it out of the sand, with the line running through his fingers. At every pellet he had to take a sounding with a small lead and line held in the other hand, and write it down on the plastic sheet strapped to his wrist. It wasn't easy. Geoff said he had just got to where the water was up to his hips, and was about to take a sounding, when he was hit in the back by what felt like an express train, and carried right up the beach. That was just the ninth wave, so he had to reel in and start again.

When he had finished his line, the moon had risen. He felt too conspicuous, at the water's edge, to go crawling up the beach, and so swam out beyond the breakers and showed his torch (carefully hooded and with a dimmed blue light) to seaward, floating in his inflated life-belt. As he was late, I had already lifted my anchor and was waiting for him. I saw the blue flicker of the torch and reached him in a few strokes. He climbed in, pretty exhausted, and we paddled out and held a short consultation. We had one more thing to do, which was to take a line of soundings from the canoe (I was not swimming this night) at the other end of the beach. So we did this, running in at one point to a depth of 3½ feet, when we were right in the breakers; and then paddled out to about a mile from the shore, anchored, and shone lights to where we thought the L.C.P. would be. To our intense surprise, all our training and practice actually worked, for the L.C.P. suddenly appeared out of the darkness within a few minutes. She was quite inaudible till twenty yards away, when we heard her bow-wave; so she would not have been heard over the surf by anyone on shore. They grabbed our rope, we climbed on board, had the canoe hoisted up on to her deck, and went to yet another position where Geoff, who was, after all, a professional hydrographer, made a view-sketch by moonlight, and an observation of tidal streams. By 0245 the view-sketch was completed, and we proceeded to meet the M.L., showing a bright green light on pre-arranged bearings.

No M.L. appeared. At 0400 we discontinued the green light and proceeded to the daylight rendezvous position, which was under the lee of a 'conspicuous hill Pk. 830ft.' shown on the chart, some miles up the coast – in Japanese-held territory, but in a completely uninhabited area, we hoped. We reached this position at 0900 and anchored four cables off shore. There was no sign of the M.L.

That was serious. Instead of all hands having a hot meal and sleeping in comfort, we spent the morning cruising up and down the coast looking for the M.L. At 1245 we steamed out to a patrol vessel which appeared on the horizon, and which went to Action Stations on our approach. They had not seen the M.L. either, so we gave them a signal to transmit to N.O.I.C. Chittagong, informing him that we were carrying on alone that night.

We had to run two lines of soundings, and would have to do it in one canoe instead of two, since the second canoe was in the M.L. – along with all our gear, clothing, and food for the second night.

At 1315 we gave everyone a dose of Benzedrine, and sailed at eight knots to raise Oyster Island lighthouse by 1800. We reckoned we had just about enough fuel in the L.C.P. to do another night's work and return to Chittagong.

At 2045 the L.C.P. stopped close inshore and Geoff and I got into our canoe again; the L.C.P. went out two miles and anchored.

We paddled to the position for our first line of soundings.

Suddenly a green rocket-flare shot up into the sky, and hung in the air, illuminating the feathery casuarina trees, the palms, the beach, and us. We froze in our canoe, thinking the Japs must have seen us. But the flare sank again and left us in deeper darkness. It must have been fired further inland than we thought, and it was not for us.

We took some soundings and found the surf began in a depth of six feet. At 2200, Geoff swam off to the beach. I retired to my waiting position, anchored, and munched a sweet, watching the stars and the dark background to the beach. There was very little sea and practically no wind. I had to be on the alert for Geoff's torch in an hour and a quarter. I wanted to have the anchor up early, to be able to get to him quickly; sometimes the anchor was difficult to get off the bottom, and the line had to be reeled in slowly and carefully, or else it got in a tangle; even the simplest things become difficult at night, when you can't see exactly what you are doing. I trailed my hand in the warm water, listened, thought, watched; drew comfort from the dependable wooden frame of the canoe, and the things in it which I knew. The time passed quickly. It was dangerous to lift the anchor too soon in case one was swept by a current or blown by the wind; only a few yards of error might carry one out of sight of the swimmer and his torch.

At 2300 I weighed anchor and redoubled my vigilance. At 2305 I thought I saw a glimmer in the water, not quite in the expected position. I took a stroke or two towards it. I saw it again; it seemed to have the bluish tinge of our torches. It disappeared. I paddled as fast as I could to where I had last seen it. Then, almost beneath the bows of the canoe, I saw the light again, and then saw Geoff.

Quite slowly, as it seemed, I realised that Geoff was not swimming, but floating *beneath* the water, and that his torch was shining on the end of its lanyard, hanging beneath him. I grabbed hold of him and then pulled in the torch and switched it off. Geoff was unconscious, but not dead: he gripped the edge of the canoe. Then we were nearly upset by a large wave: we were right in the surf. I hauled Geoff in over the front of the canoe, got the bows round, and paddled furiously, over the top of one breaking wave, and then another, and we were in clearer water. I went on paddling out. Geoff had begun to groan, and then to make noises as if he were recovering from being winded. I didn't know whether he had been shot, or caught on barbed wire, or what. When I judged we were far enough from the surf, I stopped paddling and attended to Geoff. He was now making noises like a water-buffalo giving birth.

At 2325 he climbed into the rear cockpit and sat, with his legs over the side, retching, groaning and vomiting. Between gasps he pointed out that his legs were tied together. I cut the line and he got his feet on board. He recovered quickly. Apparently he had had to swim against a strong undertow, and had got very tired. Then the reel carrying his line had broken, and very quickly he found his legs entangled, and then tied together. His life-belt was not giving him sufficient buoyancy and he found himself just out of his depth, having to keep jumping off the bottom and at the same time grope for his knife to cut away the line. He felt he would drown before he managed this, and decided to show his torch as a last resort. He had held it well above the water once or twice (which I had seen) but mostly it was awash. He had gone down twice seeing bright lights and patterns like suburban wallpaper, and the third time he went down he had lost consciousness.

In a very few minutes he said 'We must do the other line of soundings. I'm not coming back here again tomorrow night for all the tea in China. Paddle down gently until I feel a bit better.'

My own feelings were mixed. If I went swimming, would Geoff be able to pick me up? Was he rambling, in a sort of delirium, or had he really recovered so quickly? Anyway, I paddled on, and in a few minutes Geoff pulled out his paddle and we continued for about twenty minutes until we reached the second position and confirmed it with a cross-fix. Geoff now swore he was perfectly all right, and knew what he was doing: so at 0030, with considerable misgivings, I went over the side, and was in the water. I held on to the canoe for a second, looked hard at Geoff, and said was he sure he really wouldn't rather let me take him back to the nice motor-boat? Geoff's reply was short, but not specially sweet. I hastily set off swimming, and tried to remember whether it was shark that struck at white things, and barracuda at dark, or vice-versa. I was wearing grey.

After about seven minutes swimming I could see the spray tossed in the air as waves broke on the beach. Then I was in the surf, and through it, and touched bottom. The gradient at this part of the beach was much steeper than at Geoff's, which made it easier. I found 11 feet at 110 yards, which was enough, being well below Low Water Line, and swam in again, coiling the line carefully in my hand. I lay at the water's edge, studying the beach, and crawled some fifty feet up it to look at a runnel which was visible in the moonlight; but I felt too conspicuous to go any further in that brightness, and crawled back to the water.

At 0115, I showed my torch about 150 yards from the shore, and to my intense relief was quickly picked up by Geoff, who said he had not anchored, as he had not had the strength to crawl into the front cockpit. We paddled promptly to the canoe Recovery Position, anchored, had some barley sugar, and began signalling to seaward; and in half an hour the L.C.P. hove in sight and took us on board – both parties being about equally relieved to see each other. There was still no news of the M.L. and we feared she might have gone aground somewhere and be still trying to get off: but since flares were being dropped with some frequency and we could hear aircraft, we decided to retire homewards.

We reached Chittagong at 1745 after a round trip of over 300 miles: and we did not know then how lucky we had been, for we never heard of any other L.C.P. of this type doing as much as 100 miles without breaking down.

We found the M.L. at her buoy and the hands washing clothes. They had gone to the wrong rendezvous position, apparently not having consulted their orders: had seen the patrol vessel to which we had sailed out, but not seen us or thought of contacting her; and had finally returned to harbour and reported our probable loss.

We spent the next day in harbour to eat, drink, fuel, provision, rest and carry out the considerable maintenance on our gear which was necessary before another night's operations could be carried out (for instance, all waterproofed gear, such as torches, had to be re-waterproofed, a lengthy business). On the following day we sailed again, with the M.L., to do our reconnaissance of Oyster Island 'in force'.

Photographic Salon, S. India.

2 8

OYSTER ISLAND

Oyster Island consisted of rocks and a few hundred yards of sand, mostly covered with palm trees, and a tall white lighthouse, with three huts or houses at its foot. Its position off the entrance to Akyab harbour gave it some strategic importance during any invasion of that coast, which was why we had permission to investigate it. Our precise intentions were

(i) to carry out a thorough reconnaissance-in-force of the island;

(ii) to capture a prisoner, if possible, for interrogation;

(iii) to determine the nature of any apparatus employed by the enemy and capture it; otherwise destroy it;

(iv) to annihilate any enemy forces found, provided chances were favourable;

(v) to make a sketch-plan of the island in case of future operations;

(vi) to set booby traps in case the enemy returned to the island later;

(vii) to collect oysters for our Admiral in New Delhi.

The M.L. towed the L.C.P. to a position about 1½ miles away from the island, and then slipped the tow and remained in the background, ready to tow us back when needed. In the L.C.P. we had three armed Royal Indian Navy ratings on loan as a fighting reserve, and the L.C.P.'s normal crew of a Leading Seaman and a Stoker; Geoffrey Hall and myself, each with a Leading Seaman of our own party to act as paddler; the Midshipman and our commando Lance-Corporal. We ran in towards the island and when about half a mile offshore, both canoes were launched, with some difficulty, as there was a considerable swell. Geoff and his paddler went to reconnoitre one end of the island, I and my paddler to the other: we were both looking for a suitable spot for the L.C.P. to beach. About an hour later, at 2200, the canoes rendezvoused off the small iron jetty which projected on one side of the island and compared notes. Geoff reported that all his end of the island was completely rock-bound and quite unsuitable for landing. He had swum ashore and spent a considerable time stalking what appeared to be a machine-gun post; when he had got close to it, he remembered his revolver was not loaded, and had spent an agonising twenty minutes lying in the sand trying to load it silently. Then he had found it was a tree branch. He had later seen dim lights in the windows of one of the huts; but on changing his position discovered it was only the starlit sky seen through gaps in the walls.

My part of the island had also been rocky and unsuitable for landing, but I had found it was steep-to and the approach clear, so that it should be possible for the L.C.P. to get close enough to the shore for us all to swim in. Like Geoff, I had found no evidence of wire or any other defences on land. It was far too rough for us to land on the jetty.

We paddled out to the L.C.P., were hauled on board, and informed the landing party that we would have to swim. The landing party consisted of Geoff, myself, the Midshipman and our two Leading Seamen; everyone else was seasick. The fact that the Lance-Corporal was seasick (and Lucas not with us) made it impracticable to lay booby traps, which was one worry less.

Equipped with sten guns, grenades and revolvers, we inflated our life-belts, dropped overboard, and swam the few yards to the beach. The L.C.P. remained under way close to the jetty, everyone on board, except our own crew of two, being seasick.

We lay up at the water's edge until all were ready, and then, acting on our pre-arranged plan, crept slowly forward up the beach, over some sand dunes, and into the palm trees. It was vital that no one should get in front of the others, or he might be mistaken for an enemy. While we were moving through the palms, a rustle and thud behind us made everyone jump round, fingers on triggers – probably too late, if it had been a Jap. A couple of coconuts had fallen from the trees. We moved forward again, finding no signs of occupation. When we reached the lighthouse, we posted a guard on its door, and searched the huts; it was here, in the moonlight, that one of us, moving slightly apart from the others, was very nearly shot. It is so very difficult, in the dark, to know exactly where everyone is, and who is who.

Having searched the huts, we approached the lighthouse. Unthinkingly, I got there first and was not in a position to say 'after you' to the others, so found myself, to my inexpressible distaste, climbing up the stairs first. Anyone who has ever climbed up the stairs of a Japanese-held lighthouse in the moonlight will know exactly what I mean. However, not a single little Japanese hand-grenade came tumbling down, and we reached the top safely. The lantern and all its equipment seemed in perfect order. It was an anticlimax, but perhaps a welcome one.

We inspected the jetty for booby traps, and made a brief search for oysters, but none was found. When the jetty was reported clear, we went to its end and swam singly to the waiting L.C.P., and were hauled on board. Then we went out to the M.L. and found her without difficulty. The swell made transferring to the M.L. dangerous, and several severe impacts were sustained; so we took only what gear was absolutely necessary. The Leading Seaman Coxswain, Stoker and one Indian naval rating were left on board the L.C.P.; the tow was arranged and we proceeded homewards at 14 knots.

Geoff and I turned in below, in the M.L.'s wardroom, and the Midshipman elected to sleep on deck. I think we all passed out rapidly, as we were pretty tired. But our night's activities were not yet over.

I awoke, and climbing back to consciousness I wondered what had woken me. I seemed to have heard a bump. I thought the L.C.P. must have come alongside, perhaps to change personnel or adjust the tow-rope. I went on deck to see.

Peter Gimson, the Midshipman, was looking over the side, and said agitatedly to me 'Man overboard – the tow parted and we've run down the L.C.P. – I've thrown overboard two lifebuoys – over there' – and pointed. I ran up to the bridge and asked the C.O. to switch on his lights and searchlight, but he said he could not do so, as we were too near the Japanese coast. I ran back to the quarterdeck and shouted to the Coxswain on the L.C.P.; I then learned that it was the Coxswain who was overboard. He was a fisherman, but could not swim. I shouted his name and heard a faint answering shout in the water. As soon as the M.L. had lost way, I went overboard with a lifebelt and swam towards where I had heard the shout, shouting myself, but I heard no more and saw nothing; the sea was grimly empty and quiet: I cannot believe that he was still alive, as I would surely have heard him splashing or struggling. I swam back to the M.L. and was hauled on board. I found that no one had yet informed Geoffrey – I should have done it first thing – and went below and woke him. He immediately went to the bridge and asked the C.O. to show his lights; and then sent the L.C.P., with Gimson and a Leading Seaman, to search again down-wind. When she had gone about two hundred yards she turned round and came back; they shouted that they were sinking. This was the first time we noticed a large hole in her port quarter. Geoff and I jumped down into her to help save as much of the gear as possible; the canoes were unlashed and boxes of stores were passed up to the M.L., but we very soon had to get out as she was filling fast. We tried towing her, nearly awash, but very soon cut the tow, as she seemed about to founder.

Peter Gimson went into the sea, on a rope, and secured the canoes to lines, so that we could pull them on board the M.L. We were not much helped during all this by the C.O. of the M.L., who was in a fever of impatience to get away from the area. He was watching flares and lights on the coast and was convinced that we had been seen by the Japanese; and had twice sent his crew to Action Stations for what had turned out each time to be the bright planet Mars.

In a few minutes the L.C.P. disappeared from view; and we proceeded to Chittagong, which we reached at 1245 the next morning. We learned that when the tow had parted during the night the M.L. had gone back to look for the L.C.P. on a reciprocal course, at six knots; and had run down the L.C.P. just at the moment when her Coxswain had gone on to the fo'csle to examine and haul in the parted tow rope. All in all, the M.L.'s contributions to our operation had not been fortunate. The loss of the Coxswain was reported (he was not one of our own party, but had been seconded to us for duty with the L.C.P. from a base in India) and letters were written to his relatives in England.

The last I saw of Burma was a long ridge of mountains, pale slate-blue, with shadows and ravines and bright patches on them which might have been snow, but were probably sunlight on either rocks or trees; and above, an improbable sunset with dazzling streamers of rose and pink chiffon, blowing across pure cobalt blue. Three white herons flapped across the mangroves opposite us; colour drained quickly from the sky as it became night.

We reached Cocanada four days later.

29

SAILORS AFTER ELEPHANT

When Lucas, our soldier, recovered from his jaundice, he put us through a prolonged course of Jungle Warfare Training. He pored over maps, selected areas for exercises where he thought the jungle would be densest, and drove us there. They always turned out to be perfectly beautiful spots for picnics.

The first place he took us to was in the Eastern Ghats, a short distance inland from Cocanada. It was to be a Survival Exercise. There was quite a chance that one or other of us would be left behind one night in Japanese-held territory, and might either have to lie up in the jungle till someone came back to pick him up, or try to walk home. Any tips we could pick up on surviving in the jungle might be useful.

We had Army, Navy and Air Force booklets on the subject. The Army booklet was called *How to Win Friends among Wild Animals and Influence Tigers*. They all contained information which was completely contradicted in at least one of the others. But they all agreed that you could live on the jungle, if you knew how. Bamboo shoots were recommended as particularly nutritious; and of course all jungles teem with game.

Lucas took us – fully equipped for surviving in dense jungle – to a delightful grove of silver birches. We were to march on a compass course for twenty-four hours. If we survived, and our navigation succeeded, we would come out on another road where, the next day, our truck would be waiting for us. We took absolutely no rations: the jungle was teeming with game.

Twenty-four hours later, ten very hungry men staggered through the trees towards the road. We had eaten nothing ourselves, but had provided sumptuous meals for red ants and ticks, which was all that that jungle was teeming with.

We had shot at two birds, which might or might not have been nutritious, but missed them. And we had, eventually, found some bamboo, but by the time we had cut out the edible parts, and boiled them, there was not enough left to feed a kitten, let alone ten active men.

When we reached the road – our navigation, at least, had been successful – we found three ox-carts full of large tangerines on the grass beneath the trees, with their owners asleep nearby. We fell on those carts, and I personally ate seventeen tangerines – the most delicious I have ever tasted – without stopping. When we offered some money to the startled owners, who could speak no English, they looked rather doubtful, so we gave them some more. We discovered later that what we had given them was enough, by local standards, to buy all the fruit, the carts, the oxen and a wife each as well.

*　*　*

A few weeks later, Lucas decided to take me for an intensive week of jungle training. The English Superintendent of Police in Cocanada said this would be a very good idea, and we could go after the rogue elephant that had been plaguing one of his districts for years. He would lend us his .475 express rifle, and tell one of his Indian Sub-Inspectors to make the necessary arrangements. No trouble at all. All that it meant (we discovered later) was building a bungalow with bathroom and lavatory, recruiting about a hundred natives to act as beaters, and making a motorable road for eight miles through dense jungle.

The Sub-Inspector, a cadaverous-looking Indian with very thin legs, was waiting for us at his police station. When we arrived, he presented us with a rose – I wonder if he knew what nostalgia his gift would arouse – and a basket of tangerines, and climbed into our truck. It already contained two wooden beds, mattresses and bedding rolls, my suitcase, buckets, hurricane lamps, a box of food (we were taking no chances this time), two .303 rifles and the .475, and a large number of ammunition boxes with which Lucas always travelled. He packed his clothes in them as well as various kinds of explosives. Ammunition boxes were a form of spiritual comfort to Lucas.

We also had with us Passaroundyou, my Indian bearer who had insisted on coming to cook for us, although he loathed the jungle; and two of our seamen, who were driving the truck back. We had to keep stopping on the way to pick up miscellaneous policemen or villagers – we could not refuse them, as they had chickens, eggs or tangerines for us. They all piled gleefully on board for the ride, until we looked like a perfectly normal Indian bus, the vehicle itself being invisible. Every time we went over a bump – which was about every thirty seconds – the entire contents of the truck rose in the air together, and the human beings shouted. It was a riotous journey. By the time we arrived, it was amazing that anything was intact. Willing hands unloaded the truck, and our two seamen drove it away as quickly as possible, anxious to be out of the jungle before night fall.

We inspected our surroundings. This time, Lucas had picked a charming glade among large oak-like trees: just like Epping Forest, except that the leaves were darker green. Our bungalow was a single room, with a floor of dried cow-dung and walls of wattle. The roof was thatched with rushes. Our 'bathroom' – a screen made of green toddy-palm leaves – was being erected nearby. Behind our bungalow was a little two-roomed hut in which Passaroundyou quickly established himself and began preparing supper. Large earthenware jars of water were already boiling for us on a fire so we washed and then went round the room hammering in nails to use as hooks. I rigged up some codline from which to hang our mosquito nets, while Lucas got his armoury in order, and the village carpenter came and repaired one of our beds which had lost its legs in the truck. In quite a short time the Sub-Inspector brought along the village headman, who had been described to us as 'a Falstaffian figure with seven wives'. It seemed apt; he was fat and jolly, with curly grey hair, and twinkling pig eyes. He was wearing a *printed* leopard-skin pullover over khaki shorts, and a blue balaclava on his head. We made plans for the next day; we were to get up at 5 a.m. and shoot animals at dawn. Lucas in all seriousness asked the headman to lay on one Sambur deer and one blackbuck only, which would do to start with. We would go on to the rogue elephant next day. Our interpreter was a very cheerful police sergeant with a walrus moustache who spoke enough English to make us think he understood it too, which we gradually learned was not the case.

The natives of the village, Koyis and Hill-Redis, were a completely different type from those we had so far met. They looked more like Polynesians: they had round faces, yellowish skins, large eyes and fuzzy black hair drawn back tightly from the forehead and done in a top-knot. They wore moustaches but not beards. They had bamboo bows and steel-tipped arrows, and also arrows with flat wooden heads to stun birds. Their huts seemed exceedingly neat and trim.

We went for a short stroll before supper and had some target practice with the .475. The noise was tremendous and I felt the blast at a distance of twenty yards: but its kick was not so uncomfortable as I had expected. We cut a mark two inches square in a tree and both hit it at 50 yards. The sky was clouding over when we got a glimpse through the trees of jungle-clad hills around us; the sunlight and shadows on them reminded me of Scottish moors; and to complete the comparison it began to rain.

After a delicious supper of chicken, we turned in early. A native sat in a corner of our hut all night: we supposed he was our bodyguard. A fire consisting of ten long poles placed like the spokes of a wheel was made outside our doorway and burned all night. Every hour or so the watchman had to push each pole a little further in to the fire. Without the usual encumbrance of miscellaneous twigs and logs, and with a thin column of smoke rising vertically, it looked faintly magical.

*   *   *

Passaroundyou brought us cups of tea at half-past four in the morning and at five-thirty we were on the trail, in what Lucas maintained was only a heavy dew dripping off the leaves but felt to me like a steady drizzle. I thought we were being taken to a drinking-pool, where we would see a procession of wild things going down to drink just before dawn. But we cruised round apparently aimlessly without stopping and saw nothing. Once something, possibly a deer, crashed away into the jungle, but we never even glimpsed it. We could see our sights against the sky at seven o'clock and against the background of the trees twenty minutes later. At 0816 we got back to camp, and set out ten minutes later with the headman; apparently it was sheer bad luck that we had not seen any game so far, but we would certainly get some now. And it is true that something that sounded fairly big crashed away from us on this round; but we never saw it, nor did the headman. Again we came back with nothing in the bag.

After breakfast, while Lucas was reading an Army pamphlet on the Bailey bridge and I was reading *More Experiences of an Irish R.M.*, we were visited by the Sub-Inspector, the headman, and about twenty villagers carrying bundles of edible root. Passaroundyou came out of his kitchen with great hopes but was most gloomy when he looked at them. Only jungle people could eat that sort of stuff, he said, sniffing. Lucas brushed this aside, picked up the most tasty-looking root, bit a chunk off the end of it, and very quickly vomited. I tried a fragment myself, cautiously, and nearly blew the roof off my mouth; it was extremely hot and painful. We asked some of the natives to fetch the leaves of the plants, and when they were spread out with the roots, it looked just like a local meeting of the Royal Horticultural Society. I took great pains in making careful drawings of all of them; it was only later that I discovered that some knowledge of botany is essential in making identifiable drawings of plants. But they gave deep satisfaction to myself and deep amusement to three small boys looking over my shoulder.

In the afternoon we went out again to shoot. This time we were absolutely certain of a large bag, as the villagers were going to beat the jungle for us. It was most interesting; they beat the jungle no less than four times, and not an animal came out of it. Lucas had a long shot at a peacock, and missed, and I at a pigeon, ditto. When we returned, about six in the afternoon, Passaroundyou could hardly believe that we had brought back no venison for him to cook. I asked him if he liked the Jungle people. No, he said, he didn't like them at all; very ignorant people, he said. They had only just heard of saris, he told me: someone had been up to Rajahmundry (a nearby town) and seen one. Passaroundyou was definitely not at home in the jungle.

The next day we informed the headman that we were going out for a walk – not looking for game, but to look at the scenery – and could he find out where the rogue elephant was by the evening, as we thought we had better go out after it the following day.

Our plan of not looking for game worked. I first saw a glint of red: the sunlight on the coat of a deer, about a hundred yards away, grazing behind a fallen tree trunk. She was a doe, and anyway I should have tried to get nearer. I slowly raised my rifle, and fired. But my barrel was going round in circles with excitement and I missed completely. She was off up the hillside like a bolt. There was no impression of galloping – I saw only a red body moving with the steady flight of an arrow till I lost sight of her. I was glad: it was too like Bambi. Lucas sucked his teeth; but shortly afterwards he missed a sitting shot at a fat grey jungle hog, and then said he was sorry, he had been afraid of hitting me. We had honey for tea; but not out of a jar, for it was a wild honeycomb brought to us by a native on some leaves. We decided we could survive in the jungle on wild honey – if only people would bring it to us. And still we had seen no sign of the elephant.

* * *

That evening Geoffrey Hall and our Midshipman arrived in camp; and as the headman told us that the elephant was now quite close, we decided to go out and attack it in force the next day. It was, I think, the most heterogeneous elephant hunt in the whole history of naval warfare.

The headman called for us at seven in the morning, and announced that since the elephant was only four miles away, we could kill it before lunch and spend the rest of the day killing other game. To this day, I am still inclined to think that he was being serious.

We moved off in high spirits.

In the lead was the headman's nephew, as head shikari, wearing a pink loin-cloth, and carrying an ancient shot-gun, believed Abyssinian. Then came Lucas, carrying a grim expression and the .475. I followed, carrying four anti-tank bombs. Then came the Midshipman carrying our Bren gun. Then Geoffrey, with a revolver, two commando daggers, and a whisky flask. Then Passaroundyou, with the lunch. Then the Sub-Inspector, with a walking-stick, and the headman, with his double-barrelled shot-gun. After him came two of his sons, carrying bows and arrows; and behind them followed a longish train of minor characters, carrying food, water, ammunition, Dettol, bows and arrows, long knives and wide grins.

We came to a river, which we had not seen before, and crossed by a ford. On the far bank, a marching skyline of immense and wicked-looking trees clawed at the chaste white clouds. It was romantic and sinister, like a Gustave Doré engraving of medieval forests. Once inside, the sense of spaciousness was quickly lost: so was the feeling, that I had been trying to suppress all the time we had been there, that really there was not so much difference between the Indian jungle and an English wood. Now we really were in primary jungle, and it looked how jungle ought to look. The clumps of spear-grass and bamboo all seemed full of tigers; the mango and tamarind trees were vaster than anything we had yet seen, and from their

heights, giant creepers curled and dangled down. Everything was colossal vertically; there was no horizontal visibility. Like Mole in the Wild Wood, we found ourselves being elbowed and fumbled by this more hostile jungle; tripped, pushed and
scratched. Although we followed game trails, we met continual snags, great fallen
tree-trunks, spiders' webs, with the sunlight on them against the shadows behind,
tenanted by monster spiders with legs more hairy than our own, bushes spilling
carnivorous red ants, giant creepers hanging down like bell ropes, or hangman's
nooses, arms of thorn jumping up like puppies, and the rough male kiss of
bamboo thickets. The only sound, apart from the rustling of our own party, was
the occasional booming call from the depths of the forest, which we were told was
probably baboons; and the frequent rat-a-tat-tat of woodpeckers. Sometimes there
was no colour, only deep gloom and shadow; then we suddenly came on a giant
cotton-tree in a clearing, with red flowers like poppies among its leaves, and a red
carpet at its feet; or a flame-of-the-forest, a heraldic-looking tree with orange
flowers like conventional signs for flames along its branches.

'Elephant how far?' gasped Geoffrey, in basic English, to the Sub-Inspector. The
Sub-Inspector consulted with the headman's nephew out in front and came back
to reply, not very helpfully. 'Yes, sir'. After a couple of hours we halted for a pull at
our water-bottles. Geoffrey was eyeing the luncheon basket and Lucas was trying
to obtain a good Army map reference for the elephant from the headman. Suddenly the nephew came gliding back and beckoned excitedly. A few paces ahead,
everyone's pulse quickened to see a huge foot print on soft earth; then a young
bamboo-tree pulled down, and much trampled vegetation.

From there, the trail was easy. We passed a deserted village with squashed huts,
reminding me of ruined crofts in the Highlands; then a juicy tree pulled up by the
roots like a sprig of parsley; foliage broken off at an elephant's shoulder height; and
majestic piles of elephant dung, marking the way like cairns.

At noon, we halted for lunch, and made a plan of campaign. Lucas, with a first-
class elephant rifle, was to kill the beast. If he failed with his two barrels, I was to
bomb it. The bombs exploded on impact, and since they consisted entirely of
explosive, with no metal, they could be thrown at fairly close range. They should at
least stun the elephant, or halt it, while Lucas reloaded.

The Midshipman said he could not now get the Bren back from a proud native
whom he had allowed to carry it for a little. He was told to keep it pointed well away
from us, anyway, in the impending action. Geoffrey said he was quite frankly
carrying his weapons purely in self-defence. As a final piece of encouraging news,
the headman came up and told us that the elephant was now only a mile ahead,
and was in company with two wild buffaloes, probably the most dangerous
animals, apart from rogue elephants, in that kind of jungle. His faith in the Navy
was touching.

Cleared away for action, we crept forward. But the jungle was getting deeper. The sun, shining down through the tracery of trees, reached us as if through fathoms of green water. Enormous, fantastic butterflies danced in the gloom. The Midshipman began to see Russell's Vipers in every twig; leaves of spear grass waved mysteriously, when all else was motionless; and when we investigated, there was nothing there. Geoffrey swore a noose of creepers had been jerked tight around his neck. Passaroundyou was obviously vowing whole groves of coconuts to Shiva, if he ever came out of the place alive. It seemed as if we would never catch up with this elephant. We were nearly at the end of our endurance, when the nephew pointed down. Some leaves at the side of the track held a quantity of elephant's urine; and it was steaming. He whispered: 'Elephant very close. You must take off your hats.' Apparently this elephant divided up human beings into those who wore hats and those who didn't: only the former were dangerous. We took off our hats, and continued on tip-toe. The climax was at hand. Suddenly there was a sharp, terrifying noise, exactly like an infuriated and alarmed rogue elephant trumpeting, followed by a noise exactly like a rogue elephant and two buffaloes crashing away at high speed through the jungle, and gradually fading into the distance. Then silence.

We all instantly became extremely cheerful, even Lucas. The elephant had obviously gone into the next county, and we could now relax. As we walked home, I remembered how Nelson had gone down on to the ice after a polar bear. I could not help wondering how he would have got on with a rogue elephant.

I thought you said elephants couldn't climb trees …

" I've just found a place where
you can get across the river dry shod"

Sketch from the author's diary of January 1944.

Jungle warfare training.

30

DINNER WITH AN ADMIRAL

We were beginning to know, and enjoy, Southern India. The more venomous and dangerous animals and insects were, after all, rare. The profusion of harmless ones, like the frogs with suckers on their fingers and toes, who climbed walls, and the enormous beetles, bumbling about at night like frisky 4-engined bombers, were endearing. So were the citizens, as we got to know them; my bearer, Passaround-you, was an angelic man, the kindest and most faithful of servants; and in the town, we had just begun to receive invitations to the houses of Indians. We went to a wedding-feast, sat cross-legged on the floor and ate with the right hand from palm leaves. I was bitterly disappointed when a sweet, in layers of three colours, turned out to be only blancmange: but everything else was new and exotic. The women did not appear, but we knew we were being watched and could hear their whisperings behind curtains.

We drove quite often along the dusty red trunk roads, which ran dead straight for miles through avenues of trees. As we passed, the plodding men and women moved to the side, and then immediately stepped back into the middle, to the perpetual terror and fury of the following driver. I had never seen trees like the great tamarinds, often shrines, beneath which men slept with their bundles, while monkeys chattered in the branches above. Nor had I ever seen anything so beauti-ful as the saris, newly washed and spread out to dry, long slashes of bright and sub-tle colours, on the grass beside a river; or the unexpected black-and-white kingfishers flashing across it.

In the villages, tiny boys with long sticks drove immense black water-buffaloes, and gentle cows ambled clumsily among the crowds, unmolested, because sacred. In one village, I had a photograph taken of myself, being unable to pass a notice saying in execrable curly lettering, 'You Look Nice Today – Be Photographed'. The 'studio' consisted of a little room, marked 'VISITORS HALL', open on one side, with gothic windows. Judging by the result, I looked terrible, and squinted.

The birds we got to know first and best were the mynahs, the jays, the scarlet wood-peckers and the rose-pink ibises in the Godavari estuary. The Godavari river, which rises somewhere north of Bombay, had a wide delta, mostly fringed with mangroves, and we sometimes used its channels to reach an American 10,000 ton 'Liberty' freighter which had gone aground two miles off its mouth (she was bound for Calcutta, and her under-trained Captain should have taken her ten miles further out from the shore).

The huge ship lay there, emptied of her cargo, standing bolt upright on the sand, with a skeleton crew on board, waiting hopefully for the sands to shift. At low water it was possible to wade right round her: and we went regularly to run lines of soundings to see how fast the sands were moving. We reckoned they had at least a year to wait. One day I had to take out a Marine Assessor, a rather senior official from Madras, and enjoyed myself being, for once, in command of the L.C.P., as Geoffrey was away in Delhi. The return journey had to be made in the dark, so I decided to take the most direct route home, along the coast.

Since the L.C.P.'s engine had just been overhauled, and we had not made new running trials to ascertain the exact distance run at given revolutions, and since, anyway, all we had to do was to run down the coast, keeping less than half a mile offshore until we came to Cocanada Bay, I disregarded our time, being sure that I would see the entrance to the bay with my binoculars. But I missed it – as any sea-man could have warned me. I only knew where we were when some hills loomed up at the far side of the bay, fifteen miles further on. I brought the patient Marine Assessor back six hours late for his dinner; and learned another nautical lesson the hard way. The time an engine has been running at a known speed is a *fact*. What you *think* you can see – especially when it is a featureless coast-line – is not a fact.

Geoff, when he returned from Delhi, announced that, apart from there being some very pretty Wrens there, he had met an Admiral who was intending to come and have a look at us. A council of war was held to plan the sort of entertainment we should lay on for him.

Lucas's standard suggestion, booby-traps, was turned down unanimously: but it was agreed that he would be allowed to give a demonstration of sticky bombs, if the Admiral wanted to see them. ('Thank God that's over', Lucas had said, after teaching us all how to use them, 'it's the first time I've ever handled them in my life').

Our canoes and training methods would also be inspected, and the Admiral would probably want a trip round the bay in the L.C.P.; after that, we would give him the best dinner we could provide. So arrangements went forward.

I think he had a good day. He declined the sticky bombs with alacrity, enjoyed his trip round the bay, and actually caught a flying fish. As for the dinner, it was a resounding success. Passaroundyou, on his own initiative, decorated our circular mahogany dining table with the petals of white and scarlet flowers, completely covering it with a pattern as intricate as lace, and more beautiful. The main course was a curry, based on bully beef, but skilfully disguised with spices, nuts and bananas. The *pièce de resistance* of the meal was the sweet course. Among the stores we had brought from England were tins of Emergency Rations 'to be opened only on the orders of an officer', which, we had found, contained highly concentrated and delicious Fortnum & Mason chocolate. On selected occasions we dished these out to the cook and he made a superb confection know as 'Emergency Pudding', which Admiral Maund (late C.O. of HMS *Ark Royal*) found delicious, without being told its origin. The Admiral was, as Admirals often are, a man of wide culture, and talked to us by candlelight till late at night about Chinese history and literature. We enjoyed the evening and so obviously did he; it was no doubt with regret that on returning to Delhi he reported that we were installed far too comfortably. We would move, without delay, to a large Combined Operations Camp in the North of Ceylon, under a Royal Marines Colonel.

We should have given him sausages-and-mash.

31

LENT TO FRIENDS

We went to Ceylon, which took a fortnight.

We found the camp, near Jaffna, in the north of Ceylon; at least, we found the site, which was an area of sand-dunes, scrub and palm trees on the seashore, supporting colonies of monkeys and land-crabs. We were the first. We were the camp.

We installed ourselves in a Rest House, took account of the prevailing winds, drew sketch plans, and put pegs in the ground. Then a Royal Marines Colonel arrived, literally drove us out of the Rest House with a stick, and had us in tents the same night. Then he stamped off, bristling, to collect his Marines from Colombo.

We could see absolutely no way of avoiding camp life under a Marine Colonel. Then deliverance occurred unexpectedly. The Teheran Conference resulted in all plans for amphibious operations against the Japs in our theatre being cancelled for a year; all invasion forces and craft were recalled to the Mediterranean. A plan for us to walk and swim round Sumatra for a year was seriously discussed; but eventually it was decided to disband the party temporarily and lend individuals to units who would reinforce our training. I was lent to HMS *Challenger*, a surveying ship with a famous name, then working in and out of Trincomalee harbour. Owing to my defective eyesight, which debarred me from holding a watch-keeper's certificate, it was the first time in what was now over three years in the Navy that I had served as an officer in one of HM ships. The *Challenger's* readiness to accept me, a Lieutenant of quite exceptional ignorance, was, I thought, over-hasty.

On my very first day on board, which *Challenger* was to spend in harbour, I was made Officer of the Day, in order to let the other officers sleep, or go ashore. I was coached in my duties for a full five minutes after breakfast, girded with a belt, given a telescope, and pushed up on deck, to wait apprehensively for the first appearance of the Captain. Though not unkindly, Captain Wyatt was an old-fashioned seaman of the most uncompromising sort; moreover, he was senior Captain of all ships then in harbour, and his ship must therefore be even more perfect than usual. I gazed gloomily round the harbour, at the grey ships and feathery green hills.

When the Captain came up, he looked round fiercely – for my dress to be wrong, or a piece of spunyarn lying on the deck, or the ensign upside-down. All he could find was that the boom was not quite parallel with the horizon. He called my attention to it sharply, and I called the Quartermaster's to it sharply, and I forget whether they moved the ship down or the boom up, but it was corrected. After that, I was beset with such a succession of worries that I began to see why everyone in the wardroom was so happy for me to be Officer of the Day.

Would the sullage lighter come alongside while the hands were bathing? (It didn't.) Would all the M.L.s in the harbour roar past at full speed, creating tidal waves, despite the fact that we were flying the pennant that means 'Diver at Work'? (They did.) Did the Canteen Manager go ashore strictly on duty and come back drunk? (Yes.) Did the Paymaster go ashore and forget to hand over the keys of the safe? (Certainly.) Did the Signalman report that the motor-boat was returning under tow, and was this pure imagination on his part? (Absolutely.) Did the duty watch of stokers sneak out of the ship to visit the dentist, leaving the Chief Engineer leaning over the rail shaking his fist at them? (Almost.)

My culminating moment was when the Chief Engineer wanted to turn the engines over. When this is done in harbour, even if the ship is moored, as we were, between two buoys, an officer must be on the bridge. I was told what orders I had to pass down the voice-pipe to the engine-room; and when the operation was completed I had to give the orders to stop. The destroyers and submarines I had served in previously all had two engines, and on going up through the wheel-house I thought I had seen two binnacles. So when it was all over, I shouted down the voice-pipe 'Stop both!' The Navigating Officer, working in the chart-room below, and listening for my gaffes, immediately ran up the stairs shouting 'We've only got one!'

Almost my last duty as Officer of the Day was to report sunset to the Captain: I was looking forward to announcing this with due seriousness, but, to my chagrin, the Captain went on board a neighbouring ship and I performed the ceremony of sunset and colours alone.

The next few weeks were an almost idyllic (in memory) succession of days spent in small boats. Day after day I went out with one or another officer on the normal duties of surveying a coast. We put up marks, either by fixing calico in trees, or erecting poles with guy-ropes, or daubing white paint on rocks; I was deposited, from a 'pram'*, on small rocks or islands, to whose summits I had to scramble and hold a ten-foot pole horizontally, while the surveyor on shore observed subtended angles with a sextant, and the pole had to be held exactly at right-angles to the sextant, which made my job nearly as skilled as his; we walked for miles along sun-baked beaches, making sextant fixes on known marks in the harbour approaches; we ran lines of soundings by echo-sounder, and when the sounder broke down, I spent two days heaving a hand lead and wire-covered line, to the great detriment of my hands; we found turtles left deliberately on their backs by natives and righted them, but usually saw them recaptured; we cooked and ate

---

* A small dinghy with round prow.

lunches on the thwarts of our boats or on the beaches, in the company of monkeys, lizards, and crabs, all with disreputable sexual habits; and while we tramped the shore, or on long trips back to the ship, I heard stirring accounts of old sailing races, wartime adventures, and life histories.

Finally, the *Challenger* spent some days ship-sounding. For this, the bridge was in a turmoil, with the Captain plotting and calling out courses, two or three officers shouting out sextant angles and times, and the navigator writing down the soundings on the chart, while I, for this time only in my life, was Officer of the Watch in one of HM ships at sea. I repeated the Captain's orders down the voice-pipe, kept an eye on our course and safety in relation to other shipping, and noticed a whale doing his own sounding. When off watch, I retired quickly to the deck, and sat in the shade with the non-surveying officers, the Doc, the Paymaster, and the Engineer, who all professed to scoff at the panic during ship-sounding.

Apart from surveying duties, there were sailing trips for pleasure, sometimes with the Captain, in the whaler or the cutter, in broiling sun and tropical thunderstorm – once aggravated by sudden darkness, which turned out to be due to lightning having ignited the harbour's smoke defence system; there were long discussions of peace and politics and war, and parties, and sometimes music in someone's cabin, after dinner; and there were sunsets and the stars, and books, and letters to and from home. A passage from Charlotte Brontë's *Shirley* describes it:

> At last, however, a pale light falls on the page from the window; she looks; the moon is up; she closes the volume, rises and walks through the room. Her book has perhaps been a good one: it has refreshed, re-filled, re-warmed her heart; it has set her brain astir, furnished her mind with pictures. The still parlour, the clean hearth, the window opening on the twilight sky, and showing its 'sweet regent' new throned and glorious, suffice to make earth an Eden, life a poem, for Shirley. A still, deep, inborn delight glows in her young veins; unmingled – untroubled, not to be reached or ravished by human agency, because by no human agency bestowed; the pure gift of God to His creature, the free dower of Nature to her child. This joy gives her experience of a genii-life. Buoyant, by green steps, by glad hills, all verdure and light, she reaches a station scarcely lower than that whence angels looked down on the dreamer of Bethel …

Then, I was recalled. An operation was planned. On the morning I left, the spacious anchorage suddenly looked crowded; during the night the battleships and carriers of the Eastern Fleet had sailed in. The Captain of the *Challenger* was no longer senior Captain.

For me, it was back to the camp among the palm trees, now full of tents; charts and maps of Sumatra were again pulled out; canoes and weapons examined; the peaceful period was past.

Sweet shop in Badulla, Ceylon.

32

DEPARTURE TO SUMATRA

There was music on the quarter-deck, and I lay listening with my head pillowed on a steel hawser. Around us were the battleships of the Eastern Fleet. The white sails of a native canoe gleamed across the silver water; a picket boat crept under our stern with a cargo of returning liberty men, singing lustily. A green light was moving slowly past a ship near us. Thin and clear over the water came the challenge 'Boat aho-o-y' and the answer 'Pa-a-ssing'. Away to port, a searchlight flowed across a line of buoys at the entrance to Trincomalee harbour, and a launch steamed up and down, dropping small depth-charges.

But here, on the quarter-deck, was peace; the peace of the moon and stars, and of Mozart and Sibelius. I gazed at the stars. They seemed many more than the two thousand which was all, I had been told, you could count with the naked eye. 'Eine kleine Nacht-Musik' murmured the Electrical Officer, to whose efforts the gramophone recital was due; and I thought of summer time in Weimar in 1936, where I had first heard the Nacht-Musik.

The audience consisted of white shapes in horizontal positions, with a coffee cup or glass beside each. They were nearly all submarine officers, for this was a submarine depot ship. Some were asleep, some were using the music, like a beautiful view, as a background for their private thoughts, and some were actually listening. My own thoughts went constantly round the world, but returned always to the details of our departure on the morrow. We were known on the depot ship as Commandos. We were sailing the next day in a submarine, HMS *Tudor*, in order to reconnoitre a piece of Japanese-held Sumatra. My immediate responsibility, as First Lieutenant of this party, was to see that all our gear was embarked and stowed safely in the submarine. The most important part of our gear was three canoes. They had been taken down the hatch of the submarine that morning. One was on the rack which normally held a spare torpedo; the other two were triced up where hammocks were usually slung, and two sailors would have to sleep on the deck in consequence. Was there anything I had forgotten? It was like a picnic – had I packed the salt? the mustard? I could think of nothing omitted, and turned again to the music. It was almost the first that I had heard since leaving England a year before.

When I woke next morning something seemed pressing on my mind. What was it? Oh yes, we were sailing that evening in the *Tudor*. What a relief it would be when we had sailed. Our operation had been put off so often that we hardly believed it was at last to happen. Even when we had sailed we could not be certain, for the submarine's Patrol Orders were first to engage the enemy, and only secondarily to carry out our operation. This was not much comfort.

Our submarine was to sail at 1800 hours. The last day in the Depot Ship seemed very tedious. After breakfast I went down to see what was happening in the boat. *Tudor* was berthed alongside the Depot Ship, joined to her by a very thin plank. Outside her lay two more submarines just back from patrol. On *Tudor*'s casing, a bunch of the crew were sitting peeling potatoes into a bucket. They were surrounded by a pile of stores still to go down; cabbages, pommalas, grapefruit, an enormous crate of eggs, a large box of milk powder, and some tins of marmalade. The potato peelers had all their heads together and were gossiping hard like old women round a village pump. The Torpedo Gunner's Mate ('T.I.' for short) came up the hatch, coughing till he was nearly sick. 'Not effing dyin', I 'ope?' asked a peeler, kindly. The T.I. threw his cigarette stub away, wiped the sweat off his face with a rag, and said he must give up them effing things. I went down the hatch he had just come up.

Down below, the finishing touches were being put on various repair jobs. Loaves of bread from the Depot Ship were being stowed between torpedoes in the fore end; tea, as in all ships in the Navy, in whatever climate, at whatever time, was being brewed in the seamen's mess; the Duty Officer was writing a letter in the wardroom; the Navigating Officer was frantically searching the drawers in the Control Room for a part of the Tide Tables; and the periscope E.R.A. of the Depot Ship was adjusting the eye-piece of the after periscope. But I found it too hot to stay below. A submarine in a tropical harbour is a tin box with the sun beating down on it. Dripping with sweat, I wandered back on board the Depot Ship.

There was a minimum of ceremony when we sailed. 'Harbour Stations' had been ordered for a quarter to six, and we had all to be on board before that time. Our little party spent the last half-hour in the Depot Ship ante-room knocking back large iced lime juices. The bar proper did not open till six. At twenty to six we slipped away without saying any goodbyes (this rather surprised our two soldiers), and went down to the boat.

The sides of the Depot Ship were crowded with sailors looking down on the submarine about to sail. They were all naked to the waist, smoking cigarettes, exchanging witticisms with the men on board *Tudor*. Some of them had just come back from patrol, some were going out soon after us. The presence of two green berets on the bridge of the *Tudor* added interest to the occasion. ('Yus, I seed the *Tudor* go off on 'er last patrol,' they would say if we never came back.) We stared up at the rows of faces and looked nonchalant. The First Lieutenant was watching the Engineering Officer testing telegraphs. In a few minutes the Captain came on board, a tall young Lieutenant RN, who had been five years in submarines.

'Everything O.K., Number One?' He grinned at us and went back down the plank.

In a few moments everyone sprang to attention as Captain (S) the Captain of the Flotilla, stepped on board to inspect us. Our Captain came back to the bridge. There was a last minute hold-up as an E.R.A. who was feeling ill was brought before the Captain.

'How do you feel?'

'Bit of an 'eadache, sir, but I'll be all right'.

'Do you want to go back in board?'

'Oh no, sir, I'll be O.K.' (He looked anything but).

'Hm'm, – speak now, or for ever hold your peace – sure? All right.'

The Captain turned and climbed up on to a perch where he could survey the entire length of the submarine.

'In plank. Let go aft. Let go for'ard. Slow ahead both. Stop starboard. Starboard five …'

Very slowly we moved away. Captain (S) waved. Some other officers gave us thumbs up, and some gave us the V sign reversed, which is not polite. We were clear.

As soon as we were away, the Depot Ship began calling us up with her lantern. *Tudor*'s signalman watched the flickering light, replying to each word with a wink from his Aldis, and then turned to the Captain.

'From Depot Ship, sir, Good Luck and Good Hunting.' 'Make Thank you,' replied the Captain without looking round.

We passed the two other submarines which had had to cast off from the Depot Ship to let us out. Their Captains shouted 'Good Luck' to us on megaphones as we passed. Next, we passed an 8-inch gun cruiser. At the bosun's call, the row of brown bodies on the fore and after parts of the casing stiffened, and all the officers on the bridge faced the cruiser and saluted. The cruiser responded and everyone on the upper deck came to attention as we passed. We didn't pass *Challenger*; she was moored too far away for waving. The last salute was from the trawler at the gap in the boom as we passed through. Her skipper took his pipe out of his mouth and waved it.

'Fall out harbour stations.' The men on the casing came surging up over the bridge and down the conning-tower hatch. Every other hatch in the boat was now shut. It was half-past six.

Outside the boom we picked up an armed trawler which was to escort us till dawn the next day. We were doing ten knots.

'Blue watch patrol routine' said the Captain down the voice-pipe, and handed the ship over to the Officer of the Watch. From now on, although for another twelve hours escorted, we were in the war, and ready to dive any second. We looked back to the land. The evening sky was very beautiful, subdued, and peaceful. The jungle, looking like the wooded hills of home, lay purple against veils of soft yellow and orange.

'Supper is ready'.

We went below.

Cricket match in ceylon

33

THE FIRST NIGHT AND DAY

The less said about our first night the better.

Geoff, after taking ten minutes to discover how to rig his bunk, which was in the wardroom, and another ten to discover how to get into it, took only one minute to fall out of it when the ship rolled. He had omitted to fit the guard-rail. The crash with which he landed on the wardroom table caused all the rest of us to start up in terror, thinking we were being depth-charged. When we finally got settled in, with the guard-rail up and all the available ventilation directed on to himself, he got cramp (there was not room to raise one's head or one's knees more than a few inches); and then, incredibly enough, he felt cold. So he switched all the ventilation off. Alec Colson, and the submarine Sub-Lieutenant below Geoff, were far too hot, and got no air at all when Geoff switched everything off. They got very little sleep either. Colson did get some sleep when the Sub-Lieutenant went on watch. Colson, an army captain from another party, had joined us because it was decided that we might need two soldiers for this operation.

Lucas, lying on a camp bed on the deck beneath the table, had his head where the Engineer was accustomed to step when getting in and out of his bunk, and he stepped on Lucas's head three times. Also, when the boat rolled more than usual, a nearby cupboard door swung open and delivered all its contents, mostly books and games, on to his face. It did this four times until Lucas learned how to wedge it shut. When he did doze off, he woke to find an electric fan spinning like an infuriated circular saw an inch above his head. It had been rolled off its shelf, and was held from completely scalping him only by a single frayed lanyard.

I was not in the wardroom, but had been allotted the T.I.'s bunk forward; the T.I. himself slept, on patrol, beside his torpedoes. I lay and sweated and sweated, until the towel I had round me, and the blanket on which I was lying, were soaked. Still I sweated. But I was living in exactly the same conditions as the crew of the submarine, and, if they could sleep in these conditions, so could I.

As for our troops, Petty Officer Reilly had a bunk and a fan and was probably the most comfortable of any of us, but he was unable to sleep for the strangeness of it. Corporal Strong was on a seat in the seamen's mess with his head close to an electric motor running the electric machinery, and didn't sleep much either. Our two A.B.s, lying on sacks of potatoes in the fore-ends, slept perfectly all night.

During the night, my friend Edward Young passed close to us on his way in from patrol in his submarine *Storm*. If, five years previously, when we were sharing a flat in Hammersmith and pursuing the peaceful profession of typography, we could have known that we would one night pass within a mile of each other in submarines in the Far East, we would have rushed down to the Black Lion with shaking hands, to have a pint.

Despite the discomfort in my bunk, I must have dozed for, when I looked at my watch expecting it to be about 5 a.m., I found it was 7. The comparative peace of the night was now being shattered by the turning out of the seamen, whose mess was abreast of my head. Feet clumped all over the deck and a light was switched on which shone on my face. I tied my towel round my middle, rolled out of my bunk into the corridor (the only way I could get out), stood up, picked up and re-secured my towel and went along to the wardroom. It was still in darkness and everyone appeared to be asleep. I went for a wash, used a teaspoonful of water to rinse my eyes, put on a pair of cotton shorts, and obtained permission from the Officer of the Watch to go up on the bridge.

The Navigating Officer was on the bridge. The Captain of the *Tudor* made it a rule that the Officer of the Watch should never take his eyes from his binoculars while on watch. The watch was two hours, as opposed to the four usual in surface ships. So the Navigator without taking his eyes from the horizon, said: 'Slept well?' and conversation lapsed. I made myself an extra look-out and stood with my feet on the rail and my back against the periscope standards. On a level with my head were the feet of a look-out, standing on a platform which was the submarine's 'crow's nest'.

There was nothing in sight except acres of purple-blue sea, an unpleasant colour. A few clouds lay piled along the horizon, but the sky above was blue, and the air was wonderfully fresh. I took great delight in the wind blowing on my body. A bath in the wind is the next best thing to a bath in water, after a sweaty night.

I could never decide, on the bridge of a submarine, whether the view ahead or the view astern was the more interesting. Ahead, there was the narrow pencil-like deck, stretching out and ending in a bulge which looked slight but happened to contain eight twenty-one-inch torpedoes. From the bows stretched the steel jumping wire to above the bridge. I never grew tired of watching the bows falling in the sea and gathering the water over them, then lifting again, making the water cascade off. I often used to look at the bows through binoculars. These brought them into a more dramatic relief, and the glistening wet iron surface, with the heaving seas behind, became, in the lens, more dramatic than in the naked eye.

Looking aft, there was a much broader hull and a more violent disturbance of the water. Whenever we rolled, or a wave struck us in a particular way, a great column of snowy spray was thrown in the air, caused partly by a projection on the hull and partly by the underwater engine exhaust. The pattern of the water thrown up was always different, always lovely. Then there was the ordinary churning of the screws; and the white wake; it was not straight, but wandered, for we were zig-zagging almost as merrily as the rolling English drunkard.

If you looked neither ahead nor astern, but straight down the side, you could watch the sea creaming past and making myriad patterns of veined marble. Now it lapped the very base of the conning tower as we rolled over to that side; now it slid off and revealed the gleaming saddle tanks, as we rolled over to the other. It was all very seductive, and made it difficult to keep one's eyes scanning the further fields of the sea for enemies.

A submarine's motion is peculiar. It is generally affected by wind and sea in the opposite way to surface ships. If a surface ship is rolling, she rolls over further to the lee side. But a submarine rolls over further to the weather side, because the sea breaking on her weather saddle tanks is like a finger pressing her down. On this morning our motion was being affected chiefly by two things – the south-west monsoon and our zig-zag. When the long swell of the monsoon caught us on the beam during a turn, we did some particularly violent rolls. Down below, one always knew, from these rolls, the moment of altering course. But the sea was not rough.

When the message 'breakfast ready' came up the voice-pipe, I had to go down, as others were waiting to come up for their fresh air, and could not do so till I went below. If it had been a peace-time cruise, I should have asked for my bacon and eggs on the bridge.

After breakfast we did a short dive, of only ten minutes, to catch the trim. Then we continued on the surface. I was reading *Tom Sawyer*, with old-fashioned illustrations of the kind one associates with Sunday School prizes, much worse, probably, than the kind that Tom Sawyer got in exchange for his coloured tickets. The Navigator looking over my shoulder and never having heard of Tom Sawyer, kindly said that the illustrations made him sick, and the book was probably as nauseating. Later on in the patrol, when reading matter was running short, he condescended to pick it up with the intention of further criticism; but, having started to read it, he did not put it down till he had finished it – with great enjoyment. When I finished *Tom Sawyer* I began Leo Walmsley's *Foreigners*, also about a small boy.

I was allowed on the bridge twice again that day; the second time was during sunset. I saw flying fish the size of tinned sardines; and the sea, which was over a thousand fathoms deep beneath us, was a strange grey blue. The sunset was rather dull at first; then it livened up to an unearthly pink, while the sea ahead of us turned to vegetable green.

34

SUBMARINE IN THE TROPICS

On the fifth day out, we looked at Japanese-held territory through the periscope: on the horizon, dark blue mountains with wisps of cloud, and in the foreground, seemingly within an inch of one's nose, dancing glass-green waves. We identified the peaks, and then had a very fine lunch of spam, cucumber, and salad.

After lunch, Geoffrey made a view sketch through the periscope. I held the sketchbook, pencil and rubber while he moved the periscope about; as soon as he had the graticule in the eyepiece on the place he wanted, he would note the bearing, snatch the sketch book and pencil, mark in a tiny part of the line, and hand them back to me. Drawing through a periscope has to be done very quickly, as the bearings are continually changing, because the submarine is moving. It is usual to exaggerate the vertical scale two times, as in the view sketches on charts. The sketch when finished was not beautiful, but we were gratified to hear later that it helped subsequent visitors to this coast.

The officer of the watch was a nervous type, and would not let us raise the periscope for more than a minute at a time, at two-minute intervals. When the Captain came into the control room, casually raised the after periscope as well, and started taking photographs through it, he hopped up and down with anxiety, but could say nothing. There was a choppy sea, and we were nearly five miles from land; there was little chance of the 'stick' being seen.

The control room, with a lot of people in it, was about as squalid, uncomfortable and cheerful as a London tube during the Blitz. The walls and roof and the naked bodies were all gleaming with sweat. The Petty Officer of the watch was leaning up against the steel conning tower ladder, chewing gum and receiving the draught of an electric fan down his back. Under his eye, two Able-Seamen sitting on boxes were controlling the hydroplanes. Their fingers were on large slender-spoked wheels, their eyes on the needles in the depth gauges and their minds probably several thousand miles away. Both had their loins encased in evil-looking towels, held up by greasy belts; and both needed a shave, as they had already been told.

In a corner, a figure rather like King Neptune, with a flowing beard, was adjusting ear-phones on his head and slowly turning a small wheel beneath a dial which he watched carefully. He was the hydrophone operator, and he was listening to all the noises in the ocean. It was said that he could distinguish between a crab and a lobster blowing farts five miles away.

Two other ratings were on duty with note books, recording alterations of course and times of fixes etc., like everybody else, they had a job that was boring now, but would be hectic if we went into action.

The E.R.A. on the panel, who would turn the wheels to blow air into the tanks if we had to surface, had his hand on a lever, ready to lower the periscope the instant the Captain gave the sign.

In the far corner of the control room, a man was on his hands and knees, scrubbing the deck with soap and water. At half past three in the afternoon, it seemed an unlikely thing to be doing but he was under punishment. He had been awarded extra duties daily for a week, and as a result was perpetually scrubbing out the decks – generally, between one's legs, and always in the way. The more he could get in the way, the more fun it was for him. He always had a cheerful grin on his face.

The only other unusual thing in the control room was a sack of potatoes, which really belonged to the galley round the corner. Its most remarkable feature was its smell, which dominated all other smells.

We surfaced after seven, but then had to wait for supper, as the cook could not begin cooking until we had surfaced. We sat around in the wardroom, discussing personalities in the depot-ship. The Sub-Lieutenant, just off watch, had just said of somebody in a mystified tone of voice 'I don't believe he drinks', when the klaxon went. The Sub-Lieutenant leaped from the wardroom, as did the other submarine officers from their bunks, leaving us passengers rather breathless. In about forty seconds we had dived, and the needle in the wardroom depth-gauge was flickering round: fifteen, twenty, thirty, forty, fifty feet. We wondered what the alarm was for. There was a plop from the Tannoy loudspeaker: a voice intoned: 'Shut off shallow water depth gauges.' Then: 'Stop all unnecessary machinery.' Then: 'Shut off for depth charging.' All ventilation had to be stopped, including the electric fans. Apparently we were being hunted. We sat patiently, waiting to be depth charged. The temperature in the wardroom was only 93° , but the high humidity made it feel much worse. We poured sweat. It was impossible even to read a book. The First Lieutenant came in and told us we had dived because the lookouts had seen a craft overhauling us from astern, and that now we could hear the screws of two craft, probably submarine-chasers. We were definitely being hunted.

We passengers exchanged glances which said 'This would happen. But we must pretend that we're used to it, and don't care.' The Sub-Lieutenant came in and relieved the tension by giving a graphic representation of the Japanese sailors who were up above being sea-sick. About 10 p.m., supper was brought in, consisting of lovely pork chops, roast potatoes, and onions – surprisingly enough, we ate it, although it made us sweat more. It was sad to have to eat a good meal in such squalor – we tended to talk in whispers, as if the listening enemy might even hear us talking.

Never, never, never had any of us been in such acute physical discomfort. We could not think of any worse occasion, because hard times become mellowed in retrospect. The Red Sea in a troopship in August had been bad – so had certain episodes in the North Sea three years earlier. But they were all in the past. This was now. We sat rigidly still. Any movement made us sweat more. We swore never to travel by submarine again if we could help it. We sweated.

In the control room, the Captain was gradually taking us clear. Very slowly, at one knot, a hundred feet below the surface, we sneaked away. At last he judged it safe to surface. At a quarter before midnight we steamed away on the surface at full speed. The sea and sky were empty beneath the stars, and the scene was most poetic, until the chef came up and threw overboard the bread he had been baking before we dived. It had all gone sour.

Jungle trail

35

MORE NIGHT SWIMS

Next morning when we dived, I left my foetid bunk and found great solace in the grapefruit we had for breakfast. After breakfast, and after reading the submarine newspaper *Good Morning*, I could not face my bunk again, so I stretched out on three chairs in the wardroom.

This was, at last, the day of our first sortie. The nature of our operation demanded very careful planning, and a highly intricate and yet flexible time schedule. The whole operation had to be carried out in the dark, after moonset. Two canoes each carrying two men had to be launched and paddled inshore, find a certain exact position, land two officers who wished to spend as long as possible (up to three hours) in that place, pick up these officers, and then paddle back to the submarine.

The position of the submarine was all-important. Previous operations of this kind in the Med had suffered casualties, but not from the enemy. Canoes had been lost owing either to treacherous weather or to their failing to find the submarine through both parties being out of position. Some sonic and visual homing devices had been used but were never totally reliable.

For this operation our general plan was as follows. The submarine was to find the launching position, and wait submerged. As soon as it was dark she would surface, launch the two canoes, and dive again.

The canoes would go inshore, do their stuff, and return to the estimated position of the submarine. The submarine would surface at a pre-arranged time, pick up the canoes, and go out to sea. To spend several hours of the night dived was a great hardship on the submarine's crew. The batteries would be hot after a whole day's running, and the few minutes on the surface for launching would hardly cool the boat; and when dived the cooling and air-conditioning machinery could not be run.

Our schedule gave expected times for arriving at the beach, leaving the beach, and arriving at the submarine again; but, to allow for accidents, we also had to fix on final times: a final time for the landing officers to return, after which the canoes must leave the beach without them: and a final time for the canoes to return to the submarine, after which the submarine must go out to sea without them. The submarine had to charge her batteries on the surface for at least some part of the night.

If anybody was unfortunate enough to be left on the beach, we had plans for picking him up on successive nights; and, if the canoes were not recovered by the submarine during the night, arrangements had been made for them to be picked up either in daylight or on successive nights. Finally, should all these arrangements fail, each man carried an escaping outfit and would try to make his way to safety through enemy territory.

We were four officers and four ratings. If we had been able to carry out our full programme, we would have needed all this number to get through the work in the few nights available before the moon set too late to give us enough time. But our operation had been whittled down, for reasons beyond our control, and now our problem was to give everybody an outing.

The first night, Geoff and Lucas were being landed; Corporal Strong and myself were paddlers; Colson was 'Submarine Liaison', i.e. he stayed on board to look after our interests from the submarine.

We spent the afternoon in and out of the control room, looking through the periscope. Geoff was there the whole time, making fixes of our position and plotting various things we saw on the beaches – particularly some Japanese bunkers and barbed wire. The Sub-Lieutenant on watch was reduced to a state of nerves by the crush in the control room caused, he said, by useless dilettantes queueing up for a peep. The country we were looking at was very attractive. We decided to revisit it after the war. The sky was overcast and the sea smooth but with a long swell.

Our troops were busy getting the canoes ready and loading them with all the gear. The two soldiers were priming grenades and fitting sten gun magazines.

We were dived in the correct position about 1730. The operation was preceded by the order 'No moving about in the boat' to ensure its complete steadiness.

We had a meal at 1745. There could be no cooking while we were dived, so our meal was a plate of cold meat. Then we began dressing. The others were wearing two-piece gabardine suits, which contained both kapok and an inflatable life belt. I was in overalls; I would not be swimming. We carried a lot of gear on our persons. The subject of what it was necessary to carry and what could safely be left behind had been a source of argument among us for the entire eighteen months we had been in existence as a group. We all felt very much like Christmas trees, with a lot of things secured at the end of lanyards to prevent their being lost.

About 1915 the order came 'Stand by to surface'. I went along to my position in the fore ends. The wearing of a uniform loaded with gear did not conduce to comfort. When the whole team for raising the canoes was present in the fore ends, we shut the watertight door and were encased in complete and sweaty darkness. The T.I. was in charge of the compartment and, with his crew of three torpedo men, would remain down below all the time. I was in charge of the actual lifting of the canoes.

A Leading Seaman stood at the top of the ladder ready to knock off the clips fastening the hatch. There were four clips made of steel, each of which weighed as much as a cannon ball, and they had to be hammered off with a sledge hammer. I stood below, hoping he would not drop the clips or the hammer on my head. The rest of the party stood by the first canoe going up. Geoff and Lucas were aft: Geoff would be going up on the bridge immediately after the Captain to make the final decision to go ahead with the sortie.

At last we heard the air hissing into the tanks as we blew; a slight tremor in the boat indicated that we were lifting; the noise of water breaking on the hull showed we had reached the surface; and the sudden difference in pressure on the eardrums told us the conning tower hatch was opened. Then, a couple of minutes later, there came taps on the outside of the hatch that was the signal for it to be opened. An officer would be standing up above us on the casing. The Leading Seaman began hammering off the clips, each blow sounded hideously loud and the delay seemed eternal. Then the hatch was opened, the Leading Seaman was up, I ran up the ladder carrying the stern painter, and the men below bent to pick up the canoe. I settled myself astride the hatch on the outside. Over my shoulder the shore looked very close, although it was, in fact, a mile away. It was a beautiful starlit night. Up came the men dragging the canoe. There was one inch to spare on each side, so it was quite a delicate operation to prevent the canoe jamming. Four men came up pulling, two below were pushing. It seemed as heavy as a piano. Up it came and was immediately carried aft, where two stayed with it to inflate the air sausages. The rest dropped down again for the second canoe. Up it came. It stuck. I cried 'Twist it'. It was freed. It was up and carried aft; the hatch was shut, and the anxious period for the Captain, during which he could not dive, was over. Everyone left the casing (the canoes having been lashed down) and climbed into the gun platform, which was trained round to overhang our launching position. The Captain proceeded to trim down. It was necessary to bring the level of the water up over the saddle tanks so that we could launch the canoes from the casing direct into the water.

This operation involved some risk, for if the Captain reduced the submarine's buoyancy too much she might suddenly sink like a stone. Columns of spray shot in the air as the vents were opened momentarily in succession. The submarine settled down, so that the saddle tanks were awash. Our nine-foot double-ended paddles were passed up the gun hatch. Then we launched 'B' canoe, for which Lucas and Colson were waiting. It was launched according to a drill we had practised in harbour. A man at each end held the bow and stern painters, and two men were on each of the two slings. These were ropes fastened by spring hooks to rings at the canoe's four hand-holds. At the word 'Lift', the canoe was lifted and swung out and then dropped. The crew stepped down quickly, sat in the canoe, cast off the slings, took the paddles handed down to them, and pushed themselves clear. This was done without a hitch, except that they went away without their paddles, while Geoff was shouting and swearing at them, and everyone else was agonised by the noise and saying 'ssssh!'. However, they drifted back close enough for the paddles to be passed down to them. When our canoe was lowered into the water. I jumped down into the after cockpit. The swell was breaking on the saddle tank, and the canoe was one minute high and dry, and the next being woooshed over by a wave. Geoff narrowly missed overturning as he came in, and then we pushed off with our slings still attached, an amendment to the drill which we subsequently standardised. The submarine, now about fifty yards away, suddenly blew a great fountain of spray, like a whale, and sank quite slowly. In about a minute she had disappeared.

I set our course on the compass before me, and we paddled towards the shore. The night was very quiet except for the noise of the surf on the beach. The soldiers were on our quarter. Lucas made one of his excruciatingly heavy and ill-timed jokes (about was our journey really necessary) to Geoff, and received a withering reply.

After about half an hour's paddling we were four hundred yards off shore. The coast, lined with trees, was very like that on which we had trained. We paddled along close to it – far too close to it, I thought nervously – and took a sounding: twelve feet. We continued paddling along the shore until in five minutes we came to the point from which Geoff and Lucas were to swim in. They recognised it from a gap in the trees, and a building. They inflated their life-belts, tried to think of reasons for delaying, couldn't, and regretfully went over the side and began swim-ming. The sea always seems full of sharks and barracudas on occasions like this. In a few minutes their heads, two dark blobs on the grey water, were lost to sight. Colson and I paddled our canoes out a little way, and I anchored. We had both moved into the front cockpits. Colson faced his canoe the opposite way from mine, so that we could keep an all-round look-out, and we settled down to wait.

The depth was twelve feet. The sky to seaward of us was overcast, which was lucky; it reduced the distance at which we could be seen from the shore. We were to wait an hour for Geoff, and about two hours for Lucas. We had to keep a con-stant watch on the shore, and to seaward. We also had to make observations of the current, if any, to make sure we did not drift out of our position. Without taking my eyes off the shore, I washed some of my clothes which I had brought from the submarine for the purpose; and we nibbled sweets from our emergency rations.

After nearly an hour we saw a blue torch, and I sent Colson in, but weighed anchor and overtook him before he reached the swimmer. It was Geoff; I towed him out a little way, and then he climbed in. He said the surf was bloody, and took a sip from his rum flask. I said was it, and had a sip too, in sympathy. He said the canoes were invisible from the shore even at the edge of the surf.

We went out a little farther and anchored again to wait for Lucas. I looked at the stars. It was now sixteen months since I had seen my fiancée. I thought of her somewhere over there to the North West. I also thought forward, trying to imagine what this episode would feel like in memory.

After a little over two hours, Lucas's blue light was seen and Colson picked him up. He had been quite a long way inland, found what he wanted; and come back without seeing anyone; a job well done. After a little delay, while Lucas fiddled with his equipment, we set course again for the submarine. We had to cross the ten fathom line. Every five minutes we stopped and took a sounding. Suddenly we went from eight fathoms to sixteen fathoms. Having checked the sounding, we anchored. In rather less than ten minutes there was a sort of sigh, audible above the sound of the surf, and there was a dark blob on the face of the waters about a hundred yards away. The submarine had surfaced. We weighed anchor and paddled up to her. Geoff and I went alongside first and passed up our slings; but the swell was vicious. Before we could get out of the canoe, a wave capsized us. We were soon out of the water and on the submarine's casing; the canoe was emptied of water and hauled up valiantly by the casing party. No gear was lost, as it was all secured by lanyards. We gave the signal for the soldiers to come alongside. Geoff went up to the bridge to tell the Captain all was well, and I went down onto the saddle tank to help the others in. When the canoe was swept up by the swell, I was able to push it off while it was still waterborne, and steady it. Lucas and Colson scrambled out and the canoe was quickly hauled on board. The submarine turned in a wide circle and proceeded slowly (and therefore quietly) out to sea. Then she trimmed up, the forehatch was opened and the canoes struck down. The hatch was then shut, and once again she had regained her full freedom to dive at a second's notice.

I went up to the bridge. It was very pleasant there, and hateful to think of leaving the cool night air for the heat in the hull. But there was supper and iced lemonade waiting for us below. We wrote up our reports and turned in about 0400.

We slept as much as possible the next day. I did not become active till tea-time. We were doing another sortie that night, of which I was in charge. Petty Officer Reilly was paddling me, and one of our A.B.s was paddling Colson. Geoff and I spent the afternoon looking through the periscope, and found the place we were going to. There was a four hundred yard gap in the trees which was clearly visible in the periscope and on our air photographs.

The programme was the same as on the previous night. When the canoes were clear of the submarine, without a hitch, she dived, and we paddled on the course previously worked out. It was much darker than the previous night. When we reached the shore we turned and paddled along it. There were many lights among the trees; Reilly said he thought they were sentries carrying torches, and I said I thought they were fires in native villages. After fifteen minutes paddling along the shore (we had expected about ten), we found the right place. It was unmistakable, with very good marks for the canoes to maintain position on while waiting. The surf did not sound too bad. Colson and I swam in and were touching bottom after about six minutes. The surf was breaking in a depth of five feet. Colson disappeared crawling over the top of a dune at the back of the beach, and I hung around in the surf till he was clear. Then I went away to survey my own area of beach. On the way back, I saw some natives sitting round a fire. I did not attempt to get close to them for fear of causing a hue and cry while Colson was still away. I swam back through the surf. Having got through it, I was floating on my back and congratulating myself on how easy it had all been, when the seventh wave broke just behind me, threw me upside down, carried me back up the beach, and ground my nose in the sand with a sneer. I swam out farther this time before resting, and regained the canoes after showing my torch only once. There was so little set that we did not anchor again, but lay watching and eating emergency rations. The two sailors both remarked on how like an exercise it was. Reilly told me about the latest situation re his girl friend. She had not been writing to him, and he had told her he would give her another six weeks and then. Colson's light appeared about an hour after I had come back. We picked him up quickly. He had crawled across some Jap trenches, negotiated a very alarming bamboo fence, and had seen some poultry; but he had met no men. Another job well done.

We were recovered without difficulty before midnight, and proceeded seaward.

Canoeists at sea, S. India.

36

GUN ACTION

Sitting in the wardroom waiting for lunch, we gradually became aware of an unusual activity in the control-room. Within a few minutes of our noticing this activity, we were told that a junk had been sighted in the periscope. We were closing.

In a quarter of an hour, Geoff was called into the control-room. The Captain asked him to look through the periscope and give him his estimate of the junk's tonnage. We had orders to sink all junks of over fifty tons. 'About seventy, I should think?' said the Captain, hopefully. 'Eighty, at least' replied Geoff. 'Ninety,' said the First Lieutenant, after having a look himself.

A twin-engined bomber was apparently escorting the junk. This made it more interesting. The junk was fully laden, and about six miles offshore, probably making for a Japanese harbour about a hundred miles farther up the coast.

We still had some way to make up before being in a position to shoot. For the first time on that patrol we went at full speed on our main electric motors. The submarine vibrated noticeably, rather like a toy aeroplane whose elastic is fully wound. The gun's crew were told to stand by. A large man-hole in the wardroom doorway was opened, and bodies descended into the shell locker to put settings on the fuzes. We were going to surface about a mile from the junk, which was a safe distance if she turned out to be a Q ship (i.e. a merchant ship with concealed guns, used to decoy enemy ships into the range of its weapons).

About mid-day the buzzer for 'Action stations' was sounded. We sat tight in the wardroom. We were exactly underneath the gun platform. Early in the war, submarine C.O.s used not to take their guns very seriously, and affected whimsical surprise if they went off. Now it was different. Submarine gunnery was serious and highly efficient.

At last the aircraft disappeared over the land, and the order was broadcast: 'Stand by gun action; stand by to surface. Check main vents. Open all L.P. Master Blowers'. A seaman standing in the wardroom turned wheels in the ceiling and reported 'Numbers one, two and three Master Blowers open, sir'. The high pressure air was blown into the ballast tanks and the submarine floated up, while our eyes followed the depth-gauge needle swinging back. At about ten feet, the sea could be heard breaking on the hull above our heads. In a few seconds a sensation on our

203

ear drums told us that the hatch had been opened, and the pressure in the boat relieved. The gun hatch was opened immediately afterwards, and the gun's crew were up it and having rounds passed up and firing their gun all in a matter of seconds. The noise of the gun was less than I expected. Geoff had his fingers over his ears so tightly that he never heard the first four rounds.

Five minutes after we had surfaced, we had fired thirty-two rounds.

Six minutes after we had surfaced, the klaxon sounded. We submerged; and so, I gathered, had the junk.

As we dived, there was a bang, which actually was the tail clutch being let out rather quickly; but we did not know that, and thought it was a depth charge from the aeroplane. Geoff brought out a pencil and made a show of unconcernedly taking down the times of the depth charges. A few minutes later there was another bang. That was actually a stoker dropping a spanner in the engine-room, but down it went as a depth charge. Then the First Lieutenant came into the wardroom and burst out laughing at the solemn expressions on our faces. We had dived simply because the junk was sunk, and there was no sign of the aeroplane.

We in the wardroom had now to hear what had happened. The First Lieutenant had been below, watching through the periscope, for if by chance the target had fired back and wiped out the Captain, he would have had to take over the action. The Gunnery Officer had been on the gun and had had the clearest view of all. They had scored a hit with the second round, and had then hit her repeatedly, but she would not sink. She was probably laden with rice or timber. The curious thing was that there had been no signs of life on board. Not one human being had been seen. No one had jumped off her into the sea, or been seen among the wreckage when she sank. Possibly her crew had been asleep or having tiffin in the poop, and had all been killed by the first hit, which had been aft. She was a typical three-masted Shanghai junk under full sail, and they now thought she was about one hundred tons.

While we were still hearing the story, the aircraft was reported again in the periscope, circling the spot where the junk had been, with a puzzled frown on its radiator. 'Look hard, my friend, but you won't see us' murmured the Captain. He admitted that a junk was unfairly easy game, but said that (a) it had been under air escort, and (b) the morale of his crew was much raised by the action. This was their first Far Eastern patrol, and it was important to have a success; submarine crews do not thrive on uneventful and fruitless patrols; they had joined submarines to hit the enemy.

This was testified by the gleam in the eyes of the wardroom steward (No.3 on the gun), when he came in to lay the table for lunch.

37

THE WAY HOME

The Captain's orders gave him permission to return to harbour when our operation was completed. And as that was now the case, we cheerfully looked forward to a speedy run home, and imagined that we should see the Depot Ship in about three or four days.

On the way home, the Captain decided to take a roundabout route and pass between two islands where he might find some Japanese shipping to attack. That meant that we would have an extra week on board. A week may not sound a long time; but when you have to spend it sitting in a submarine's tiny wardroom, doing nothing all day long, and when it is the third week you have so spent, then indeed the minutes and seconds ebb out slowly.

But just before tea-time, some bouys with red flags, seen in the periscope, roused the Captain's suspicions. Four minutes later, he came into the wardroom and announced that we were in the middle of a minefield. Back in the control room, he said to Geoffrey, standing beside him, 'Are you married?' Geoffrey admitted that he wasn't. 'Well, I am!' replied the Captain grimly. Apparently our mine-detecting units gave contacts all round us. We turned, using our screws (which gave a smaller turning circle than our rudder alone) and began to thread our way out. The Captain, who was steering, described the following hour in his patrol report as 'hair-raising'. But we got out. A signal was then made to our base reporting the minefield, and we left the area. We would get a cooked supper after all.

Periodically we tried to tidy up the wardroom. With four extra inmates, it was unusually chaotic. The naval custom is to stow all gear that is left sculling into a 'scran-bag', from which the owners may redeem their property at the cost of a piece of soap per article. Whenever the First Lieutenant started to pop the books and odd articles of clothing into a bag, everyone jumped up and tried to save his own property, lamenting that he, personally, had so little space to stow his gear compared with the amount that everyone else had. After about an hour's pandemonium, peace returned, and the wardroom really looked quite nice. But, as with a small boy whose hair, having been brushed, begins to rise slowly out of position as soon as the brush has left it, so with the wardroom. In an hour or so it was as bad as ever.

Boredom beset only our party, for the submarine officers were watchkeeping, and their routine of watch, eat, and sleep made a satisfying rhythm, and was their job. They boasted of the long patrols they had done, and of the even longer ones they would like to do. They were keen to stow extra food along the passage ways and in all the compartments, and patrol in the Pacific till the fuel ran out, and then be fuelled at sea and continue on patrol. British submarines operating from Britain or in the Mediterranean do not usually patrol for longer than three weeks; but American submarines, which are reputed to be so comfortable that the men live in them in harbour, often patrol for five or six weeks. The thought appalled us.

We each showed the strain in different ways. Geoff became gradually more and more restive. After reading in a fidgety manner for half an hour or so, he would suddenly punch Colson or me on the shoulder, and hope we would punch him back. He was careful not to punch Lucas, for Lucas's idea of a playful punch was not ours.

Lucas became more and more deeply involved in his own thoughts, and was really calmer than any of us. But he used to spend hours every day in the heads (lavatory) which was the only place where he could find solitude for prayer. This caused great fury among the others, who wanted to use the place quickly before turning in or going on watch.

The Midshipman sank deeper and deeper in apathetic gloom: partly caused by the fact that he was constipated, but chiefly because he had come to the end of his mental resources. He simply could not think any more thoughts, or read any more books, that did not bore him completely. He just sat all day in a coma, pathetic to watch.

I do not know how I showed to the others, but I felt the strain in my head, as if it were a bottle of fermenting liquor that might burst at any moment. I moved about the submarine as much as possible, talking to various people; the most healing moments of each day were those I spent looking up the conning tower at the sky. We were still in enemy waters and not allowed on the bridge. I felt as if I should burst very soon with a loud report, if I could not get out of the submarine, and I did not know how I was going to live through those last seven days.

Our troops were given various jobs by the Coxswain of the submarine, and we kept them busy with mending and maintenance of weapons and other articles of gear. They grumbled at this, so we assumed, rightly, that their morale was not suffering.

The detour which the Captain made to cross Japanese shipping routes did not produce any results, so our boredom was not relieved by any excitements whatever. A few events on board made welcome disturbances. One was the day on which the batteries had to be topped up with distilled water. Some of the cells were beneath the wardroom, so all the floor had to come up. We had to vacate the place completely for several hours as Jock, the steward, made this an opportunity for a thorough scrub-out. We therefore asked the First Lieutenant to conduct us round the boat. It was the first time that either Lucas or the Midshipman had properly explored her. The stokers, who lived near the engine room in the after ends, were living in even more cramped quarters than we were. It was quite impossible to stand up in their 'house'; but the ventilation was better, and while the diesels were running, it was almost cool with them.

In the electricians' mess, we stopped (a) to look at their pin-up girls, and (b) to watch their 'factory'. In nearly all ships there are some craftsmen who while away long voyages by manufacture. Usually the things made follow fashions. For one period the fashion is for metal-work. Everyone is making marvellous brooches, rings, trinkets, elaborate picture-frames, cigarette-boxes etc. Another time the craze will be for turning out model ships or animals in wood, or fluffy toys, or coloured portraits of mothers and sisters and wives. On this patrol the industry was in leather goods, and some miraculous sandals, belts and braces were being produced. The men offered to sell, and Lucas lived up to his reputation as a pessimist by buying a belt and braces.

One other important item was being made on board during the voyage home. This was the submarine's 'Jolly Roger'. It is the traditional right of a submarine returning from enemy waters to fly a black flag bearing the skull and cross-bones, with a symbol added for each ship sunk or other success of the patrol. So the signalman was sitting cross-legged, like a tailor, sewing on to the submarine's black flag a small white square for the junk, and a dagger, to indicate our operation. Some submarine commanders, used to sinking large tonnages in the Mediterranean, and having sunk only a few junks on their first Far Eastern patrol, thought that they had not earned the right to fly their Jolly Roger merely for junks, and had not flown it. But they had been reprimanded by the Captain of the Flotilla, who had pointed out how important junks were to the Japs in those waters.

As we gradually drew away from enemy waters, we were allowed to have the wireless on more often. The news was exciting, for the allied armies had just begun their sweep through France in 1944. I shall never forget listening to the eye-witness account of how De Gaulle visited Notre Dame amid turbulent scenes, in a Paris once again free.

We did have one job on our homeward voyage. Wishful thinking made us imagine that the Supreme Allied Commander and numerous senior staff officers would be biting their finger nails with anxiety and impatience until we returned safely and rendered our report. Geoff's plan was to complete the writing of it while we were at sea, and then proceed straight to headquarters the day after we arrived (allowing the first night for the customary celebration). At HQ we would install ourselves in the best hotel, borrow somebody's office and the best-looking Wren we could see, put the finishing touches to the report, get the Wren to type it, make our drawings, hand over the completed report, bow deeply, and whizz off on leave: preferably with the best-looking Wren aforesaid.

So we wrote and wrote, and checked bearings and distances on chart and map, read each others' reports, annoyed Geoff by criticising his English (of which he was secretly proud), and goaded Lucas into writing a paper entitled 'How to be Happy in a Submarine', of which the gist was that it was impossible to be happy in a submarine. It was amazing to see how long the report gradually became – and there was no padding in it.

Then we made plans for leave, so far as it was possible to plan leave without a telephone or Post Office on board. Geoff's plans definitely centred on the best-looking Wren. Mine were to get away as quickly as possible from all naval and military officers. Lucas's were to jump an aeroplane going to Burma and join his young brother, probably in a fox-hole. The Midshipman – well, he was at such a low ebb of morale that he was incapable even of looking forward to leave. Like the young man in Newbolt's poem, he sat all day in a dream, untroubled of hope. The only way to rouse him, even temporarily, was to criticise his torso, or to try to pluck the few hairs which it boasted. He apparently had no girl to dream about, and I think his most passionate dreams were of his motor-bicycle.

During the return journey, I discovered that by piling the wardroom chairs on the table I could make room for another camp bed on the deck; so I did this and spent the remainder of my nights in what was, by comparison, comfort. The chairs piled on the table made it slightly difficult for the table to be used after about 10 p.m., which was a pity if an urgent secret cipher arrived and had to be deciphered by an officer. The ciphers were usually passed to the Chief Engineer, and when he was roused out of his bunk he would tread lightly on Lucas's face as he got up, and heavily on mine as he sat down at the table. He would then drop on me a continual dew of papers, books and pencils and rubbers till he was finished; but he never actually complained that he had not enough room. For me it was heavenly comfort compared with my previous modes of sleeping in the submarine. But it still reminded me of the squalid days and nights of 1940 that I had spent in the air raid trenches of Portsmouth Barracks.

Gradually we neared port. The great question became whether the fresh water would last out. The Chief Stoker, carrying a greasy old exercise book full of figures, made a report each morning to the First Lieutenant in such gloomy terms as: 'Used over 80 gallons yesterday, sir. Have to start rationing soon,' or: 'Can't last out at this rate, sir – only 200 left now'. We dreaded the day when the water would be shut off except for half an hour in the evenings. At the First Lieutenant's request, I made a series of little posters advocating the use of less water. One showed an inebriated Commander holding a bottle of whisky, another a promising blonde up to her shoulders in a bath. They were stuck up above all taps in the submarine, and had no effect whatever. So the First Lieutenant made an appeal over the Tannoy, but, as he spoke in a completely unemotional and monotonous RN voice, no one thought he believed in what he was saying, and all went on as before. Then, on the last day but two, the Chief Stoker presented his book to the First Lieutenant with an expression of unparalleled and almost inspissated gloom, and announced that he'd been forgetting to count X tank, which had another 100 gallons in it, so we should be all right, easy.

The last excitement in a submarine's patrol is usually the rendezvous with the escort vessel that will take her back to harbour. Has the navigation been perfect, and will the escort be sighted dead ahead at exactly the predicted time? In this case the rendezvous was at midnight with two M.L.s. Much to their annoyance, our look-outs sighted them before they sighted us. This was a triumph, for a submarine at night is a much bigger silhouette than a M.L. Our Captain was justly pleased and rewarded the successful look-out with five shillings.

The Midshipman, when he heard that we had met our escort and would arrive in harbour next morning, went to bed wearing what we had not seen on his face for nearly ten days, a broad smile.

Next morning I awoke about seven. The boat was quite silent and still; the diesels were not running; everything was peace. I asked permission to go up the conning tower onto the bridge, feeling that it was like a request to go up from a rocket that has already been lit.

Luckily, the answer from above was 'Yes, please'. When I arrived on the bridge, I found we were at anchor in a large bay. The shore line swept round in a great circle to the far side, on which was the narrow entrance to another bay, in which the Fleet lay anchored. The sides of an aircraft-carrier shone in the sun, and behind her were a cruiser's tall funnels and the white tripod masts of battleships. Behind and round the ships rose low hills covered in feathery jungle; but it was not virgin, for here and there poked out wireless or radar masts and signal stations. Across some of the hills moved cloud shadows, like the pools of shadow on the downs at home.

1 asked the Officer of the Watch why we could not go straight in. He said that we would go in about 0900, but had to do noise trials first. And, just as he spoke, a small motor boat came through the outer boom and headed for us. When she came up, she had the noise party from the Depot Ship on board, and she lay off, waiting for us to say we were ready. Our Captain was roused and came up on the bridge. It was not his first sight of the land, but it had been dark when he brought us in. Noise trials were a routine for submariners returning from patrol. They had to carry out a number of evolutions on the surface, and submerged, with the noise boat listening and making recordings and assessments of the noise. Then, if any trouble had developed on patrol, it could be repaired immediately.

It was tiresome having to do more dives, with all cooling machinery switched off, but it was necessary. We packed frenziedly while the boat was on the surface, and sat rigid whenever we dived, as movement then became too uncomfortable.

At last the trials were finished, and the submarine's nose was pointed for the harbour entrance. The Jolly Roger was run up between the periscope standards, and a large clean ensign fluttered bravely above it. Poor old Lucas, who had been looking forward to this moment during the entire patrol, now found he had lost his green beret, and therefore decided that he could not go up on the bridge for entering harbour. He could not disgrace the bridge by appearing bare-headed (despite the Captain's assurance that it would not matter), and he refused kind offers of a sailor's cap, a tin helmet, and a fez. So he stayed below, while we went up above and drank in the joy of living, through our eyes, ears, noses, and the pores of our skin.

Our submarine's officers were now all in immaculate white. We were in khaki, and the ratings in clean white shorts, bare torsos, and beards.

First, we passed the Boom Defence vessel. The skipper, just out of his bunk, appeared in an orange sarong, and waved a banana.

Then we passed the destroyers, all still asleep, and then the cruisers, just waking up, and then a battleship in which everyone had probably been up and working furiously since dawn.

At last we approached our Depot Ship. Very smartly, and at what seemed to us much too high a speed, the Captain brought us alongside. A few familiar faces peered down at us from the decks above: the officer of the day, the Commander, and the Senior Engineer. Most of the submarine officers were still fast asleep. Heaving lines snaked out, fell short, were thrown again and caught. We were secured.

It was not long before the various necessary tasks were completed, like removing our gear from the submarine, and filling in and signing victualling check lists, and saying au revoir to the various submarine ratings who had looked after us so well. Within a very short time, we were revelling in the luxuries of hot water and a three weeks' accumulation of mail. 'Now open that envelope – now wash this elbow – now that airgraph – now soap just here – heavens, there's an O.H.M.S. letter going down the plug-hole …'

We set foot on shore the next day. It was a very beautiful country to come back to, I thought, as we looked again at the feathery palm trees, the hedges gay with scarlet hibiscus blossoms, the paddy fields green as a green flame … it was not its fault that I longed for a grey drizzle in the Woodstock Road.

38

THE COAST OF CHINA

The voyage home from Colombo was in the *Christian Huygens*, a luxury liner turned into a troopship, in which the barman was said to earn more than the captain.

On sunny evenings we sat on deck with the girls also returning to England, and made up rhymes. One of our favourite girls was Maggie, and I wrote for her:

> *As we took our evening noggin*
> *Maggie fell into the 'oggin.*
> *As she slowly dropped to leeward*
> *I rang the bell and called the steward;*
> *And with a faltering voice I said:*
> *'Make that last order ONE instead'.*

Geoff and Doreen

Kay and Maggie.

Up on A deck, Margaret Thomas
Writes a lot, but with no commas
With her head against a stanchion
Kay can't think of ANY scansion.

As we approached England, the Germans were invading the Ardennes, and it was rumoured that we would all be thrown into the front line; but by the time we arrived, in early January 1945, it was happily all over.

*   *   *

I looked at my diary. It was about 0930 on Thursday, the fifteenth of November 1945. I was sitting at a desk in an Oxford College, reading the *South China Sea Pilot*. Before me lay spread out an Admiralty chart of the coast from Pen'tung to Ho'Wei, with five air photographs taken at forty thousand feet, and a magnifying glass. There were also the tide tables for Hong Kong and a pencilled note on the telephone pad which read '7 lb 2 oz'.

I was now back again in ISTD; and the unit in which I was serving had just started to write up the coast of China. Two of the other Naval Officers had been to China, but not that part. I had just come back from the Far East, and knew what a mangrove was, if the Chinese had them. When we started, the Army was swarming across Burma and would no doubt be wanting to land on China at any moment. There was some urgency in the matter. The material we had to work on was hopelessly inadequate, but still we pressed on.

Then, in August, the war had ended.

In January, five months later, we were still writing up the coast of China, as if nothing had happened; still poring over the occasional air photo where a pilot happened to have crossed the coast with his camera open; still guessing the exact nature of ten miles of coastline which occupied one inch on a seventy-year old chart.

We were getting paid for it. Some of the others, who wanted jobs in the department, were hoping very much that the Admiralty would think of sending someone out to actually look at the ground on the spot. The coast of China was, to them, like the famous Hole in the Road; they saw no reason why they shouldn't keep it open for a very long time, and even pass it on to their sons. And after the coast of China there was, of course, the coast of Russia.

But I had a pre-war job to which I wanted to go back. There was also this matter of 7 lb 2 oz. When I had made that note, during a telephone call from a hospital in Liverpool, my son was already about 120 minutes old. I was not really interested in what he weighed. The full impact of those small figures had not yet struck me.

I had spent five years in the Navy, sailed on or under five oceans, and walked on three continents. I had seen the Aurora Borealis over Norway and the Southern Cross over Sumatra. I had worn seven different kinds of hat, carried (but never used) six kinds of gun, and been issued with an Instantaneous Death Tablet. I had been cursed by four Gunner's Mates and kissed by one Admiral (but he was French).

Yet the whole period had amounted to very little more than a series of rather pleasant meals taken out of doors, or on shipboard. Ever since I had walked through the gates of the Royal Naval Barracks in Portsmouth, five years earlier, I had – it was beginning to dawn on me – been living a sheltered life.

It was time I faced up to some realities – and here was the first of them, weighing 7 lb 2 oz. Peace at last? I had my doubts!

Room in the Officers' camp, with Haggis.

APPENDIX

NOTE ON MY DOG, HAGGIS

Bacchus is mentioned a lot in this book, but so far I have not mentioned my own dog, Haggis; she appears on p.186, lying beneath my seat.

I inherited Haggis in Ceylon from a sailor who was no longer allowed to keep her on board. She moved happily into the tent I was sharing with Lucas. She was in fact a very good and affectionate mongrel, with a pale brown and yellow coat. When I took her for walks in Colombo, I had her on a very long white lead, intended to encircle any attractive Wrens we might meet.

Prior to going home to Britain in the *Christian Huygens*, we were sent to live in a luxurious officers' camp, planned by Lord Louis Mountbatten, on the banks of the great river, Mahaweli Ganga, close to Colombo.

Each officer slept in his own room in a line of cabins made of wood. In my neighbouring 'basha' I had a peppery army major who owned a black retriever as his pet. One day I was told that the retriever seemed to be interested in Haggis, which worried me. When I asked the major, he said that his dog wouldn't dream of touching an uncouth mongrel like Haggis. I wondered.

Then Haggis started to make herself a 'nest'. I provided her with some blankets to lie on beneath my bed. A few mornings later, I heard squeaks. I looked below and there was Haggis with three puppies, all light brown. So at breakfast I told my major that everything was all right, there were no suspicions about his dog.

When I went back to my cabin, there was Haggis, with four more puppies, all jet black.

Experts decided that two puppies were enough for Haggis, and the four black ones and one brown were quietly put to sleep. I then had to leave the camp and join the ship going home. I learned later that the two puppies made such a continuous noise that the other officers could not sleep. Someone then threw them both into the crocodile-infested Mahaweli Ganga. Four days later, the two puppies turned up in the camp, a bit wet, but wagging their tails delightedly. After that they were heroes, and moved in with the cook.

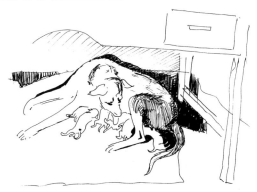

215

INDEX